Advance

Living as a Man of Valor will be on... reading list for men and leaders of men! I've followed Brad and his MOV team as they have been faithfully following the Lord's command to "go and make disciples" around the world for many years. Their specific focus on helping men 'know who they are so they know how to live' has produced much fruit. They've now captured their well-researched and organized conference content in a practical book that will encourage and mobilize even more men. Read this book with a friend or a small group and grow together!

—Mike Young
Founder & Executive Director, Noble Warriors
Former President, National Coalition of Ministries to Men

Living as a Man of Valor is one of the most practical and down-to-earth guides to being a man I have found. Brad Smith and his team have put together a fierce tool for strong, gentle, and responsible manhood. One of the greatest needs in the world is responsible men and this book will be a blessing for families, communities, and churches all around the world."

—Brandon Brewer
Global Outreach Pastor, Temple Bible Church

Brad Smith and his team at Men of Valor have compiled an excellent tool for guiding ministry to men in the local church. This manual is written by real life practitioners, not ivory tower academics or armchair quarterbacks. Thanks for giving us more ammo for the fight, more tools for the trade, and more courage for the conquest. The only thing better than the information provided is the model you have given with your lives!

—Dr. Jack Elwood
Cofounder, Washington Area Coalition of Ministries of Men
President, Heal Africa

There are many voices in the world today telling men what their role in society is and how to fulfill it. In the midst of these conflicting and confusing voices, can a man find the truth concerning his roles and responsibilities in life? Yes! The correct answers come from the One who created man and did so according to His plan and for His purpose! *Living as a Man of Valor* is a valuable tool to help men around the world discover God's design for their position, priorities, and practices. Reading and applying the biblical principles found in this book will give men important guidance in order to live a fulfilling, fruitful, and God-honoring life!

—Dr. Billy Ross
Vice-President, World Hope Ministries International
Director, World Hope Bible Institute

After nearly fifty years of ministry, I had no idea how much scripture speaks into the hearts of men. This book is an eye opener and should find its way into the hands of all men who call themselves Christ followers. You will be shaken out of apathy and given a clear biblical path to follow that will shape you into the man God wants you to be.

—Rev. Mike Minter
Founding Pastor, Reston Bible Church
Author, *A Western Jesus* & *Stay the Course: A Pastor's Guide to Navigating the Restless Waters of Ministry*

Brad Smith has written a must-read resource for anyone seeking to understand the best way to minister to men. As you read this book you will be learning from one of the internationally known speakers and experts in men ministry. The book is also a guide to those men who seek personal development as leaders, fathers, and husbands.

—Dr. Leonard Wambua, PhD
Executive Director, Eagle Rise Girls Center and School
CEO, Africa Capacity Building Initiatives
Senior Lecturer, Management University of Africa
Consultant, USAID Nairobi

Now more than ever, our world needs to hear the ideas and disciplines in this compelling new book from Brad Smith. If you are interested in becoming the man God destined you to be, this is a must read. Brad has written the ultimate how-to manual to get you through every challenge the world has brought and will bring your way.

—Clair Hoover
Executive Director, National Coalition of Ministries to Men

Living as a Men of Valor is a book that will grab you and keep you reading from start to finish. It is not a long read and well worth your time! This book coaches us in the various responsibilities that God gives us. It helped me see weaknesses that I can work on to better balance my journey as a husband, father, grandfather, and leader. As a former soldier, general contractor, hunter and outdoorsman, I appreciate "manly men" lifted up; many young men and even boys need to have manly, Godly men to emulate. I encourage young and old alike to lace up your boots, grab your pack, and head out on an adventure to do what it takes to complete your journey as a man of valor!

—Warren Jenkins
Cofounder, Jenkins Restorations, Inc.

Living as a Man of Valor presents God's ongoing heart for men. Brad Smith presents God's call to men, equipping of men, leading of men, and provision for men in the face of the world's desire to discourage, frustrate, and isolate men. This book presents a practical guide and useful material in starting a new group or energizing men's ministry.

—Paul W. Bice
Executive Vice President, BCT—The Community's Bank

Anchored in the Bible, with clear practical principles for true manhood, Brad Smith's *Living as a Man of Valor* will rejuvenate every reader.

—Rev. Steve Njenga
Founder & Director, Camp Brethren Ministries, Eburru, Kenya

My dad taught me by his example how to be a man in the eyes of God, but not every man has had that blessing. The Lord has led Brad Smith and others to present us the role of a biblical man based on the Word of God to address this need.

—Jamie Jackson
President Reagan Board appointee, Federal Home Loan Bank
Former President & CEO, Commonwealth Mortgage

The Church is not equipping men for spiritual battle—maybe because there has not been a biblical training manual. But now there is! Brad Smith's *Living as a Man of Valor* is a comprehensive text for manhood training.

—Chris Van Brocklin
Ambassador, No Regrets Men's Ministry
Board Member, National Coalition of Ministries to Men

"Brad Smith and his team have done a great service in the battle for the hearts of men. They present a strategic and tactical plan for the "why?", the "how-to?" and the "so what?" of reaching and discipling men. I enthusiastically recommend this volume to your careful study.

—Rev. Marty Granger
Cofounder, Washington Area Coalition of Ministries of Men
Founder & President, Ministry Alliance

LIVING

AS A

MAN

OF

VALOR

*When you know who you are,
you'll know how to live.*

Living as a Man of Valor © 2023 Brad P. Smith

ISBN: 978-1-959544-05-0

Phial Press
Austin, TX

This edition printed & distributed through KDP.

Cover Design by Travis McSherley, 400 West Media, 400west.com

Photo credits Shutterstock, Lightstock. All rights reserved.

Phial Press is an imprint of Wootton Major Publishing, LLC
www.woottonmajorpublishing.com

Bible Translations Used

AKJV	American King James Version
AMP	Amplified Bible
BSB	Berean Study Bible
ESV	English Standard Version
GNT	Good News Translation
ICB	International Children's Bible
ISV	International Standard Version
KJV	King James Version
NASB	New American Standard Bible
NKJV	New King James Version
RSV	Revised Standard Version
WEB	World English Bible

The NASB and ESV are the Bible translations most commonly used by Men of Valor International. We sometimes use the KJV/NKJV or RSV, less often other translations, and only when their word choices assist with understanding but do not harm original meaning, intent, and accuracy.

Foreword

When the Lord appeared to Gideon and announced, "The Lord is with you, you mighty man of valor," (Judges 6:12), it was meant for more than reassurance. God was outlining a plan—He was equipping Gideon with His calling. Every man wants to know that someone believes in him, that he has someone right there with him. But God goes even further than human brotherhood in His Word when He says, "*I* am with you." These words of affirmation cut straight to the heart and are words that every man wants and needs to know. These words strengthen and equip men to live out their calling as men of valor— their calling to live godly lives in their marriages, work, and communities. Because "If God is for us, who can be against us?" (Romans 8:31)

These thoughts come from the first chapter of the book you are about to read, *Living as a Man of Valor*. This book is not a harangue of what men are doing wrong, but rather a calling and encouragement to all men that God is with us and *already* sees our potential as men of valor.

In my work as a pastor, I do a lot of counseling. Once, the leader of a wives' study group asked me why it always seemed to fall on the wives to set everything right in marriage.

"For example," she continued, "here we are studying your book about how to love our husbands, but the fact is as a group we've read half a dozen books on marriage. At best, our husbands have *started* maybe one or two."

Another wife added, "I gave my husband the best marriage book I could find and told him how much it would mean to me if he would read it. The bookmark hasn't moved in two months!"

Apathy in marriage and family grieves more than our wives; it grieves our God. The apostle Paul tells husbands to love our wives as Christ loved the church. (Eph. 5:25) To love as Christ loved is to be the initiator as Christ is the initiator in His relationship with the church. We were estranged from God, but Jesus came from on high to bring us back. He didn't wait for the church to approach Him. He didn't expect that the bride, as the "relational" one, would be more invested in the relationship and plead with Him to come back.

Which means, men, that to be like Christ, the glory of God (1st Corinthians 11:7) is to be the ones who chase after our wives. If things go bad, we are responsible for setting them right. We should be the ones having marriage study groups. We should be the ones saying to our wives, "We need to talk." We should be the ones who buy the books or sign up for the marriage conference or initiate getting away from the kids for a while, or who researches the best marriage counselor.

Living as a Man of Valor is not just about marriage. It discusses all aspects about being a man of God. It is a book the church needs and one I would love to see men's groups go through. As a pastor and counselor, I particularly appreciate that *Living as a Man of Valor* appropriately calls men to Christ's kind of love. In a world where even the definition of "man" is up for debate, it takes commendable boldness to talk about the God-given *roles* of men, but these authors do it courageously and powerfully. Every woman and child will be blessed if their husband and father take these words to heart.

As part of His love, Jesus wasn't just the lead initiator; He also became the lead sufferer. He "took the bullet" so we didn't have to.

That was the attitude of our Savior, and that's the attitude of a man of valor toward his family. If suffering must come, let it begin with me. If someone needs to get a second job, it's me. If someone needs to speak up to my parents or in-laws about undue meddling, it's me. If someone needs to have the painful conversation with a child about who they're dating, it's me. If someone needs to say "No" to more requests so that there's more time for marriage and family, it's me.

This doesn't diminish our wives—we know they are capable of all of the above—it's done in an attitude of *service* to our wives. We honor them by welcoming their input and gifts. My wife Lisa can do many things much better than I can, so when she takes the lead it's a matter of strategy and honoring her superior gifts. That's a much different dynamic than forcing her to lead because I'm being afraid, lazy, or apathetic.

Living as a Man of Valor calls men to go to war for our families and to be willing to "take the first bullet." Chapter after chapter calls us to prayerfully reflect on our calling and position. So we have to ask ourselves, "What can I do for my wife? What burden is she carrying that I should carry? What action has she been forced to take that I should be taking? How can I be the father my daughter and son need? How can I be the man that my church, work place, and community needs?"

The truths in this book are life-transforming, but embrace them with an attitude of *humility*. For example, if we've been passive in marriage and suddenly come on too strong, our wives might think we have been disappointed in how they have been handling things. Instead, we need to be repentant, explain what's going on, thank them for stepping up when they did, but then offer to at least help carry the burden from now on and be the man of valor God says we are.

Paul's words are simple, and powerful, and profound: Look at Christ on the cross, and let's *love our wives* like that. Look at the life Christ modeled and the things He taught, and let's *live our lives* like that.

Knowing that the Lord is with them, men of valor settle for nothing less.

—Gary Thomas

Author, *A Lifelong Love*,
Making Your Marriage a Fortress,
Sacred Marriage,
& *Sacred Parenting*

Table of Contents

The 'Men Problem'

Patrick Morley

Much has been made about the "men problem".

School teachers can barely educate on the heels of it. Social services are overwhelmed because of it. Employers are stumped by it. Law enforcement feels the brunt of it. Many jails and prisons are full because of it. Politicians don't know what to do about it. Candidates avoid it. Divorce courts are at capacity because of it. Families are ripped apart by it. Wives soak their pillows with tears as a result of it. Children grow up in poverty as a consequence of it. Teenagers experiment with drugs and sex to cope with it. A lot of money gets spent to treat symptoms of it.

We open teenage pregnancy centers [and abortion clinics], establish substance abuse centers, increase budgets for social services, build homes for battered women, authorize more jail space, put extra beds in our homeless shelters, increase the number of law enforcement officers, and fit our schools with metal detectors to deal with it.

Everyone is concerned about it. Many address the consequences of it. Yet very few people are doing anything that will change the root of it. It is among the most pervasive social, economic, political, and spiritual problems of all time. Men have become one of our largest neglected people groups.

—excerpt from *Pastoring Men*

**Now that you understand the "men problem,"
I invite you to explore the "men opportunity."**

—*Brad Smith*

Introduction

Brad Smith

Why Men?

"And I sought for a man among them who should build up the wall and stand in the breach before me for the land... but I found none."

Ezekiel 22:30 (ESV)

When we were fairly new to our church in the late 1980s, I saw an announcement about starting a "men's ministry." I had never heard of a men's ministry and had no idea what it was. But they talked about hosting breakfasts and events, and I knew I could help with organizing. I was looking to serve somewhere, so I volunteered. Besides, what guy doesn't like hanging out with other guys?

I was in a lot of roles for that ministry over the years, but what was most meaningful for me was the personal growth I experienced while doing it. Yes, I attended the breakfasts, Bible studies, dinners, retreats, and other various outings, and over time I organized, led, or spoke at most all of them. But the biggest deal for me was the personal impact.

I discovered that normal men sharing real stories of how they worked through problems in their lives, work, neighborhood, or in their marriages and families—and what I learned from them—was ten times more important than my service. During many dark days of unemployment, discouragement, and marriage and family challenges, the fellowship, camaraderie, occasional hand on my shoulder accompanied by words of affirmation or a written note, was huge, having major impact on my outlook, perspective, and obedience.

Over time I had the blessing of giving back to other men by mentoring, discipling, and influencing men for Christ. Serving men was and remains an incredible joy.

Nothing Like That Here

At one point, I was invited to India to help a group of national pastors and itinerant evangelists with strategic planning (my vocation). These men traveled extensively around India for their ministry, visiting and teaching at churches, conducting open-air crusades, etc. During the breaks, I talked with one of the attendees, Pastor Johnson Duvakumar from Chennai. He asked what ministry I was involved in at my church, and I told him about the men's ministry and the activities, friendship, and growth in Christ we experienced and the service we did together. While most of the previous conversations we shared were animated, two-way, give and take, I noticed that while talking about the subject of ministering to and through men, he was quiet.

So I asked, "What does your church in Chennai do for the men, and what have you seen being done for men in your country's churches?" He did not respond. Thinking it would help to provide some examples, I stuttered, "...you know, men's Bible studies, retreats, pancake breakfasts...?"

He answered, "I haven't seen anything like that in my church, nor have I seen or heard of that in any of the churches that I've been in."

I was shocked.

No Life Sharing

I became a Christian in high school; I attended a Christian college and majored in Bible; but it was when I was living life with the men at my church, with all of its joys, pains, sorrows, and support, encouragement, and successes in the midst of real-world, life-on-life reality, that I finally began to experience the abundant life Christ offers. With men—men of God. And I thought, *The Christian men in India do not have of any of this?! They don't know the joy and benefit of sharing life with other men like I've known?!*

So when Johnson said that he knew of nothing going on for men throughout India, all I could think to ask was, "How many men are in the churches?"

To me, it seemed obvious: If there is no consistent, organized, dedicated teaching and ministry to and through men, why would the men go to church?

Maybe you have read or heard of David Murrow's 2011 book, *Why Men Hate Going to Church*. There are some lighter reasons and some heavy reasons that Murrow offers, and I encourage you to read it if you haven't already. But in my experience, there are about five main reasons (further discussed later), and one of them is very simple: Churches are often only focused and budgeted towards ministries to and for women and children. Why? Well, that's who responds. That's who comes to church!

> **If there is no consistent, organized, dedicated teaching and ministry to and through men, why would men go to church?**

God Established His Church for Everyone

But God established His Church to teach His Word and His truths to everyone! The Lord of the Church has made it clear in His Word how very important *men* are. Men have a high calling to leadership and service. They have a vital, immensely important role. Men have an enormous impact on the family, in the church, and in the society.

This matters! Men are essential, not just to the church's ability to do its Kingdom work, but to its survival and ability to flourish.[1] When men don't attend church, they don't hear the truth that saves and transforms them, impacting their marriages and families.[2]

> **Men are essential to society's survival and to the church's ability to flourish.**

Granted, men are difficult to reach. They often don't respond... at least to the normal methods of "outreach". But if we give up on them— if we do not make an effort to reach and teach men—we are making a strategic mistake. We are playing into Satan's hand.

This mistake is not just impacting the church: we see damage from ignoring men everywhere. Families are falling apart. Men are not involved in their children's lives, and kids are getting into trouble— some serious and life-impacting. Societal norms are eroding— sometimes dramatically. Communities are decaying. Let's face it: Most of the problems in the world are because men aren't living their God-ordained roles.[3]

> **By ignoring men, we are playing into Satan's hand. And we see the damage everywhere.**

It's because men don't see the importance they have. They feel that they have no purpose.[4] Feeling hopeless, they often seek to drown their problems in alcohol, drugs, porn, and other idols, fixations, and vices. If the church doesn't reach and disciple men, who will?[5] Where do men learn how to live properly? How do they understand their position in Christ and their priorities? How do they pursue practices according to God's clearly successful blueprint? It can only come from the church!

So it was no surprise when, in answer to my question "how many men are in the Indian churches?" Johnson said, "I don't know, but not many."[6]

I suggested that I bring a team back to India to teach pastors some basic biblical truths about how to reach and disciple men. The first Men of Valor conference was in 2005 in Assam, India, hosted by the Boro Baptist Association. Forty part-time rural pastors attended.

Over the next two decades, Men of Valor went on to lead conferences in almost thirty countries and established national teams in several. Thousands of men have gone through the teaching, and we continually receive reports of men's discipleship groups forming and multiplying, men living for Christ, marriages healing, families restoring, and churches growing after each conference. Why? Because when a man learns that God sees him as a man of valor, he starts to live differently.

The World Could Look Very Different

If men understood who they are in Christ and what God says should be their priorities and their practices, the church would be a very different place. If each man knew that he was a man of valor, he would live differently. I believe more marriages would flourish. I believe children would live in a world of love. I believe workplaces and communities around the world would look very, very different.

> **When a man learns that God sees him as a man of valor, he starts to live differently.**

I want men to fully understand their deep value in God's eyes. I want them to know how important they are to God. I want them to see that He has equipped and called them. And to understand and follow what He expects from them.

Men matter. Reaching and discipling men is not simply just the right thing to do. It is not simply that it is because we are losing one-half of God's human creation. We need to reach and teach men because it is God's *plan.*

Why men? I offer four reasons.

1. God's Model. When you compare great leaders of the Bible, what is the one thing that they have in common? Think of Adam, Noah, Moses, Joshua, Gideon, Samson, Samuel, David, Solomon, Elijah, Elisha, Nehemiah, Isaiah, Jeremiah, Ezekiel, Daniel, John the Baptist, Stephen, Paul, James, Peter, John, and the list goes on.

You might point out their compassion, bravery, strength, or humility. You might say they were filled with the Spirit.

Those characteristics are all generally true of biblical leaders. None of them were perfect. They weren't all the most respectable people. They weren't all the best decision-makers. They weren't all even the best leaders.

But they were all men.

Pastor and author John Piper writes,

> God has revealed himself to us in the Bible always as King, not Queen, and as Father, not Mother. The second person of the Trinity is revealed as the eternal Son. God appoints all the priests in Israel to be men. The Son of God comes into the world as a man, not a woman. He chooses twelve men to be his apostles. The apostles tell the churches that all the overseers—the pastor/elders who teach and have authority (1st Timothy 2:12)—should be men; and that in the home, the head who bears special responsibility to lead, protect, and provide, should be the husband. (Ephesians 5:22-33)[7]

Now, God did (and does) also use women leaders, but He primarily appointed men.

To be clear, we are not saying that women cannot or should not be in positions of spiritual leadership. There are many examples of wise, gifted women in the Bible who did God's work and filled essential roles—Esther, Ruth, Mary, Rahab, Manoah's wife, Hannah, Abigail, Phoebe, Lydia, Priscilla—to name just a few. And there's Moses' sister, Miriam; Anna; and Philip's four prophetess-daughters. (Exodus 15:20; Luke 2:36-38; Acts 21:9) Paul mentions a prayer meeting of women on the riverside in Philippi in Acts 16:13; surely they had a woman as leader—no men are even mentioned. Deborah was an important national leader: She was anointed as both judge and prophet in Israel—a distinction that only one other person, Samuel, had in the nation's entire history! People came from all over to hear her judgments. (Judges 4:5)

From the day Jesus began teaching, women have been drawn to Christianity in part because its teachings elevate and honor women more than any other major world religion. The Bible tells men to love and honor their wives, to give themselves up for their wives, to live with their wives in an understanding manner. Galatians 3:28 says that when it comes to salvation, "there is neither Jew nor Greek, there is neither slave nor free, there is no male and female, for you are all one in Christ Jesus." (ESV) Men and women are equal in God's sight. Jesus Christ clearly loved and respected women, teaching them as well as the men, and even allowing them to travel with Him. (Luke 8)

> **Men and women are equal in God's sight,**
> **but He is calling men to lead.**

Deborah did the job God gave *her*, but she had to rebuke Barak for not doing the job God gave *him*: leading the army against the king of Canaan who was oppressing them. Barak wanted to step back and let her do his job, too. (Judges 4)

> **The biblical model clearly shows**
> **that men are to lead.**

But God has and is calling men to do their jobs. And He is calling them to lead. When you read Scripture, the biblical model clearly shows that men are not to shirk or avoid leadership. They are to lead.

Lest we think this puts women in a less enviable position than men, we have to remember that it is men who are ultimately responsible to God and held accountable for the state of the church.[8] God asked, "Adam, where are you?" because, at the crucial moment when Eve took the fruit, Adam did not take leadership. (Maybe she did the deed, but Adam, *you're* responsible). And God still wants to know: Men, where are you?

As Dr. Tony Evans points out,

> God created Adam before Eve because Adam was to be responsible to both rule and lead. Adam was given his calling to cultivate and guard the garden before Eve was even created. And, as a result, it was Adam whom God sought when both Adam and Eve had disobeyed Him. This is because Adam was ultimately responsible. As a man you are ultimately responsible for those within your domain.[9]

That's the first reason why churches must go after men—they are pivotal. When men aren't leading, we lose more of them because men tend to follow men, not women.[10]

2. God's Design. In Genesis 2, we see the order of God's creation and His original intentions for the humans that He made in His own image: Adam was created first, and no helper suitable for him was found among all the rest of God's creation (2:18). So God created Eve out of one of Adam's ribs to be his companion, his *ezer k'negdo*, "a help, an ally, appropriate for, corresponding to him."[11]

Right here, in the beginning of the Bible, we see that it was God's original design in marriage for the man (husband) to be the leader and initiator and the woman (wife) to be the helper. Though these roles have been reversed in many homes, churches, and cultures, that was never God's plan.

Let's take a look at Paul's writing in his first letter to the Corinthians:

> "But I want you to understand that the head of every man is Christ, the head of a wife is her husband, and the head of Christ is God. ...A man...is the image and glory of God, but woman is the glory of man. For man was not made from woman, but woman from man. Neither was man created for woman, but woman for man...Nevertheless, in the Lord woman is not independent of man nor man of woman; for as woman was made from man, so man is now born of a woman. And all things are from God." (1st Corinthians 11:2-3, 7-9, 11 ESV)

Woman was made for man (11:9), is subject to her husband's leadership (11:3), and is his glory (11:7). None of this, by any means, gives men a higher position or the right to dominate their wives, who are also made in the image of God. (Genesis 1:27) But what this passage does say to us, men, is that we are to reflect God's glory. Verse 7 states that we *as men* are called to exemplify the glory of God.

Pastor Albert Barnes, a respected Bible commentator from the 19th century, defines *glory* as "splendor, brightness, that which stands forth to represent God, or by which the glory of God is known."[12] A man's actions, demeanor, attitudes, words, and tone are to give the world a glimpse of God... to reflect God's glory.[13]

**Men are God's representatives;
they are to reflect God's glory.**

When Moses came down from the mountain, the people were afraid to come near him because the skin of his face shone. He put on a veil because the glory of the Lord was too bright. (Exodus 34:29-35) *That's how we should reflect God's glory!*

In Revelation 21: 22-24, New Jerusalem's light is the glory of God. By its light, by the glory, the nations walk in the city. God's glory guides them. God's glory helps them see where to go. The glory of God lights people's way. The glory of God as shown by you, man of valor, should light your family's way.

Wives reflect their husbands' glory. We *as men* are to reflect God— because she will reflect us. Pastor Barnes also wrote, "But the women are the glory of the man, the honor, the ornament. All her attractiveness, all her beauty, her loveliness, and purity are therefore an expression of his honor and dignity, his integrity, his caring for her and the family, his stature, his respect."[14]

Let me tell you something I've learned; it's taken me many years to see this. When my wife is discouraged... if for a few days she looks sad or is quiet... I no longer ask her what's wrong. I ask God. I ask God what I have done that has made her sad and discouraged... because she reflects me.

Men of valor, we are called to love our wives as Christ loves the church.[15] (Ephesians 5:25) That's not easy for us to do; it is humbling, and challenging. God doesn't tell his bride what to do in a harsh, demeaning, or abrasive manner; neither should we. God tells us to be His glory. He calls us to reflect His brightness and His splendor so that our wives can reflect that glory in turn.

As my former pastor often said, "Show me a husband who loves his wife as Christ loved the Church, and I'll show you a wife who has no problem submitting to her husband." When we're right with God, our transformed lives can blaze a powerful trail for the changes we want to see in our families, churches, and communities.

3. God's Leaders. In 1st Timothy 2:12, Paul says, "I do not permit a woman to teach or to exercise authority over a man; rather, she is to remain quiet." (ESV) With the great respect that the Bible shows for women, how does this fit?

Here's what Pastor Stephen Kendrick said to help explain this verse: "God will not give men the chance to step back in His church."[16]

If a man sees a woman leading, he'll say, "Fine—you do it," and he'll sit back and take a nap. When a man is not presented with responsibility, it is his nature to be passive. If he does not feel needed, he won't make himself irreplaceable. He will not rise to a challenge if none is given to him. He will not take his place if his place has been taken from him.

So we see that God is not putting women down. He simply wants men to fulfill their role.

God is not putting women down.
He simply wants men to fulfill their role.

When women lead, men step back, and that is clearly not God's plan. But, having said that, *in order to lead properly, men must be trained by the church and given the opportunity and tools to grow spiritually.* No one wants to follow an ignorant or abusive leader.

The biblical calling of men is very important. God wants and commands men to lead. I believe that women assume roles of leadership not always because they should and not necessarily because they even want to, but because the men are absent or unengaged. Praise God for the women who have stepped in when men did not or could not lead![17] Advocating for men is not about diminishing women. But God is still calling men to be the leaders. His plan has not changed.

4. God's Church. A study done in the United States by Hartford Seminary showed having just a few men in a church is one factor that is strongly linked with low numbers of attendance and involvement for all genders and ages. Additionally, a higher proportion of women in the congregation is associated with decline rather than growth.[18] On the other hand, the involvement of men in the church is directly associated with church growth, health, and unity.[19] In short, "a man shortage is a sure sign of congregational paralysis and decline."[20]

Real-life stories bear this out. David Murrow, in *Why Men Hate Going to Church*, points out that two of the largest churches in the United States began by concentrating on and targeting men. When the church leaders went door to door to announce the start of the new church, they focused on talking with the men in each home.

John Chellah, one of the pastors I worked with in Zambia, turned the attention of his church to reaching men. Three years later, he announced to a group of pastors that the involvement of more men had helped increase the size of his church from 200 to 700 members.

Murrow would not be surprised. He believes that if you focus on men, your church will grow. If you personally disciple men, your church will explode.

Pastor Russ Sawyers explained his church's outreach strategy like this: "We asked, how do we reach the most people? And it seemed that if we could reach the husband or dad, then we had a good shot at reaching the rest."[21]

> **Churches that have as many men as women are three times more likely to be growing.**[22]

Studies have also shown that when churches have more women than men in the congregation and in leadership roles, the churches tend to turn inward.[23] The church tends to look only at itself and not the world around them; the focus becomes more about safety, security, self-preservation, and self-care—and less about outreach.[24]

Is an inward focus totally wrong? No, it's not. The church is a spiritual hospital, but that's not all it is. If women are in the majority—if the church focuses inward—it will eventually shrink in numbers. It will feminize and become more of a place for women than for men over time. It will lose its boldness, its daring. That will drive men away.[25]

Lastly, the New Testament tells us that elders and pastors are to be men. (1st Timothy 3:1-7; Titus 1:5-9) If we do not reach and build men, if the numbers of men continue to dwindle in churches worldwide, we will lose the leadership of His church—at least as God intended.[26]

God's Plan

Why men? Why do men matter? Why should we reach and build men? Because reaching and building men is God's plan: His model, His design, His leaders, evidenced in His church.

For years, I have enjoyed the camaraderie and challenging example and influence of godly men, inspiring me to pursue love and good deeds. (Hebrews 10:25) Most men around the world are not experiencing that. And we see the results.

If we want to build the church, if we want to restore families, if we want to reach and revive communities, and bring sanity to our world, we must intentionally proclaim the gospel to and disciple men. That's how we'll change the world!

MEN OF VALOR INTERNATIONAL
MENOFVALOR.ORG

What Do We Teach Men?

Men of Valor International first teaches men their position in Christ and then, building from that, their biblical priorities and practices. We start with understanding our strength in the Lord and bring a positive, inspiring message, because knowing how God sees us, and knowing that He is constantly with us, makes the battles of life winnable. What follows in this book is what we have taught to thousands of men in more than two dozen countries around the world.

There is material here that you may have seen or heard before, but Men of Valor International has learned that far too many men are not hearing these truths. In conference after conference, men approach us and say, "We've never heard this before!" The sad reality is that few churches are reaching out to men, and fewer still are teaching biblical truth specifically for men.

We hope you are inspired to read on—and learn how God sees you and why you matter to Him.

Notes & References

[1] "There is no movement of God without men of God. If you want the Lord to move in your church, go for the guys."
Kenny Luck, *Sleeping Giant* (B&H Publishing Group 2012) 143

[2] "Church involvement is the most important predictor for marital stability and happiness. It's… correlated with less depression, more self-esteem, and greater family and marital happiness. Religious participation leads men to become more engaged husbands and fathers. Teens with religious fathers are more likely to say that they enjoy spending time with their dads."
David Murrow, *Why Men hate Going to Church* (Thomas Nelson 2011) 23

[3] "Society's very survival has always depended on men who would fulfill their roles."
Murrow, *Why Men Hate Going to Church*, 39
"Men are God's instrument… And Satan understands that, and that's why he attacks men so."
Pastor Fred Richard of Northwood Church, Summerville, NC. Quoted by Michael Zigarelli, *The Man-Friendly Church* (Michael Zigarelli 2018) 13

[4] A man without purpose often becomes wicked. See Proverbs 6:12-15 and 29:18: "Where there is no vision [no revelation of God and His word], the people are unrestrained." (AMP)

[5] "The institutional church is God's appointed means—the first responders—to help men become [real men]. A disciple-making church offers the only systemic solution to what ails us."
Patrick Morley, *Pastoring Men* (Moody Publishers 2009) 25-26
See also Chapter 2, "What is a Real Man?"

[6] Since then, I've learned that the number of men compared to the number of women attending or involved in churches in India is about 20-25%. According to pastors and church leaders, Africa only has 15-20% men. In Japan, missionaries report the churches are at about 10% men compared to the number of women. A national U.S. ministry told us that in Thailand it is an appalling 3%. Can you even picture that—having 100 people in your church, and only three of them are men?

[7] John Piper, "The Value of a Masculine Ministry," *The Journal for Biblical Manhood & Womanhood* (2012) 10

[8] See for example Ephesians 5:22-33 and its comparable teaching, Colossians 3:18-21. These passages speak much more to the man's duties than to the woman's; men have a great responsibility–and a high calling!

[9] Tony Evans, *Kingdom Man* (Tyndale 2012) 18

[10] For more, see 'Why Men Don't Go to Church'

[11] *The Strongest Strong's Exhaustive Concordance of the Bible* (Zondervan 2001)

[12] Albert Barnes, *Notes on the New Testament* (Kregel Publications 1962) 754

[13] "Ninety-nine percent of a husband's leadership is leadership in character. His call is to surge in holiness, to be obsessed with godliness, to stop at nothing to grow in righteousness."
Tim Challies, "Accept Your Leadership" (2017)
https://www.challies.com/articles/lead/

[14] Albert Barnes, *Notes on the New Testament* (Kregel Publications 1962) 754

[15] Ephesians 5:21-33 affirms God's pattern. "Since Paul has told wives to 'submit to your own husbands,' we would naturally assume that as he turns his attention to husbands he will tell them, 'Husbands, lead your wives.' But he doesn't. He assumes a husband will lead but is aware that without further instruction this leadership will be harsh, selfish, or inadequate. To counter this, he carefully defines the quality of the husband's leadership. Such leadership is to be gentle and tender, to imitate the love of Jesus Christ for his church."
Challies, "Accept Your Leadership"

[16] Stephen Kendrick, speaking at the NCMM National Leader's Conference in Rockville, MD, 2014

[17] "That's exactly what Deborah did in a time when men had lost their way. The book of Judges records some of Israel's worst days, and the absence of male leadership is a strong reflection of the time. While serving as judge, Deborah affirmed the rightness of male leadership, not only looking to Barak to lead but letting him know this was what God wanted. Nevertheless, sadly, Barak didn't step up."
Nancy DeMoss, "When Men Don't Lead: A Look at the Life of Deborah" (Online: 2011)
https://www.reviveourhearts.com/podcast/revive-our-hearts/season/when-men-don-t-lead-a-look-life-deborah/

[18] C. Kirk Hadaway, *FACTs on Growth: A New Look at the Dynamics Of Growth and Decline in American Congregations Based on the Faith Communities Today 2005 National Survey of Congregations* (Hartford Institute for Religion Research, Hartford Seminary, 2006), 18

[19] "When churches ignore their men, they soon find themselves without many. Donations, volunteerism, evangelism, and attendance all suffer. But give men a little attention, and they respond. The church grows."
Murrow, *Why Men Hate Going to Church*, 131

[20] "The Gender Gap and Your Church" at
https://churchformen.com/men-and-church/#

[21] Russ Sawyers, quoted in Zigarelli, *The Man-Friendly Church*, 6

[22] See "The Gender Gap and Your Church" at
https://churchformen.com/men-and-church/#

[23] Retired Dallas Seminary professor and church strategy consultant Dr. Aubrey Malphurs, describes most American churches as "The Family Reunion Church". Their unifying value is fellowship; the pastor's role is Chaplain; the key emphasis is 'to belong'; and the desired result is a 'secure Christian'. If most churches around the world have more women than men, then it follows that his description is accurate.
Aubrey Malphurs, *Advanced Strategic Planning* (Baker Books, Grand Rapids, MI, 2005) 107
David Murrow goes one step further, saying that churches with a vast majority of women will die within 30 years. See "The Gender Gap and Your Church" at
https://churchformen.com/men-and-church/#.

[24] Yet, "...healthy churches...without exception...are externally focused: their goal is to make a significant... difference in the lives of people around them."
Murrow, *Why Men Hate Going to Church*, 203

[25] For more, see "Chapter 7: Victoria's Secret... When We Lost the Men" in *Why Men Hate Going to Church*.

[26] We will also lose men in general. "U.S. studies have found 37% of liberal congregations, representing more than 17 million Christians, are now led by women. ...with more than three in four of all Americans convinced females should be permitted to be clergy. At the same time, however, many worry about the so-called 'feminization' of the Christian church. Both genders are concerned that...the rise of women in the church is not working for a huge number of men. Have women won the rights battle in many churches, while losing the war?"
D. Todd, "With Four in Five Members Female, Churches Want to Again Reach Men," *Vancouver Sun*, Dec. 15, 2012

PART I: A Man of Valor's Position

God "has given us everything we need for life and godliness" (2nd Peter 1:3), but most of us feel defeated by circumstances or by our own perceived inadequacies. Gideon certainly did. (Judges 6:15) The key to overcoming your inadequacies or your obstacles starts with knowing who you are.

The problem is that many of us do not know who we are. Those that do, don't act as if they believe it.

In dealing with trouble, or a challenge, obstacle, or problem, we are fully entitled—even commissioned—to face it, to go forward in strength. We have Almighty God in us, and "...greater is He who is in you than he who is in the world!" (1st John 4:4, NASB)

Greater is He that is in you than any trouble. Greater is He that is in you than any challenge we may encounter. Greater is He that is in you than any obstacle we face. Greater is He that is in you than any problem! He gives us His mighty strength and His incomparable great power. We are made in His image and share in His nature.

When you know who you are, you'll know how to live.

Chapter 1

Brad Smith

A Man of Valor

"And the angel of the LORD appeared to him and said
to him, 'The Lord is with you, you mighty man of valor.'"
Judges 6:12 (RSV)

Many years ago, there was a young boy named David who chased and killed lions and bears. When a predator snatched one of the sheep he was tending, he'd grab its beard and kill it with his bare hands. (1st Samuel 17:34-35)

David spent most of his youth tending sheep alone in the wilderness. He saw to the care and growth of the sheep, defending them from the elements and from wild animals using a hand-made sling from which he successfully threw stones at predators. He also spent many hours getting to know God. Out in the wilderness, the shepherd boy who would someday be king of Israel became brave, fearless, and strong... in the Lord.

> **Alone in the wilderness, David became brave, fearless, and strong... in the Lord.**

One day when he was about fourteen years old, David's father asked him to take food to his older brothers who were involved in a battle against the Philistines, Israel's enemy. When David arrived, he immediately saw that the armies were not fighting; they were merely facing one another across a valley. He learned that each morning the Philistines sent a giant of a man named Goliath to stand out in front of his kinsmen. And a giant he was! About 10½ ft. (3.2 m) tall! Goliath carried a huge shield and a spear as big as the trunk of a tree and he was covered in armor. No man could stand against him and hope to live. Every morning this giant shouted, "Come on, you cowards! Who dares to fight against me? Come out and I'll crush you with my hands! I defy you, Israel. Give me a man to fight!"

When David heard these words, he became angry. His anger was not just for the cowardice of his brothers' army, but because Goliath was defying the armies of the living God—David's God, the God who had always granted him victory out in the wilderness.

"God always helped me in the wilderness—why not here, too? Why not now? God is still God!" So David volunteered to fight Goliath. He didn't use the king's armor; he only took his sling and five smooth stones. Then he walked out to the edge of the valley.

Goliath was filled with scorn when he saw David. "The soldiers refuse to come, and instead they're sending this little boy to attack me? I'll tear him to pieces!"

David Was Not Afraid

But David was not afraid. There is nothing in the account to indicate that David had any fear as he faced Goliath. Hard to believe, and a tall order for most men! There is no record of his feelings at this point other than courage. Real courage. But even if there was fear, he did not allow his feelings to overcome his faith; he did not allow his fear to keep him from doing what he knew was right. And what he knew was that the Lord was with him.

In the Lord's strength, and with the skill gained from killing animals in the wilderness, the brave young man yelled to Goliath that he was about to kill him in the name of the Lord. "You come to me with a sword and with a spear and with a javelin; but I come to you in the name of the Lord of Hosts, the God of the armies of Israel, whom you have defied." (1st Samuel 17:45, RSV)

And then he started *running* toward the giant.

> ### "God always helped me in the wilderness—why not here, too? God is still God!"

Have you ever run toward the giants in your life? Have you ever run toward the problems? That's what David did. He didn't run from the giant, he ran right at him!

The biblical account says that David picked out just one of the stones, swung his sling, and hurtled the stone at the giant—while he was running! It hit Goliath in the forehead and sank in. Goliath fell face forward to the ground. He was knocked out and probably dead. The very first stone David threw felled Goliath. But just to be sure the fight was over, the young shepherd boy jumped onto the giant and cut off his head—with the giant's own sword. (Remember? David didn't bring one!)

That boy did what an army of 10,000 men could not do! Because of his faith in a God greater than giants, the young shepherd boy accomplished a mighty victory.

The Philistines were stunned and silent. So were the Israelites at first. But then picture this: A Hebrew soldier shouts, then a few more. Then one starts running down the side of the valley toward the Philistines, and then another, and then another and another... soon the entire army is running at the Philistines, yelling and attacking. The battle gets louder and louder, more and more men join in. The entire army leaves their places of hiding and safety—because David's victory makes them feel like they can win! As one man, they say, "If little David can kill Goliath, then *we can take this army!*"

> **Through faith in a God greater than giants, a boy accomplished a mighty victory.**

Meanwhile, David picks up the head of Goliath and walks back to the king. As the battle rages, David presents his trophy to Saul. And what does Saul say to him? "Congratulations, young man!" Or, "You're our hero!" Or perhaps, "I'll honor you with a feast and a medal, and I'll invite all of Israel!" Or even, "Thank you"?

No. Saul asks David whose son he is.

What?

Now of course David respectfully answers that he is the son of Jesse. But...

Does Saul really care about David's father?

Was that what he was really asking?

No. Saul is asking: "Who are you? Where do you come from? What is your family background? What village did you grow up in? What is your occupation? How did you learn to fight? How did you get to be so brave? *Who are you??*"

Who Are You?

This is not an unusual question. Whenever a stranger mysteriously appears and does something amazing, spectacular, perhaps even lifesaving, it is the first question people ask. "Who is this guy? Where did he come from?" We don't want to know just about the brave act; we have to know more. We want to understand. We want to know the hero's background, his training, where his strength and skill come from, who he was.

Who are you?

Sometimes you might stare in the mirror and ask yourself that question. Who am I? What you see may be a patchwork of failure, imperfections, mistakes and brokenness. You may be struggling to understand your purpose in life, or if you even have one. You may be wearied by the daily grind of work, commuting, family responsibilities, and the problems you face. Deep down, truthfully, honestly—who are you?

Deep down, truthfully, honestly—

who are you?

I'm going to give you an answer to that question. It's an answer that is found in the Scripture, one that has everything to do with the kingdom of God. It shows us men what the purpose of our lives is. It's all you can be, it is who you are—in just 10 words. And it is in the book of Judges.

The Calling

The sixth chapter of Judges gives us a glimpse into what Israel had become not very long after it had conquered the Promised Land. The nation of Israel, made up of the people God had chosen to display His glory and salvation to the world, had fallen into an appalling cycle of sin and rebellion. Over and over again they grew complacent, forsaking their covenant with God and His laws as they pursued and served foreign gods, doing what was evil in the sight of the Lord, and every man doing "what was right in his own eyes." (Judges 21:25 ESV)

The first several verses of chapter six tell us that God responded to yet another instance of the Israelites' sin by allowing the nation of Midian to oppress them. The Midianites lay the land waste, consume all the Israelites' harvest, and either take or kill the livestock, leaving no food. Things got so bad that the Israelites hid themselves in caves and dens. And then they cried out to the Lord for help.

God hears their cry. He does not leave them alone: He raises up a deliverer. But not a known warrior and hero... a nobody.

God hears their cry. He does not leave them alone: He

raises up a nobody.

Judges 6:11 introduces Gideon. This young man is beating out wheat in a winepress to hide it from the Midianites. The winepress was an enclosed space, a hole in the ground, with little if any wind. It was hot. He was sweating. The work was difficult and aggravating. Gideon was irritated. And on top of all that, he was wondering if the God who had done so much for Israel in the past is still around or even really cares anymore.

It is at this point that the angel of the Lord comes up to Gideon. Look at this: Gideon is alone, he's frustrated, he's discouraged, he feels like he cannot do anything... and out of the blue, out of the air, an angel appears. Without warning the Lord arrives.

Maybe you've had times like that. When the Lord sends a message—maybe not an angel—but a brother shows up and encourages you when you least expect it; when you think things will never change, when you've lost all hope... the Lord appears.

"And the angel of the LORD appeared to him and said to him, 'The Lord is with you, you mighty man of valor.'" (Judges 6:12 RSV)

When you think things will never change, when you've lost all hope... the Lord appears.

Wow. Where did that come from? Why would the angel of the Lord say this?

Well, I think it is far more than comfort. It is more than an attempt to ease Gideon's fears or angst. God is outlining a plan.

He's equipping Gideon... and giving him a mission.

God With Us

Let's take a closer look. The words "the Lord is with you" empower and equip the man of God to do His work. God—the God of the universe—says, "I am with you." David knew that; it was the reason for his bravery. He learned it in the wilderness and lived it out the rest of his life. God prepared and helped David to face Goliath and God will prepare you and help you to face your battles and problems, too.

Over and over in His Word, the Lord affirms that He is with you: "I am your helper," (Psalm 118:6), "I will save you," (Jeremiah 15:20), "I will fulfill my purpose for you," (Psalm 138:8), "You shall not be shaken," (Psalm 62:6), "I am your guide," (Psalm 73:24), "I am your keeper," (Psalm 121:5), "I know the plans I have for you," (Jeremiah 29:11).

The God of the universe says, "I am with you."

Every man wants to know that someone believes in him. Every man wants to know that he has someone right there with him. All men need this; it's not something to be ashamed of. God made us to need one another, to stand together.

But God goes even further than human brotherhood in His Word. He says, "*I* am with you." Every one of us needs to know that there is a God in Heaven and that *He* is with us. He is at our right hand! He will take care of us. He will look out for us. He is our helper, our Savior, and our guide. God promises every believer that He will be with us always and will never leave us. (Matthew 28:20)

These are words of affirmation that cut straight to the heart, words that every man wants and needs to hear. Words that every man needs to know and believe. These words strengthen and equip. "If God is for us, who can be against us?" (Romans 8:31)

An Equipping Presence

Scripture is full of examples of how knowledge of the Lord's presence has empowered and emboldened men to live out their callings. Genesis 39:2-3 tells us that the Lord was with Joseph and caused everything he did to succeed. Even when Joseph was wrongfully accused and sent to prison, the Lord was with Joseph and showed him unfailing love (39:21). Joseph went on to serve the Lord faithfully in all circumstances—first in prison, then as interpreter of Pharaoh's dreams, and finally as second-in-command over all of Egypt. It was God's ongoing presence with Joseph that enabled him to find success and favor in the situations he encountered.

When God appeared to Moses in the burning bush, Moses reacted with fear and hesitation. In fact, he gives multiple reasons why he is the wrong man. (Exodus 3:11- 4:16) Who am I, he wanted to know, that I should go to Pharaoh and bring the people of Israel out of Egypt?

God's reply answered Moses' fears: "I will be with you." (Exodus 3:11-12) Moses went on to lead his people out of slavery, through the wilderness, and to the edge of the Promised Land. God's presence with Moses was the only factor that enabled him to become a great leader.

I will be with you.

Moses' successor, Joshua, was commissioned by God after Moses' death to lead the Israelites the rest of the way. God exhorted Joshua to meditate on the Law and promised success if he was careful to keep the covenant. And God promised something more: "Just as I was with Moses, so I will be with you. I will not leave you or forsake you...Be strong and courageous. Do not be frightened, and do not be dismayed, for the Lord your God is with you wherever you go." (Joshua 1:5, 9 ESV) Joshua led his people to victory over their enemies, and led them to settle in their new home in the Promised Land.

Before his death, David, the shepherd boy who first understood God's presence in the wilderness and then acted on that understanding the rest of his life, passed on words of exhortation to his son Solomon. As Solomon prepared to oversee building the Lord's temple, David charged his son to "be strong and courageous...do not be afraid and do not be dismayed, for the Lord God, even my God, is with you. He will not leave you or forsake you, until all the work for the service of the house of the Lord is finished." (1st Chronicles 28:20 ESV) Solomon went on to complete the temple and is known as the wisest man who ever lived.

Finally, one of the most powerful assurances of God's presence recorded in Scripture is found in the Great Commission. "And Jesus came and said to them, 'All authority in Heaven and on earth has been given to me. Go therefore and make disciples of all nations, baptizing them in the name of the Father and of the Son and of the Holy Spirit, teaching them to observe all that I have commanded you. And behold, I am with you always, to the end of the age.'" (Matthew 28:18-20 ESV)

> ### I am with you always, to the end of the age.

Jesus Christ—God in the flesh—gave His disciples an unshakeable reason not to fear, a purpose and calling, and the promise that He would be with them. The disciples took Christ's word to heart. What they went on to do in God's power and presence would change not only the world of their age, but the very course of history. Many would not be reading this today if the disciples had not obeyed and believed that the Lord was with them.

What do all these passages tell us? What is God so carefully and repeatedly saying to you and to me? If these men needed to be told this...if *these* mighty men of valor needed this encouragement... we are *all* in good company.

The key to your success as a Christian, as God's child, is to realize and believe that the Lord is with you—and then act on it.

> **The key to success is to realize and believe that the Lord is with you—and then act on it.**

Now, you probably won't be called by God to lead a nation out of slavery. You probably won't be called to conquer a land. But when you need to...

- ✓ Love your wife and honor her even when you are angry—**The Lord is with you.**
- ✓ Teach your children—**The Lord is with you.**
- ✓ Resist a women's temptation—**The Lord is with you.**
- ✓ Stand up to an oppressor in your community—**The Lord is with you.**
- ✓ Do what's right when everyone around wants you to do what's wrong—**The Lord is with you.**

In the services in some churches, people turn to one another and tell each other, "The Lord is with you." My daughter once pointed out, "That sounds just like a nice little saying. Everyone says that." Maybe some people say it too often, forgetting the importance of its meaning. But most people don't say it enough!

The *Lord* is with you.

The Lord *is* with you.

The Lord is *with* you.

The Lord is with *you*.

The Lord is with you all the time. Men, because God is with you all the time, no place is any closer to God than the place where you are right now.

> **Wherever you are, whatever you are doing, God is with you.**

A Call to Act

Why does knowing that matter? What difference does it make? Let's go back to the story of Gideon.

First, the Lord equips Gideon with Himself. But He doesn't stop there; He also gives Gideon a call to action.

The Lord declares Gideon a "mighty man of valor." Other versions read "mighty warrior," "valiant warrior," "mighty hero," or even "mighty man of fearless courage." The Merriam Webster dictionary defines valor as "strength of mind or spirit that enables a person to encounter danger with firmness and bravery."[27] The Hebrew word used in this passage, *khah'-yil*, means strength.[28]

But wait... what is this about? Gideon is a refugee, a war victim, destitute and desperate. He's just beating wheat. He's even hiding while he's doing it. He's not a warrior. He's definitely not a leader of men. Why would the angel of the Lord call this cowardly nobody a "mighty man of valor?"

Because He's calling Gideon to more. By using the words "you mighty man of valor," he is placing a call on Gideon's life. God is giving Gideon a divine sense of something beyond what he has known or been. God is commissioning Gideon. He is saying, "I have a job for you."

Now, don't just glide through these words—there is something very important to notice here. What do we know about Gideon before this statement, before the angel visited him at the wine press? What do we know about who this man is or what he has done?

Nothing.

Look at this: the Lord calls Gideon a mighty man of valor before Gideon does any mighty work, before he accomplishes any significant deed, before he has done anything noteworthy at all.[29]

> **The Lord calls Gideon a mighty man of valor before Gideon does anything noteworthy.**

No Olympic runner is given a medal before he runs across the finish line. No sports team gets the trophy before they score the winning points.

But God does not work like that.

We are told in Matthew 3:17 that when Jesus was baptized, a voice from Heaven said, "This is my Son, whom I love; with Him I am well pleased." Before Jesus had begun His ministry, the Father gave His unconditional blessing. Before Jesus "proved" Himself or publicly accomplished anything, God publicly affirmed Him.

In the same way, the Lord did not first watch Gideon for several years and say, "Aha! I found him! What a great warrior this is. I'll give him a calling so that I can use his talent to deliver Israel from the Midianites." No—Gideon was not a mighty warrior who had already proven himself. He was not a great man that the Lord happened to discover. Gideon was a mighty warrior because the Lord was with him. He was a man of valor because that's what God said he was. That's all!

> **Gideon was a man of valor simply because that's who God said he was.**

Gideon received his life that day. He was given his calling before he picked up a sword or learned how to be a soldier or even knew how to be a man. That day, hidden away on his father's property, Gideon learned and embraced who he was. He began to understand that he was loved, that he wasn't alone, and that he had a mission. When the angel called him, he became a man. When he finally understood and believed that what God said about him was true, that he was already a man of valor, it transformed his life.[30]

This truth can transform your life, too.

No One "Qualifies"

Gideon's past did not qualify him for the call. Gideon did not have to accomplish anything before God called him. The same is true of you.

At the moment of salvation when you receive Jesus into your life, God welcomes you into His family. He gives you a new life, He promises you the presence of His Holy Spirit, and He gives you a calling. He gives you something to do in His kingdom, for His purpose. He even gives you the ability to do it, just like He did for Gideon. If you've accepted Jesus Christ as your Savior, He has equipped you—and He is telling you who you are. You are a mighty man of valor. We are all mighty men of valor!

You might be thinking, "You are not talking about me here! I'm no Gideon! I sin too often; I have failed so many times; I've made mistakes in my marriage, with my children, or in my church."

Well, we're all like that. I've been involved in men's ministry for more than twenty-five years. I've had the privilege of hearing a lot of great teaching from godly men. But I'm just another worker in the United States. I'm just a husband and dad who has made many mistakes. I struggle with sin. I get angry and impatient with co-workers, my wife, my kids, and with God.

But just like Gideon, when I kneeled and gave my heart to the Lord, God told me to rise. He told me to get up out of the winepress—out of the hole I was in, where I was sweating, angry, irritated, alone, and afraid. And He's telling each of you as well:

Get out of the hole you are in: Rise up! Rise and be the mighty man of valor that you are in Christ!

Get out of the hole you are in: Rise!

No One is "Worthy"

If you feel inadequate, if you say, "I'm no man of valor," then welcome to the club. None of us is sufficient by ourselves. We have done nothing to merit God's calling, His favor, or even His salvation. But, you are not an accident. Your life has a purpose and meaning—you are one of God's greatest achievements. A unique man that God created for His purposes. God was at His very best when he created *you.*

Here is the amazing truth: our salvation comes solely from God—as a gift—when we are still in a helpless state. Scripture assures us that "God shows His love for us in that while we were still sinners, Christ died for us." (Romans 5:8 ESV)

In Ephesians 2:8-10, we read:

> "For by grace you have been saved through faith; and that not of yourselves, it is the gift of God; not as a result of works, so that no one may boast. For we are His workmanship, created in Christ Jesus for good works, which God prepared beforehand so that we would walk in them." (ESV)

We do nothing to earn the free gift of salvation. Yet the Lord saved us from our sin. He has something prepared for us to do, and He's even equipped us with the ability to do it. We don't have to be perfect and strong before God calls us—and, in fact, we *can't* be. Our sufficiency, our worth, and our ability come solely from God. In 2nd Corinthians 12:9, God tells us, "My grace is sufficient for you, for *my power is made perfect in weakness."* (ESV)

God has something prepared for you to do, and equipped you with the ability to do it.

Think about it: Gideon wasn't a perfect man before the Lord called him, and he wasn't a perfect man after the Lord called him. He was weak in his faith and unprepared, maybe even incapable, by human standards. But he was still a mighty man of valor.

Why does this matter so much? Because if you had to earn the right to be God's child, if it were true that only the best and the brightest become sons of God, then you would have to fight every day to prove yourself. You would always be anxious, never certain that you were meeting the standard or living up to God's expectations. Every time you failed, you would get so discouraged that you would feel that your worth, your importance, maybe even your usefulness, is gone. Really, you would have no hope. No chance to succeed. After all, you are just not good enough.

But praise God—in His kingdom, you don't have to do *anything* to earn the right to have a valuable place and a gift of service that fits in with His eternal plan for the ages. We are all equally valuable in God's sight! We are *all* mighty men of valor.

Of course we have our faults. Of course we've made mistakes. But no matter where we are today or what we have done, the Lord sees us as who we are in Christ. You don't have to believe just what you see in the mirror anymore. God has given you a new identity; you *are* a man of valor.

God Can Use Anyone

Gideon was less than perfect, but his is not an unusual case: God works with very imperfect people. He has used many men who made mistakes, some of them very big mistakes. He has used men with broken, messed-up pasts.[31] Consider the following examples:

- ✓ Abraham was an old man. He lied more than once, putting his own safety above his calling to protect and cherish his wife. But James says he was God's friend. (James 2:23)
- ✓ Later in his life, David committed adultery and murder, but in Acts 13, he is remembered as a man after God's own heart.
- ✓ Elijah was moody and got depressed, but he regained strength and joy to serve God. (1st Kings 19)
- ✓ Peter had a temper, spoke without thinking, and denied Christ, yet he was called by name to feed Christ's sheep. (Mathew 16, John 21)
- ✓ Saul opposed Christ and persecuted Christians, yet after a dramatic conversion, God used him to establish and strengthen His church. (Acts 8-9)
- ✓ John Mark left Paul and Barnabas when they needed him. He was a quitter—uncommitted and unreliable. But Barnabas took John Mark under his wing, and he became a valuable worker who later wrote one of the gospels. Even Paul later acknowledged his value. (2nd Timothy 4:11)

And there are more: Noah got drunk. Jacob was a liar and a skilled deceiver. Moses was a stuttering, fearful murderer. Samson was a womanizer who couldn't control his lust or his raging anger. Jonah was a proud and stubborn prophet who ran from God. Timothy was timid, and too young. John the Baptist, Thomas, and even His own brothers doubted Jesus at times. And when Jesus told them to watch and pray, the disciples fell asleep. And Gideon was a nobody.

The Lord used these imperfect people in His service to accomplish His purposes. *They weren't already qualified or equipped; He equipped them with His call.* That equipping, that call to action, is what launched Gideon on his journey of valor.

God acts when people make a total commitment, not when their lives are totally perfect.[32] God moves when a man realizes who he is and acts on it. And what God starts in a man, He is faithful to finish: "And I am sure of this, that He who began a good work in you will bring it to completion at the day of Jesus Christ." (Philippians 1:6 ESV)

And He wants to use you.

| **God acts when I make a total commitment—** |
| **not when my life is totally perfect.** |

Do You Know Who You Are?

Men, do you know who you are? How would you answer if someone asked you, "Who are you?" What goes through your mind when you stare in the mirror and wonder, "Who am I?"

You don't have to wonder anymore. God tells you exactly who you are if you have received Jesus Christ as your Savior. According to His Word, you are:

- ✓ Chosen by God (Ephesians 1:4)
- ✓ Totally forgiven (Colossians 2:13)
- ✓ Loved (Colossians 3:12, Romans 1:7, 1st Thessalonians 1:4)
- ✓ Made holy and blameless (Colossians 1:22)
- ✓ At peace with God (Romans 5:1)
- ✓ Freed from condemnation (Romans 8:1)
- ✓ Totally accepted (Romans 15:7)
- ✓ A new creation (2nd Corinthians 5:17)
- ✓ Complete (Colossians 2:9-10)
- ✓ Given all things (2nd Peter 1:3)
- ✓ Righteous (2nd Corinthians 5:21)
- ✓ Qualified (Colossians 1:12)
- ✓ More than a conqueror (Romans 8:37)

> **Who are you?**
> **A mighty man of valor!**

Where the Life of Valor Begins

But I have some bad news. All the truths you've just read don't apply if you have not accepted Jesus Christ as your Lord and Savior.

You have to know the Lord before you can become His man of valor. You have to follow Him before you can be equipped or called by Him, the ultimate man of valor.

> **You have to know the Lord before you can become His man of valor.**

Jesus Christ died and rose again from the dead so that you might live eternally in Heaven with Him. When He died, He took all your sin—everything that you've ever done wrong—on Himself. He could do this because He is perfect and without sin. His sacrifice opens the door not only for you to be saved and forgiven, but for you to find freedom and purpose in Christ.

Titus 3:3-6 says,

> "For we ourselves were once foolish, disobedient, led astray, slaves to various passions and pleasures, passing our days in malice and envy, hated by others and hating one another. But when the goodness and loving kindness of God our Savior appeared, He saved us, not because of works done by us in righteousness, but according to His own mercy, by the washing of regeneration and renewal of the Holy Spirit, whom He poured out on us richly through Jesus Christ our Savior, so that being justified by His grace we might become heirs according to the hope of eternal life." (ESV)

Brother, give your life to Him. He's calling you, and He has a mission for you. This is where your life of valor begins.

Romans 10:13 says that everyone who calls on the name of the Lord will be saved. That includes you. Will you commit your life to Him and step into His purpose for you? Will you become the man of valor He intends you to be? Take a few minutes and talk to God. Right now.

Beyond the Mirror

Even if you've already made that commitment, you may need a fresh start. Maybe you've known the Lord for some time but have become discouraged. Maybe you are struggling in your marriage, with your family, or at work. Maybe you are a pastor or church leader and your ministry has worn you down and you feel that you are not making an impact.

All of us must come to the place where we stop focusing on who we think we are, what we think we can do, and on all those things that are holding us back and causing us to stumble. We need to fill our minds not with what we see or feel, but with what God sees. So look in the mirror and ask yourself this question: What does God see when he looks at me?

> **Fill your mind not with what men see and feel, but with what God sees.**

God looks at you and at me and sees His new creations. We are His men of valor.

Do you now know who you are?

Do you believe who you are?

We have to trust not what we see, but what we are: that God can and will do mighty things through us. Why? Because He is with us. Because He has more for us. Because, by His grace alone, *we are men of valor*.

The Lord is with you, mighty man of valor!

+ + +

Knowing who you are in Christ is the starting place. He is in you. You have Christ's name, His character, His strength, His power. He has given you dominion, He speaks to you, and He works in and through you... to become a real man. A man of valor!

Next, let's read about the power behind our position.

Make it Practical

1. Why was Gideon called a mighty man of valor?

2. How do you see yourself? What is your identity built on?

3. What hinders you from believing that you are a man of valor? What can you do about it?

4. Does it change your outlook to understand that even now, right where you are, God is with you? How could this truth change the way you live your daily life? How would it affect your interactions with your family, your co-workers, your fellow churchgoers, and other members of your community? How would it affect your work habits? How would it affect the way you spend your time?

5. Reflect on this statement: "God acts when people make a total commitment, not when their life is totally perfect." Are you withholding yourself from God? Are you waiting until you "get your life together" in order to offer yourself fully to be used by God? Or are you ready to fully commit your imperfect life to God, trusting that He can, will, and wants to use you to accomplish mighty deeds?

6. Have you chosen to follow Jesus Christ? To pursue His mission for you and for His Kingdom? If not, do it now. Talk to Him ... just like you are talking to a good friend.

Notes & References

[27] https://www.merriam-webster.com/dictionary/valor

[28] *The Strongest Strong's Exhaustive Concordance of the Bible* (Zondervan 2001)

[29] "Gideon, in human reasoning, was not a likely candidate for the job of delivering Israel. ... His station in life was not impressive ... he was only an obscure farmer busy hiding things from the Midianites. There was nothing in Gideon's life to indicate to the natural eye that he was a "mighty man of valor" [and] at that time Gideon had not demonstrated any discernible valor."
John Butler, *Gideon: The Mighty Man of Valor* (Scripture Truth, 1992), 28

[30] There is much, much more to Gideon's story. One of the best resources that we have found for further study is *Gideon: The Mighty Man of Valor* from John Butler's "Bible Biography" series.

[31] "...one important reason God often calls those into His service who, like Gideon, appear deficient is that He, not the servant, will get credit for the work. Because of his lowliness, people would see that it was not Gideon but it was God who worked though Gideon. That is exactly what God wants. The focus needs to be on God and His glory, not on man's greatness." *Ibid.*, 29
See also: 1st Corinthians 1:27-29

[32] "God calls a lot of folk into service who may not at the time of the initial call evidence much promise that they will be God's gallant servants. But it is not the man in himself that makes a gallant worker for God; it is what God can make that man which is the key to service. Let any person simply submit to God's plan and purpose for their life, as Gideon... did, and God will make them what they need to be in order to do His work." *Ibid.*, 28

Chapter 2

Bruce Campbell

What is a Real Man?

"I am crucified with Christ: nevertheless I live; yet not I, but Christ lives in me..."

Galatians 2:20 (AKJV)

Mighty men of valor, the Lord is with you! We have highlighted our amazing calling from the Lord Jesus Christ. The Lord is with us and calls us mighty men of valor before we have done or accomplished anything. Being mighty men of valor has nothing to do with our performance but with who He is: God of all, maker of heaven and earth, all wise, all powerful, the only Savior, the Lord Jesus Christ.

The Men of Valor ministry focuses on the importance of being real men—men of valor—and reaching out to men with the saving Gospel of Jesus Christ.

What Is A Real Man?

We have this title "Mighty Man of Valor" that goes with our position as sons of God. When we know who we are it becomes clearer how we are to act. But before we talk about actions let us consider the core of what a real man is.

> **When we know who we are,**
> **it becomes clear how we are to act.**

In cultures around the world, a real man is defined in terms of what he does, his duties, and his performance. He is defined by abilities, accomplishments or in what class he was born into. Some might say real men don't change babies' diapers, they don't cry, they rarely apologize. They are supposed to be athletic and macho, telling others what to do. They can out-drink women. They are aggressive; they are fighters. In order to be considered a real man in a gang, one might have to commit crimes or actually kill someone from a rival gang. To join a fraternity or a secret organization, a "real man" may have to do certain silly, embarrassing, disgusting, lewd, or abased things; or succeed at a dangerous, possibly life-threatening requirement. Why? Because that's what a real man does!

Even the world's religions define a "real man" by a list of do's and don'ts. They might have to pray a certain number of times each day in designated places, repeating memorized lines. They might have to perform certain sacrifices in order to be accepted. Maybe they are never to smoke or eat certain foods. Maybe they can't associate with those outside their religion or even worse, taught to kill an infidel.

But in contrast to how cultures and religions define a "real man"– performing and craving significance, pursuing independence and self-sufficiency, or executing stupid, unlawful, or perilous acts—there is how God views a "Real Man".

How God Views a "Real Man"

"And God said, let us make man in our image, after our likeness..." (Genesis 1:26 KJV) The word *image* does not mean exact duplicate. It means resemblance. The first man, Adam, was created with the essential nature of God. He was equipped by God that as a real man he would reveal the very glory of God: the man's glory was completely dependent upon the presence of the Creator within the creature.

When God created Adam, he lived in unconditional love. Adam didn't do anything to earn or deserve God's love. God's love was constantly present because God is love. Adam didn't know what un-love was. He didn't know evil, rejection, or failure. He wasn't trying to prove anything to God. His fellowship with God was constant. He knew he was loved and significant because he was made in God's image and loved by Him. There was nothing he could do to be more significant or more secure.

He had available to him all the limitless resources of God for accomplishing the purposes of being fruitful and having dominion over the earth. Adam's authority to exercise dominion came exclusively from his submission to God's authority.

Adam was equipped by God to reveal the very glory of God as a real man.

Ian Thomas wrote, "God always intended that He should indwell us: so we might be a physical, visible expression on this earth of the God who is invisible."[33] God alone is righteous, and in order for us to evidence righteousness, God himself within us must produce it.

The "Natural" Man is Not a Real Man

The "natural" man, or who we are in the flesh, does not have righteousness or any true spirituality. 1st Corinthians 2:14 states, "The natural person does not accept the things of the Spirit of God.... he is not able to understand them because they are spiritually discerned." (ESV)

Ian Thomas explains: "The natural man is not normal. He is not what God created and intended man to be. In his fallen condition he is destitute and alienated from his Creator."[34]

We all know well that the soul of man, un-enlightened by the Holy Spirit, will rationalize until even wrong may seem right and right wrong. Therefore he is not a "real man." He might be moral, good, even a heroic man. Admirable acts or right behavior can be performed by any man. But man's "righteous" deeds do not earn the favor and blessing of God. Man's best intentions will never produce God's fruit. God intended men to be His men and only in that relationship, empowered by the Holy Spirit, is any man a real man by God's definition.

> An oil lamp needs oil to produce light. Why? Because the lamp was made to function in that way. A car needs gasoline to go. Why? Because the car was made to function in that way. Why does a man need God in order to be functional? Because we were made in that way.
>
> Man cannot produce righteousness on his own, any more than a car can go without gas or an oil lamp can shine without oil. Trying to light an oil lamp with no oil is foolish and useless. You will remain in the dark. Trying to drive a car without gas is likewise futile. You will end up getting out and pushing it only as far as your physical strength allows, bringing you to exhaustion.
>
> The same is true with men. Simply urging them to be good; telling them to draw upon their personalities; trying to legislate their actions with rules, regulations, and religion; and threatening them with punishment or prison can never succeed in producing righteousness.[35]

Life in Jesus Christ is not conformity to external rules of behavior that are imposed upon you from without; it is the reintroduction by the Holy Spirit of a Holy God from *within*. The problem is not that Christians don't have the Holy Spirit—all do, from the moment of new birth. The problem is that many do not let the Holy Spirit have *them—* we don't allow the Holy Spirit to work in and through us.

> **Why does a man need God to function?**
> **Because we were made that way.**

It Takes God to Be a Real Man

To get light from an oil lamp, fill it first with oil. To get a car to provide you with transportation, fill the tank with gas. To get man to be what he was made to be, he must be filled with God. Oil in the lamp, gas in the car, and Christ in the man.

It takes God to be a real man, and it takes Jesus Christ to put God back into a man. Jesus rose again and ascended in order to send God the Holy Spirit into us. "Don't you know that your body is the temple of the Holy Spirit, who lives in you and who was given to you by God?" (1st Corinthians 6:19 GNT)

This is called the new birth, being born again as our soul is awakened by God's spirit. Consequently, those who are born again by the grace of God are real men. They are men of valor. Scripture says that all other men, though living, are spiritually dead in trespasses and sins. (Ephesians 2)

> **Men who are born again by the grace of God are real men.**
> **They are men of valor.**

So then, as real men, we have Christ's life within us so "He can teach our minds, control our emotions, and direct our wills, governing our behavior as we let God be God."[36]

It's Like Instinct

If you take a stick and poke a wasp nest, you will discover that wasps have a highly developed emotional capacity to get very angry. You will also see they have a highly developed capacity to determine exactly who is poking the nest. And you will find they have a will to seek vengeance on their enemy.

Animals are like men in that they have the capacity to think, react, and decide. But, God did not create animals to be inhabited by their creator as man was. God built a unique mechanism into animals called instinct. That is the means by which they are protected and their behavior governed. Because of instinct, the behavior patterns are repetitive and predictable, but there is no moral relationship between them and God as there is between us and God. They do what they do because they must. There is a law within them that compels their mind, emotions and directs their will.[37]

> **Instinct is indispensable to animals;**
> **the Holy Spirit is indispensable to men.**

We are uniquely made to be governed by God himself living within us so he can teach our mind, control our emotions, and direct our will.

Utter Dependence

God has created us to be real men as we live in utter dependence upon Him. The only evidence of this dependence on Him is our obedience to Him. What allows God to be God in a man is our love for Him, dependence upon Him, and obedience to Him.

This is exactly what Jesus Christ expressed before God the Father. His love for the Father resulted in his total dependence upon the Father and total obedience to the Father. That is why in John 5 he says that without the Father he could do nothing.

For men to be "real men," the same relationship that existed between Jesus Christ and God the Father must also be the relationship we pursue between ourselves and the LORD Jesus. Jesus said, "...apart from me you can do nothing." (John 15:5 ESV)—meaning nothing of lasting worth or eternal benefit.[38]

The Great Exchange

"Son of Man" was the Lord's most common designation of Himself. Although it's a prophetic title referring to the Messiah (Daniel 7:13), Christ used it repeatedly as a sign of His identification with humanity. Jesus took the title "Son of Man" to Himself as affirmation that, in human form, He was representative of all mankind; He is the example of how Adam originally lived, how a real man is supposed to live: gentle and humble, completely dependent on God the Father.

A man of valor understands that being a true man is to engage in the ongoing process of exchanging his old way of handling life (what the Scripture refers to as the flesh), for God's life.

The essential ingredient of the life we live is to be Jesus Christ, Himself. Not our personality, our willpower, our gifts, our talent, our money, our education, our dedication, our sacrifice, or our anything.

Paul said in Philippians 1:21, "For to me to live is Christ." (ESV) In Galatians 2:20, Paul stated, "I am crucified with Christ: nevertheless I live; yet not I, but Christ lives in me: and the life which I now live in the flesh I live by the faith of the Son of God, who loved me, and gave himself for me." (AKJV)

'Well, It Isn't *Just* Me'

"I live, yet not I, but Christ lives in me." Everything that was unique to Paul, his upbringing, training, personality, gifts, etc., make up the "I" part of this verse. But, he immediately follows that with "well, it isn't *just* me, but Christ living in me." He is saying that after he was born again, he became a real man, available to the Lord, since the Holy Spirit of Jesus Christ lives inside him and is united to his life.

Not all Him;

Not all me;

But Him *in* me, working in me to will and do His good pleasure.

Paul knew that Christ was living through Him. He was now living as a real man in spite of the persecutions, hardships, and poverty that is part of his experience. He was a mighty man of valor, and so are you. The same Christ that was strong in Paul is strong in you.

> **The same Christ that was strong in Paul is strong in you.**

Be Careful

The sad thing is that a man of valor might be too impressed with himself and his own ability. Even though he says that Christ is in him, he might not understand the personal relevance of the indwelling presence of Christ. He might think that sounds "too religious" or "too mystical" and would rather pride himself on being a practical man of action. Thus, like Esau, he might despise his birthright (Genesis 25) and reject his dependence on Christ.

Perhaps you're asking, "How do I make this real to me?" You want Christ to live his life through you, but you just don't feel it happens much. The answer is both challenging and simple: consistently present your body as a living sacrifice to God, offer Him praise and thanksgiving, and focus your mind on who you are in Christ. Then the transformation will take place. (Romans 12:1-2, Hebrews 13:15)

So, remember your position, mighty man of valor, since all the practices, priorities, and actions discussed in this book flow from this reality. "God can do anything through a man who will admit that he needs everything from God."[39] "The Lord is the strength of our life." (Psalm 27:1 KJV)

The Lord is with you, mighty man of valor!

> **God can do anything
> through a man who admits
> that he needs everything from God.**

+ + +

A fundamental aspect of being a real man, of being a man of valor, is leading as He did. In our next chapter, we'll learn what that looks like.

Make it Practical

1. How does the title "man of valor" help you to know how to act?

2. What did a "real man" look like in your elementary and high school years? What does it look like today among your co-workers, neighbors, and friends?

3. "God always intended that He should indwell us. This is so we might be a physical, visible expression on this earth of the God who is invisible." What is your reaction to these sentences? What are the consequences of this?

4. How does Bruce define "life in Jesus"? What is required for a man to know this "life"?

5. How does Bruce define a "real man"?

6. What is the ultimate intent of our existence? How do we strive toward it and maintain it?

Notes & References

[33] W. Ian Thomas, *The Indwelling Life of Christ* (Multnomah 2006) 17
[34] *Ibid.,* 18
[35] *Ibid.,* 20-21
[36] *Ibid.,* 22
[37] Bruce credits Ian Thomas for this concept
[38] *Ibid.*
[39] *Ibid.*

Chapter 3

Bill Wilcox

A Man of Valor
is a Servant Leader

"The good shepherd lays down his life for the sheep."
John 10:11 (RSV)

A mighty man of valor is only that because God says he is, not because he accomplished anything. He understands that his highest calling as a real man can only be fulfilled as he allows God's Spirit to indwell and control him. Jesus wanted the men who followed Him to be leaders—but not like the leaders around them who sought power, status, and material wealth for themselves. Jesus wanted his leaders to lead by serving others. And He led by example.

> **Jesus wants his leaders to lead by serving others.**

Look what He did in John chapter 13:

> Jesus... laid aside his outer garments, and taking a towel, tied it around his waist. Then he poured water into a basin and began to wash the disciples' feet and to wipe them with the towel that was wrapped around him. He came to Simon Peter, who said to him, "Lord, do you wash my feet?" Jesus answered him, "What I am doing you do not understand now, but afterward you will understand." Peter said to him, "You shall never wash my feet." Jesus answered him, "If I do not wash you, you have no share with me." When he had washed their feet and put on his outer garments and resumed his place, he said to them, "Do you understand what I have done to you? You call me Teacher and Lord, and you are right, for

so I am. If I then, your Lord and Teacher, have washed
your feet, you also ought to wash one another's feet. For
I have given you an example, that you also should do just
as I have done to you. Truly, truly, I say to you, a servant
is not greater than his master, nor is a messenger greater
than the one who sent him."
(John 13:3-8, 12-16 ESV)

Full-Time Server

Serving others can be very difficult. Using your energy and
resources to help other people can be exhausting. Yet the most effective
leaders are servants, and no one demonstrated servant leadership
better than Jesus. Alone with His disciples on the night before He was
crucified, Jesus did the unthinkable: with no one available to wash
their feet, Jesus became the foot washer. The Master became the
servant. The greatest and most high became the least and the lowest.

Jesus could do this because He was secure in His Father in Heaven.
He knew who He was and where He was going. But Jesus also served
His disciples because He loved them.

The Lord had another reason, too, for washing the disciples' feet.
When He had finished, He explained to His disciples that He had set
an example for them and they should do for others as he had done for
them.

Note that the Lord did not tell them to do *what* He had done. He
commanded them to do *as* He had done. The disciples were not told to
become full-time foot washers; they were to become full-time servers
of men and women.

If we are followers of Jesus, if we desire to be excellent disciples of
Jesus, then we must commit every day to do "as" Jesus did and use all
of our energy in service to others.[40]

Men of valor are full-time servants.

Not a Warrior Leader

Around 700 years before Christ was born, the Lord spoke through
the prophet Isaiah about Christ as a suffering servant. (Isaiah 52-53)

The Jews were looking for a powerful Messiah. They were wanting
and expecting a warrior leader who would deliver them from the
bondage of Rome, and they overlooked the prophecies of the suffering
servant—the suffering servant who would deliver them from the
greater bondage of sin and guilt.

This is the reason that Jesus, after His resurrection, rebuked two of His disciples on the road to Emmaus. Luke 24:25- 26 says, "And he said to them, 'O foolish ones, and slow of heart to believe all that the prophets have spoken! Was it not necessary that the Christ should suffer these things and enter into his glory?' " (ESV)

As the Suffering Servant who was prophesied by Isaiah, Jesus clearly communicated His purpose for coming to this earth. Mark 10:45 says, "For even the Son of Man did not come to be served, but to serve, and to give His life a ransom for many." (NASB)

In His sacrifice on the cross, Jesus gives us the ultimate example of servant leadership. Should we not take up the infirmities of others? And carry others' sorrows? A man of valor is willing to be a suffering servant.

Servant leadership in the biblical context means carrying out Christ's mission of making disciples as we serve others, helping them in their weaknesses, lifting them up in their grief, and putting their well-being ahead of our own comforts. We must start in our homes with our wives and children and then in the workplace, at church, and in our communities.

Men of valor make disciples through serving others.

All Service is to God

[Jesus] asked them, "What were you discussing on the way?" But they kept silent, for on the way they had argued with one another about who was the greatest. And he sat down and called the twelve. And he said to them, "If anyone would be first, he must be last of all and servant of all." And he took a child and put him in the midst of them, and taking him in his arms, he said to them, "Whoever receives one such child in my name receives me, and whoever receives me, receives not me but him who sent me." (Mark 9:33-37 ESV)

The service we render to others is really a measure of the service we render to God. The disciples argued over who is the greatest among them. Jesus must have been greatly dismayed at their selfishness. As they fought for the highest position in the coming kingdom, Jesus strove to turn their thinking upside down. The way of God's children must be different than the way of this world.

Earthly rulers seek power, control, and material wealth. But men of valor must be the very least and the servant of all.

In Matthew 10:39 we read, "Whoever finds his life will lose it, and whoever loses his life for my sake will find it." (ESV) This verse is not just about martyrdom; we can "lose" our life every day by giving it away in service to others. As we give our lives away—as we lose our lives—we find our lives as Jesus lives His life through us.

Men of valor find life in Christ by giving up their own.

Service is the Path to Legitimate Leadership

> Jesus said to them, "You know that those who are recognized as rulers of the Gentiles lord it over them; and their great men exercise authority over them. But it is not this way among you, but whomever wishes to become great among you shall be your servant; and whoever wishes to be first among you shall be slave of all. For even the Son of Man did not come to be served, but to serve, and to give His life a ransom for many." (Mark 10:42-45 NASB)

In his 1970 essay, "The Servant as Leader," Robert Greenleaf made a wise observation about how an attitude of servant leadership begins and what kind of results it can produce:

> The servant leader is a servant first. It begins with the natural feeling that one wants to serve, to serve first. Then conscious choice brings one to aspire to lead. This person is sharply different from one who is leader first. For such it will be a later choice to serve—after leadership is established. The leader-first and the servant-first are two extreme types. [41]

So how do we know whether a leader is genuinely serving? I really like Mr. Greenleaf's answer to this question. He said,

> The best test and the most difficult to administer is: Do those served grow as persons? Do they, while being served, become healthier, wiser, freer, more autonomous, and more likely themselves to become servants? [42]

Let's look at Jesus in this light. Jesus didn't merely talk servant leadership: He lived it. And His inner circle of disciples became better people in every conceivable way after He had met them than they ever were before He met them. Look at these examples:

✓ **They preached boldly.** The disciples all fled in fear as Jesus was arrested the night prior to his crucifixion. Yet following His resurrection and ascension into heaven, we see them acting in ways far different. Peter and John (Acts 4) were arrested for preaching about Jesus and the resurrection from the dead. When threatened by the Sanhedrin to stop preaching, they said, "Whether it is right in the sight of God to listen to you rather than to God, you must judge, for we cannot but speak of what we have seen and heard." (Acts 4:19-20 ESV)

✓ **They suffered happily.** In Acts 5, Peter and the apostles were arrested for preaching the good news and for healing. They were miraculously released from prison and went to the temple to preach. Again they were arrested, beaten, told not to speak in the name of Jesus, and then freed. They rejoiced "that they were counted worthy to suffer shame for His name." (Acts 5:41 NKJV) Additionally, James and John had sought to be seated at the right and left hand of Christ when He came into glory. Later they rejoiced that they could suffer shame for His name, demonstrating the humility they had learned from Christ.

✓ **They died for others.** Ultimately, according to historical records, all of the apostles except John (who apparently died an old man as he cared for Mary),[43] willingly suffered martyrs' deaths. These same apostles who had fled at Christ's arrest, and especially Peter who had denied Christ three times, now demonstrated immense faith and courage as they faced martyrdom and illustrated how their time with Jesus had made them far better men and disciples.

Jesus showed that His mindset was unquestionably "servant-first." And He refocused His disciples' thinking to align more closely with the servant-first model.

Men of valor let Jesus change and use them.

The World's Leadership

Look again at how Jesus described worldly leadership in Mark 10:42: "You know that those who are considered rulers of the Gentiles lord it over them, and their great ones exercise authority over them." (ESV)

Worldly leaders display their character in a variety of ways, from verbally abusing or humiliating their family or subordinates and sometimes even physically beating them, to more subtle mistreatment like maintaining "lordly" attitudes.

I served as an officer in the US Navy for 27 years. During that time, I worked for one Admiral in the Pentagon who mocked me because I'd made coffee for the people who worked for me. He said to me, "You shouldn't be making coffee!" He believed that military officers should have everything done for them.

We can become prideful in subtle ways as well. After I had worked at the Pentagon for a few months, I began to notice that virtually none of the senior officers ever spoke to, or even acknowledged, the cleaning staff. It was as though they were invisible. The Lord convicted me about this, so I made it a point to greet the cleaning crew and treat them with respect and concern.

Men of valor must not pride themselves on their position or expect that they deserve others' service.

God Ordains and Bestows Leadership

In another instance of when the disciples were vying for power, Jesus reminds them "just as My Father has granted Me a kingdom, I grant you that you may eat and drink at My table in My kingdom, and you will sit on thrones judging the twelve tribes of Israel." (Luke 22:28-30 NASB)

Here Jesus' instructions clarify His role in the power structure. His words were intended to remind the disciples of a perspective they had apparently forgotten: Jesus was the One who would grant them a kingdom. Jesus held that power because the Father had bestowed it to Him.

Man of valor, remember who really holds the power. It is God who ordains and bestows leadership, and the most successful leaders live God's kingdom values and act as servants to those who follow. Here are two examples:

1. Timothy the Servant Leader

> I hope in the Lord Jesus to send Timothy to you soon. ...For I have no one like him, who will be genuinely concerned for your welfare. ...you know Timothy's proven worth, how as a son with a father he has served with me in the gospel. (Philippians 2:19-24 ESV)

Timothy embodied three principles of servant leadership:

✓ **Timothy knew what he wanted to produce.** Timothy had genuine interest in the welfare of others; therefore, his leadership would result in care for them. By contrast, a worldly leader expects privilege or prestige—he expects to be served.

> **A man of valor takes genuine interest in the welfare of others.**

✓ **Timothy knew Whom he served.** When you are serving God, you will be accountable both to others and to God. Timothy served Paul by serving those whom Paul had commissioned him to lead. Worldly leaders lose sight of their accountability and thereby fail to lead. For the servant leader, loyalty to both his leader and his followers are absolutely essential. If a leader is disloyal to his leader and speaks poorly of his leader in front of his followers, he will find that before long his followers will become disloyal to him. Without loyalty up and down the leadership structure, any organization and any leader will fail!

✓ **Timothy focused on serving, not on gaining power.** True servant leaders are rare. Paul knew of no one else like Timothy. Jesus taught that the greater the service, the greater the leader. If you want to be truly unique and truly valuable, be a leader like Timothy who served Paul and the church first by helping his followers to succeed in being mature disciples of Christ.

2. Barnabas the Servant Leader

> Joseph, who was also called by the apostles Barnabas (which means son of encouragement), a Levite, a native of Cyprus, sold a field that belonged to him and brought the money and laid it at the apostles' feet. (ESV)

✓ **Barnabas gave.** In Acts 4:36-37 we discover why:
A leader will either be a giver or a taker. A leader who is a taker takes from others as many benefits and privileges as possible. The taker sees others as existing to provide him a title, a job, status, and service. A giver, by contrast, seeks to evaluate what he can put into others and what he can contribute. The giver's passion is to meet its people's needs. Barnabas was a giver. He believed that he existed for the good of the church and the glory of His Lord rather than that the church existed to serve him. Barnabas gave encouragement. Man of valor, give encouragement to your wife, your family, your church leaders, your fellow men in Christ, and your co-workers.

✓ **Barnabas mentored.** Mentoring is an essential leadership function. Men who are discerning enough to spot young and older men with potential and who are confident enough to assist them with visibility and exposure are fulfilling a key leadership role. Barnabas was one of those leaders. Barnabas sponsored Paul at a time when everyone distrusted and rejected him. Paul had tried to destroy the church, but after his miraculous conversion, Christians refused to believe that he had genuinely become a follower of Christ. Paul was only introduced to the church because, as we learn in Acts 9:27, Barnabas took him in and brought him to the apostles. Later Barnabas moved to Antioch. As a result of his contagious witness, many people came to believe. When the work became too much for one man, Barnabas brought Paul to Antioch, and together they grew the church. Barnabas was never upset that Paul grew greater in reputation. In Acts 13:2, we learn that Paul and Barnabas were chosen for a mission trip that turned out to be quite difficult but very successful. During this trip, John Mark, a younger member of the team, deserted the effort and went home. When Paul and Barnabas organized a second journey, John Mark wanted to rejoin the team, but Paul refused to take Mark with them. Barnabas had a decision to make: should he go with the highly effective, rising young star that he had launched (Paul)? Or should he help another young man that others had written off (John Mark)? For Barnabas, the choice was simple. His character was marked by a refusal to abandon good people who needed sponsorship, encouragement, and development. Acts 15:39 tells us that Barnabas took Mark and sailed for Cyprus...and into obscurity...while Paul became famous.

> **A man of valor does not abandon good people who need mentoring and encouragement.**

Did Barnabas pick another champion in Mark? Did his mentoring and investment in Mark pay off? Peter thought so, referring to Mark later on as "my son Mark" in 1st Peter 5:1. Amazingly, so did Paul. Near the end of his life, Paul requested that Mark come to him in Rome. In 2nd Timothy 4:11, we read that Paul asked Timothy to get Mark and bring him along, for he was useful to Paul for ministry. Mark even wrote one of the gospels! Barnabas didn't pick someone who was already a champion; he helped turn a young man who had walked away from a commitment into a champion. A great mentor doesn't win by starting with winners—a great mentor sometimes turns losers into winners. God always needs leaders with the vision and commitment to do that.

In my Navy career, I had no greater joy than seeing men that I had helped to train take command of Navy units. And, as a Christian, I find great joy in seeing men that I have mentored starting to minister in the lives of other men. Mentoring is a critical element of being a servant leader.

> **Great mentors don't succeed by starting with winners.**
> **Great mentors turn losers into winners.**

Men of valor remember Whom they serve. They do as Christ and His apostles did: they encourage others, sincerely care for them, and build them up through mentoring.

Only Two Things Matter

My former pastor used to say, "There are only two things on this earth that last into eternity: people and the Word of God." This relates very closely to servant leadership. Invest your life in people and the Word of God, and you will lay up treasure in Heaven.

The only reason Jesus came to earth was to serve God the Father and, through His death and resurrection, to serve humanity. Likewise, a man of valor serves God and serves humanity.

The Lord is with you, mighty man of valor!

+ + +

A man of valor represents God—in his behavior and his words. It is a distinguished position, a privileged position, a role of honor. Wherever we are and whomever we are with. We'll see in the next chapter that a man of valor is not a representative of himself; he is an ambassador of a ruling authority.

Make it Practical

1. It wasn't the action of washing feet that Jesus was asking His disciples to do. It was an attitude, a mindset of serving others. What examples of servant leadership have you seen?

2. Sometimes we describe someone as having the "gift of service." But like evangelizing, Jesus commands that all of His followers should serve others. In Jesus' teaching, serving is not so much a specific, planned event as it is a lifestyle. Where and how do you serve others today? Is it a lifestyle for you?

3. "Making disciples" to many Christians usually brings the image of speaking or teaching doctrine and the core elements of the faith. Jesus spoke *and* served. Bill wrote "A man of valor makes disciples through serving others." Is that a surprise to you? Can you envision how this could be successful?

4. Service may look like bold preaching or caring for someone with a contagious disease. Or, it may be as simple as acknowledging and thanking the trash collectors for their work. How do you serve your wife and children? Your neighbors? How do you serve those who report to you? How do you serve your team members?

5. Do you regularly do what you expect others to do? In your home? At work? In your neighborhood? At church?

Notes & References

---

[40] "The foremost call in leadership is love. Christian leadership is not first charting vision or giving orders, but modeling and expressing godly character. Christian leadership is not concerned first with the leader but with the one being led." Challies, "Accept Your Leadership",
https://www.challies.com/articles/lead

[41] Robert K. Greenleaf, *The Servant as Leader* (The Greenleaf Center for Servant Leadership 2015)

[42] Ibid.

[43] According to *Foxe's Book of Martyrs* (1563)

Chapter 4

Bruce Campbell

A Man of Valor
is an Ambassador

"For the sake of this gospel I am an ambassador..."
Ephesians 6:20 (GNT)

W e have been considering our position because we belong to Jesus Christ. We are mighty men of valor before we have done or accomplished anything. In order to function as those who were created in the image of God—as real men, as servant leaders—we must be born again, having the life of Jesus Christ by His Holy Spirit living inside of us.

Men of valor are also ambassadors of Jesus Christ: "He died for all, that those who live might no longer live for themselves but for him who for their sake died and was raised." (2nd Corinthians 5:15 ESV)

"Therefore, if anyone is in Christ, he is a new creation. The old has passed away; behold, the new has come. All this is from God, who through Christ reconciled us to himself and gave us the ministry of reconciliation; that is, in Christ God was reconciling the world to himself, not counting their trespasses against them, and entrusting to us the message of reconciliation. Therefore, we are ambassadors for Christ, God making his appeal through us. We implore you on behalf of Christ, be reconciled to God." (2nd Corinthians 5:17-20 ESV)

Paul explains in this passage believers' fundamental role in the furtherance of His kingdom. Not because we are "qualified" to be ambassadors. It is just who we are. As with being servant leaders or exhibiting the fruit of the Spirit (Galatians 5:22-23), we are *malachis*,

God's messengers. And like the prophet Malachi in the Old Testament, the Lord is with us!

We are going to address our position by considering:

1. The Meaning of an Ambassador
2. The Mission of an Ambassador
3. The Message of an Ambassador

1. The Meaning of an Ambassador

In the Old Testament, the Hebrew word *mal'ak* means "messenger" or "agent."[44] The nations on various occasions and for various purposes used ambassadors to make alliances, (Joshua 9:4) to ask for favors, (Numbers 20:14) to set things right when wrong had been done. (Judges 11:12) Additionally, to do injury to an ambassador was to insult the king who sent him. (2nd Samuel 10:5)

Today, ambassador is more commonly used and understood to be a person of high rank employed by a government to represent it and transact its business at the seat of power of another government.

A Personal Representative. At the time Paul wrote his letter, each Roman province was governed either by the Roman Senate or the Roman Caesar. When a province was peaceful, it was ruled by the Senate. But when a province was filled with conflicts and confrontations, factions and frictions, then the unruly province was governed by a personal representative of the Caesar, who was called an "ambassador." Ambassadors were the representatives of the Caesar to work with provinces where significant conflict existed.

Corinth was a city in Greece under Roman rule. A portion of Paul's letters to the Corinthians deals with conflicts in the congregation. There were factions, conflicts, and confrontations. There were conflicts about worship; whether or not women should wear veils; whether food sacrificed to pagan idols could be eaten; etc. There were also conflicts about whether or not a particular sexual sinner should be disbarred from worship, and even whether Paul was a true apostle or not.

So in the midst of all this conflict and confrontation in the church at Corinth, the Apostle Paul called for new people who were reconciled with God and thus able to reconcile with each other. They were called to be ambassadors of peace and reconciliation amidst the conflicts around them—something they would clearly understand in their cultural environment.

A New, Distinguished Position. When a person is in Christ Jesus, he becomes a new person. The old qualities in him pass away.

He becomes controlled by the love of Christ. In fact, that person becomes the goodness of God in human form. In becoming a "new creation in Christ," there are three "no longers" for men of valor:

1. No longer do we live for ourselves.

2. No longer do we regard other people from a human point of view. We reject thinking like this:

> *When they are popular, or rich, or have something I want—I will be their friend.*
> *When they are sick, or needy, or strangers, or their skin is a different color than mine—I will avoid them.*

3. No longer do we put the sins of others to their account. We don't keep a running list of others' sins; we do not take pleasure in rehearsing others' sins—for the sake of gossip or to make us feel better about ourselves.

We are now ambassadors of Jesus Christ, which means we occupy a very distinguished position.

A Privileged Position. The world is full of ambassadors. Most governments on earth send ambassadors into other foreign lands for representation. When you are in an embassy, everyone is informed that when the ambassador comes into the room, all are to stand and stand formally at attention in order to honor the position of the ambassador. Now, prior to the ambassador's arrival there are several other people coming and going from that room, and you don't bother to stand for any of them. But when the ambassador comes in, everyone stands up at attention. It doesn't matter whether you agree with the views of that country's policies or not. You are to stand and stand formally, because this is an ambassador. This is a representative of a government and that government's leaders. This is an important person, and you are commanded to formally stand before him or her.

Being ambassadors for Jesus is a great privilege. As mighty men of valor, it is the highest honor to be chosen to be ambassadors and represent the greatest and only God there is. God has made all the magnificent beauty of things in heaven and on earth, and it is incomprehensible that we are an ambassador of this Creator. It is the most humbling honor to represent the God who died for us on the cross. Therefore, we are not ashamed of His gospel, because it is His power for people to be saved.

Please remember we are not ambassadors of ourselves, of other Christians, of the Church we attend, or of organizations; we represent God. There might be times when we are ashamed of ourselves or of something a church or other Christians have done. But as an ambassador of Jesus Christ, we need never apologize for His life or His words. We serve in a privileged role.

Men of valor are not ambassadors of ourselves, other Christians, or the Church we attend.

We represent God.

---

2. The Mission of an Ambassador

The mission of a country's ambassador is to be a personal representative of the government; a man of valor is the personal representative of Jesus Christ.

✓ *An ambassador is not elected, but appointed.* We are appointed (called) by Christ. (2nd Corinthians 5:18-20) Everything we do and say reflects on the one who sent us. We are representatives of the King of Kings. Ambassadors don't speak in their own name but on behalf of the ruler who appointed them, whose messenger they are. In the same way, we don't speak in our own name but in the name of the one who bled and died for us. Remember Peter's statement recorded in Acts 3 when speaking to the lame man who lay at the gate of the temple? "Silver and gold I do not have, but what I do have I give you: In the name of Jesus Christ of Nazareth, rise up and walk." (Acts 3:6 NKJV)

Each of us is the personal representative of Jesus Christ.

Everything we do and say

reflects on the One who sent us.

✓ *An ambassador only acts or speaks as he has been authorized.* He speaks wholly for his king, or his government. He is the mouthpiece of his sovereign. He never utters his own thoughts; he never makes private personal offers. He doesn't give personal promises; he doesn't make personal demands; he doesn't accept personal gifts or bribes to change his message. He represents his sovereign. It is not our own dignity that lends weight to our ambassadorship; it is the dignity of the One we represent. The ambassador simply says what he has been commissioned to say. Even so, as we are ambassadors of Christ, God entreats through us. We speak only that which our sovereign has told us to speak. We are to speak and act as we have been authorized. "If anyone speaks, he should speak as one conveying the words of God... that God in all things may be glorified through Jesus Christ..." (1st Peter 4:11 BSB)

✓ *An ambassador does not speak to please his audience, but to please the ruler who sent him.* On several occasions, Jesus spoke non-pleasing words to the religious leaders of His day.[45] Paul did the same in several letters.[46] As an ambassador, Paul said in 1st Corinthians 2 that his speech and preaching were not with enticing words or man's wisdom, but in demonstration of the Spirit and of power so that their faith would not rest in the wisdom of men, but in the power of God.

✓ *An ambassador does not take rejection personally.* He is accepted or rejected not on his own merit but because of who he represents. At the end of Paul's second letter to Timothy, he said Demas had forsaken him, having loved the present world. He also said that Alexander the coppersmith did him much harm, and no man stood with him, but all men forsook him. He prayed that God would not put it to their account. (2nd Timothy 4:10-16) Likewise, Peter and John "...left the Council, rejoicing to have been considered worthy to suffer dishonor for the sake of the Name." (Acts 5:41 ISV) And "...Jesus said, 'Father, forgive them, for they know not what they do.'" (Luke 23:34 ESV)

> **An ambassador is accepted or rejected not on his own merit, but because of who he represents.**

✓ *An ambassador is a representative under all circumstances.* There is no place in the country where the ambassador is assigned where he can go to escape being the ambassador. Likewise there is no place we can go and escape being God's ambassador. (Jonah 1-3)

> **There is no place we can go to escape being His ambassador.**

✓ *An ambassador is not a citizen of the country where he is sent.* He is in a foreign land. His loyalties are to where his citizenship resides. Scripture says a man of valor's citizenship is in Heaven. (Philippians 3:20) Our loyalties belong to Jesus; His Kingdom is our true home. We are aliens and strangers in this world.

✓ *An ambassador is a temporary resident.* He lives there, but it is not his home. For we know that when we die, "we have a building from God, a house not made by hands, eternal in the heavens." (2 Corinthians 5:1 NASB) An embassy is a home away from home for an ambassador. He is appointed to represent his country for a period of time and then return to his homeland. Likewise, a man of valor is appointed to his position during this temporary life, knowing that his eternal home awaits.

3. The Message of an Ambassador

The ambassador's message is the beliefs, views, and positions of the one he represents. It is his duty to proclaim those messages to others. An ambassador needs to know his government's policies and positions on a variety of issues.

We need to know the fundamental message and commands of Jesus Christ so we can go and make disciples teaching them to observe whatsoever Jesus commanded. (Matthew 28:18-20)

An ambassador is given written instructions. Our written instructions are summed up in 2nd Timothy 3:16: "All scripture is inspired by God and profitable for teaching, for reproof, for correction, and for training in righteousness, that the man of God may be complete, equipped for every good work." (RSV) Consequently, we must be students of Scripture, knowledgeable of God's words and view point, forming our response to our world from His perspective and commands.

The Message of Jesus' Ambassador is Reconciliation

In the passage we opened with, what is the primary message? Jesus died so that in him, we might become the righteousness of God. The great miracle of reconciliation is that God chose not to hold each of us accountable for our sin, but instead to lay the penalty for our sin on Jesus.

2 Corinthians 5:18 makes it clear that reconciliation is by the will of God. God is the reconciler. In verse 20, God is imploring *through* us. In every sense God is the source, God is the initiator, and God is the reconciler.

To put it another way, reconciliation with God is not something we accomplish when we stop rejecting Him. It is something He accomplishes when we accept His free offer of grace, initiated by His divine sovereignty. He is the source of reconciliation. So when we are proclaiming the message of reconciliation, we are fulfilling our ambassadorship and participating in God's redeeming work.

> **The ambassador's message is the beliefs, views, and positions of the one he represents.**

We are blessed to share the message of reconciliation—to tell others what God has done in Christ and to encourage them to be reconciled to God. We are privileged to continually live the role and character of His ambassador. If you and I are going to be effective ambassadors for Christ, others—our wives, our children, our co-workers, our friends—need to see the peace and presence and power of God at work in our lives.

We Are the Means by Which God Speaks

God makes his appeal to others through us. Who ever heard of an ambassador who was tongue-tied or refused to speak His sovereign's message? Jonah tried to refuse—look where that got him! (Jonah 1)

So an ambassador both knows the message of God and speaks the message of God into a particular situation. We counsel, urge, ask, plead, admonish, exhort to get people to be willing to reconcile to the God who is willing to reconcile with them (v.20). Why is this something we have to beg people to do? Because, as Jesus said, men love their sin. They love darkness rather than light because their deeds are evil. They run from the light. (John 3:19)

> **An ambassador *knows* the message of God and *speaks* the message of God as instructed.**

The mandate that every man of valor has from God is to proclaim and engage in the ministry of reconciliation, thereby being an ambassador for Christ.

The Lord is with you, mighty man of valor!

+ + +

We've just learned about a man's position: enveloped and enabled by the Holy Spirit, a servant-leader and a capable and willing ambassador of the King—a real man of valor. That's who you are. When you know who you are, you'll know how to live. So let's go there next—let's look at how we are to live as a man of valor.

God's Message of Reconciliation
(2nd Corinthians 5:15-21)

Why did Jesus die?

He died so that we might be reconciled to God.

How are we reconciled to God?

Jesus is sinless, completely holy, enjoying the benefits of an unrestricted relationship with God. Jesus lived fully in righteousness—a right relationship—with God. 2nd Corinthians 5:21 informs us that God made Jesus "to be sin" even though he knew no sin. God treated Jesus as if He were sin itself, banishing Jesus from His own holy presence. This happened as Jesus was crucified. Because of the death of Jesus we can experience that right relationship with God.

Yes! God is willing to forgive all our sin, all the sins we have committed in the past, all the sins we might be currently committing, and all the sins we will ever commit. He will forgive them all forever. Bury them in the depths of the deepest sea, remove them infinitely as far as east is from west and forget them. This is freely available to us. But we have to choose it. We have to choose to receive it.

Ephesians 1:7-8 says, "In Him we have redemption through His blood the forgiveness of our trespasses, according to the riches of His grace, which He lavished upon us." (ESV)

Make it Practical

1. What did being an "ambassador" mean to the Corinthian church members?

2. Is it an honor for you to be an ambassador of Jesus Christ? Why or why not?

3. Does realizing that you do not represent yourself, other Christians, or your church make your interactions easier or harder?

4. An ambassador does not always please his audience. Sometimes his authorized message is displeasing to the listener. How do you feel about being an ambassador in that situation? Knowing your audience may react negatively, would you speak the words that you've been told to say?

5. Read Matthew 10:25 and John 15:18-25. Why did Jesus say that the disciples will be hated? Bruce reminds us that the messenger—the ambassador—only speaks what he was told to say by His sovereign. Therefore, the reaction to the message should not be taken personally by the ambassador. Can you do that? Why or why not?

6. "God makes His appeal to others through us." In your own words, write out the message of reconciliation that you have been entrusted to deliver.

Notes & References

[44] Robert Young, *Young's Analytical Concordance to the Bible, Revised Edition* (Wm B Eerdman's Publishing Company 1991)
[45] See Mathew 15:1-16; 21:12-13; 23, and Luke 11:37-52
[46] See 1st Corinthians 5; 11:17-22 and Galatians 3:1-5; 4:8-11

Preface to Parts II & III

A Man of Valor Has Everything He Needs

Now that you know you are a man of valor, you may have a tendency to think: "What can I do to make this happen?" or "What are the six steps I must take to make this work?!"

Keep a couple of important facts in mind:

1. Gideon was called a mighty man of valor before he did anything; you and I are mighty men of valor before we do anything. In other words, by accepting Jesus Christ's shed blood and payment for your sins, you already are a mighty man of valor.

2. The apostle Peter wrote under the inspiration of the Holy Spirit: "His divine power has granted to us all things that pertain to life and godliness..." (2nd Peter 1:3, ESV)

Now we need to learn how to apply who and what we are—because, 2nd Peter 1:3 continues, we are granted all things..."...through the knowledge of him who called us to his own glory and excellence..." Gideon had things to learn. We have things to learn. Philippians 2:13 says, "for it is God who works in you ... in order to fulfill his good purpose." (ESV)

Open the Lock

Do you know what a padlock is? What do you do with it? Where would you use it? Well, if used properly, it keeps things locked up. It keeps valuables safe.

How does it work? You thread the hook through two parts of a clasp on a door frame or metal box. Then you press the hook down into the cylinder and click it shut. If shut correctly, it does its duty by staying locked. But by itself, it doesn't have much use. By itself, you can't get your valuables back. It is just a useless hunk of steel—a dead weight, or worse, an obstacle—and that is not what it was designed for.

The lock looks complete. It is functional. But it cannot do its full job by itself. That's because the lock is useless without the key. It can only fulfill its purpose with the key.

Jesus is the Key

Here's the point, man of valor: our lives find meaning only in knowing God. Without understanding that He sees you as a man of valor, that He's already given you everything you need, your life is like a lock with no key. You look complete; you are functional, but without the key, you are not useful for His purposes. The key—Jesus—is required for you to carry out what you were made to be and do. He is the vine, we are the branches—apart from Him we can do nothing. (John 15:5)

With the Key, Fulfill Your Purpose

You have already been given everything you need for life and godliness. Now let's learn how we are to live like it. Let's learn how to apply what we already have. It's not about working it out; it's about living it out—living out your priorities (Part II), and then your practices (Part III).

You cannot do that without having the right key... without knowing the key, its shape, its proper fit, and how to use it. We'll start then with some suggestions about how to get to know the key, Jesus, through His Word.

PART II: A Man of Valor's Priorities

A man of valor's abundant life is achieved by keeping his priorities in order: (1) God, (2) Marriage, (3) Family, and (4) Work/Ministry.

Work for many men becomes the most important aspect of their lives. Maybe they find their identity in their job. Maybe they don't want to be around their wife and kids. Or maybe they just don't want to take the time to study God's Word. No matter the reason, they easily get their priorities messed up.

But only when our walk with God is healthy and strong—because we know and obey His word and we talk with Him frequently—when we truly know God, do we have *any* hope of loving our wives as Christ loved the church or providing proper, perceived love and guidance to our children. Keeping our walk with God at the forefront also guarantees that He will help us to succeed at work.

Keep the most important thing, the most important priority, man of valor! And then serve and lead your wife, kids, and in your workplace—in that order!

Priority #1: Personal Walk with God (Chapters 5-7)

A man of valor's walk with His God is first. Everything about life and godliness is only learned through consistent study and application of the Word of God. You cannot know the power of God or lead a successful life without knowing and applying the Word of God.

Equally important for the man of valor is prayer. In Isaiah 1:18 God calls out to His children, "Come now, and let us reason together." (NKJV) That doesn't sound like a distant, dictatorial God; that sounds like a friend. In fact, Jesus calls us friends. (John 15:15) Friends talk, listen, and share feelings and observations. Friends enjoy one another, spend time together, and take walks together. If you want a strong prayer life, you need to give Him time like you would any other friend.

Time spent with God, studying His Word and praying, leads to familiarity, and hopefully, love. That love, as Jesus stated, leads to willing obedience. Jesus said, "If you love me, you will obey my commandments." (John 14:15, GNT) The Greek word for love here is 'agape', which means to love deeply and unconditionally. If we have that deep love, obeying becomes second nature, even a delight—not a burden.

Without a deeply personal, consistent walk with God, the man of valor cannot hope to see success with the rest of his priorities!

Priority #2: Marriage (Chapter 8)

If the man of valor is married, his second priority—*after* God—is his wife. She needs to know that he cherishes her. He needs to nourish her, build her up, and love her as Christ loves the church. He needs to be willing to die for her. He needs to lead, protect, provide, teach, and be a friend to her.

Priority #3: Family (Chapters 9-10)

If the man of valor has children, he is blessed! But they are his third priority. A father of valor makes it clear that after God and his wife—above his work or ministry—his kids are everything to him. Your work or ministry is not more important than your children. Do not shame the name of God by causing your children to resent or reject Him because Daddy was never around for them due to unending work or ministry needs. In the end, you'll deeply regret it. Remember the old saying, "No man said on his deathbed, 'I wish I had spent more time at work.'"

Priority #4: Work / Ministry (Chapter 11)

The man of valor's last priority is his work (for church leaders and workers, insert "ministry"). Many men not only place their work or ministry above all else in their lives, they find their complete identity in it. But, a man's service is the outpouring of God's gifts, not his reason for being.

Chapter 5

Brad Smith & Bill Wilcox

A Man of Valor is a Man of the Word

> "...that the man of God may be complete, equipped for every good work."
>
> 2nd Timothy 3:17 (RSV)

There was a man living in California whose dream was to fly. He joined the US Air Force, but his poor eyesight disqualified him from becoming a pilot. After he was discharged from the military, he sat in his backyard watching jets in the sky.

After watching for a few weeks, he decided that he was going to find a way to fly. He purchased forty-five weather balloons from an Army surplus store, tied them to his lawn chair, and filled the huge balloons with helium. Then he strapped himself into his lawn chair along with a pellet gun, and some sandwiches and beer. He figured he would shoot a few of the balloons when it was time to descend.

Larry planned to lazily float to a height of about thirty feet above the backyard, where he would enjoy a few hours of flight before coming back down. But things didn't work out quite as Larry planned.

When his friends cut the rope tying the lawn chair to the ground, Larry did not float lazily up to thirty feet. Instead he soared into the sky as if shot from a cannon, pulled by the lift of the 45 huge helium balloons!

He didn't stop at 100 feet or at 1000 feet. After climbing higher and higher, he finally stopped at 16,000 feet—almost 5,000 meters—up in the sky.

At that height he felt he couldn't risk shooting any of the balloons lest he unbalance the load and really find himself in trouble. So he stayed there drifting, cold and frightened, with his beer and sandwiches for more than fourteen hours. He crossed the primary approach area of the Los Angeles airport, where airline pilots radioed in reports of the strange sight.

Eventually he gathered the nerve to shoot a few balloons, and slowly came back down. The hanging ropes became caught in a power line, causing an electrical power blackout in a neighborhood. Larry carefully got out of the basket up there in the power lines and climbed to safety—and was promptly arrested for violating commercial airspace. As the police led him away in handcuffs, a reporter asked him why he had done it.

Larry answered, "A man can't just sit around!"[47]

That is kind of a funny story, but Proverbs 14:12 has a good description of a man like that: "There is a way that seems right to a man, but its end is the way of death." (NASB)

> **"There is a way that seems right to a man, but its end is the way of death."**

On our own we tend to do stupid or even sinful things; we become misguided; we make things worse when we think we're helping; we go the wrong direction. Or like the man in the story, we are simply foolish and just might end up dead. The fact is, we can't trust our own judgment.

The Bible Shows Us the Right Way

Only God's Word is truth and is able to give us our position and direction, showing us the right way to live.

During a time when the various tribes of Israel were fighting with each other, we read in Judges 21:25 that Israel had no king and everyone did as he saw fit—what was right in his own eyes. And the result was chaos. When every man is doing as he sees fit and no one is following the Word of God, fighting, stealing, and immorality become rampant. In Jeremiah 17:9 we read, "The heart is deceitful above all things, and desperately sick; who can understand it?" (ESV)

We cannot trust feelings or personal desire, because left to ourselves, we can justify *anything*. Nor can we trust what others may say. It is only God's Word that provides a solid foundation for decisions. When we take our eyes off of God's truth, we won't make wise decisions. Like Larry, the lawn chair guy, we'll do what feels right at the moment. It may even be fun for a while, but at some point we'll cause lots of trouble and have a rough landing. We might even die. By following our own deceitful desires, we'll never find the abundant life that Christ wants to give us—more and more of Himself. (John 10:10, 14:6)

> **When we take our eyes off of God's truth, we won't make wise decisions.**

Hunger

Have you ever gone a long time without food? Do you remember what you felt like at the end of that time?

I have asked many people this question. When teaching a group of about a hundred churched and unchurched men recently in Mzuzu, Malawi, I asked who had gone the longest without food. Several hands went up with typical responses: Two days. Four days. Even seven days. But then one man answered, "30 days."

"Really?" I asked. "What did you feel like at the end of that time?"

"Listless, tired, dull, 'in a fog'. No energy, and intensely hungry," was his response.

Did you know that Jesus once went without food for forty days and nights? Can you imagine how weak He was, how He craved food? It was in this weakness that Satan came to Him and tempted Him to make bread out of the stones. What did Jesus do?

Now, I would have used my power to make bread. Instead, He quoted verses from the Bible to Satan. He used the power of the Bible to fight Satan. If Jesus fought Satan using the Bible, then how should we fight Satan and temptation? Obviously in the same way—by using the Bible.

But how can we fight Satan if we don't know the Bible?

Why is using the Bible as our guide so important? It is because the culture of every village, city, and nation tries to say what is right and wrong—and culture changes over time and from place to place. If we follow the culture, we will change our ideas, too, and not truly know what is right and what is wrong.

> **What should we do when facing a difficult situation, or when we are tempted to sin?**

Look in the Bible—or remember what we've learned there—and bring it to mind to fight Satan or to make the right decision.

The Word Helps Us Overcome Temptation

When Satan tempted Jesus, telling Him to prove He was the Son of God by telling a stone to become bread after He had fasted, Jesus answered, "It is written, 'Man shall not live by bread alone.'" (Luke 4:4 ESV) Jesus turned away Satan's temptation by referring to Scripture.

The Old Testament verse Jesus referenced was Deuteronomy 8:3, "And he humbled you and let you hunger and fed you with manna, which you did not know, nor did your fathers know, that he might make you know that man does not live by bread alone, but man lives by every word that comes from the mouth of the LORD." (ESV)

The man of valor understands that the Word of God will help him turn away from temptation that a foolish man would embrace.

1 Corinthians 10:13 says, "No temptation has overtaken you that is not common to man. God is faithful, and he will not let you be tempted beyond your ability, but with the temptation he will also provide the way of escape, that you may be able to endure it."(ESV)

So, let's look at some examples of how we might find the way of escape:

✓ When your culture tells you it is okay to have sex with a woman you are not married to, what do you do? **Go to the Bible.**
Hebrew 13:4: "Let marriage be held in honor among all, and let the marriage bed be undefiled, for God will judge the sexually immoral and adulterous." (ESV) This means you should only have sex with your wife—no one before marriage and no one outside of marriage. By knowing this verse, you can fight the temptation.

✓ When your culture tells you it is okay to get drunk, what do you do? **Go to the Bible.**
Proverbs 20:1 "Wine is a mocker, strong drink a brawler, and whoever is led astray by it is not wise." (ESV) Ephesians 5:18: "Do not get drunk with wine, which will only ruin you; instead, be filled with the Spirit." (GNT)

✓ When your culture tells you it is okay to be lazy, what do you do? **Go to the Bible.**
Colossians 3:23-24: "Whatever you do, work heartily, as for the Lord and not for men, knowing that from the Lord you will receive His inheritance as your reward. You are serving the Lord Christ." (ESV)

✓ When your culture tells you it is okay to hit or to be disrespectful to women, what do you do? **Go to the Bible.**

Colossians 3:19: "Husbands, love your wives, and do not be harsh with them." (ESV) Jesus showed love and care for all women and set an example to treat them with respect.

✓ When your culture tells you it is okay to hate or fight someone because they have hurt or insulted you or your family, what do you do? **Go to the Bible.**

Matthew 5:38-39: "You have heard that it was said, 'An eye for an eye and a tooth for a tooth.' But I say to you, do not resist the one who is evil. But if anyone slaps you on the right cheek, turn to him the other also." (ESV) If someone mistreats you and you treat them with love and respect, God is glorified, and you help the person realize how great and loving our God is.

✓ When your culture tells you that homosexual marriage is okay and promotes it, what do you do? **Go to the Bible.**

Leviticus 18:22: "Do not lie with a male as with a woman; it is an abomination." (ESV)

✓ When your culture tells you it is okay to change your gender, from boy to girl or girl to boy, or man to woman or woman to man, what do you do? **Go to the Bible.**

Genesis 1:27: "So God created man in his own image, in the image of God he created him; male and female he created them." (ESV)

Men of valor make their decisions in light of God's eternal truth.

Men of valor make decisions in light of God's eternal truth.

The Power of Knowing the Bible

Think for a minute about Jesus' parable of the four soils found in the Gospels. A sower went out and scattered the seed of God's Word on four kinds of soil: a hard path, rocky terrain, thorny ground, and good rich soil.

Most men today would recognize themselves in the first three soils where the seeds don't grow, yet they honestly want to be like the good soil where the fourth seed fell. Well, we can be that soil! Matthew 13:23 encourages us to be men who hear God's Word and understand it. *Those* men produce crops yielding thirty, sixty, or a hundred times what is sown.

What is keeping your life hard, rocky, and choked with thorns? After all, God created us for more. In John 10:10 He says that he wants us to live His abundant life.

Jesus gave us an insight about why our lives can be hard in His discussion with a group of confused religious men. In Matthew 22:29 He said, "But Jesus answered them, "You are wrong, because you know neither the Scriptures nor the power of God." (ESV)

Do you understand what Jesus said to these religious men? He made a direct connection between knowing the Bible and leading a powerful life. Many men are in error because they don't know the Scriptures and therefore don't know the power of God. Men of valor truly hear, understand, and apply God's Word and therefore produce a harvest. Digging deeply into the Word of God is one of the most important factors for men to live powerful lives.[48]

Men of valor truly hear, understand, and apply God's Word and therefore produce a harvest.

Acts 17:11 states that the Jews in Berea "...were more noble than those in Thessalonica; they received the word with all eagerness, examining the Scriptures daily to see if these things were so." (ESV)

What does this mean?

The Berean Jews listened to the Word with enthusiasm, studied it, examined it, and compared Scripture to Scripture—day after day. They diligently reviewed what they heard to see if it was true—just like you need to do when you hear a preacher or a teacher of the Word.

The Bereans understood what Paul later wrote in 2nd Timothy 3:16-17: "All Scripture is breathed out by God and profitable for teaching, for reproof, for correction, and for training in righteousness, that the man of God may be complete, equipped for every good work." (ESV)

The Word of God (The Bible) is the Key to a Man of Valor's Success

Teaching is instruction about the core elements of the Word of God. It explains the path to follow.

Reproof is a rebuking from the Word that points out when you are off the path. Sometimes you know when you are off the path; sometimes you need someone to tell you! When a man of valor is in the Word of God and is rebuked, "...reproof gives wisdom..." (Proverbs 29:15, RSV)

> "For the word of God is living and active, sharper than any two-edged sword, piercing to the division of soul and of spirit, of joints and of marrow, and discerning the

thoughts and intentions of the heart." (Hebrews 4:12, ESV)

But the Word of God doesn't just teach and rebuke, it also corrects. Correcting is how the Word of God assists in getting the man of valor back on the straight and narrow path. Correction means to put right or fix a situation or a behavior. You may have done something wrong, but now the Word can repair a situation and take what may be wrong and turn it into something right.

Finally, Paul says the Word of God trains a man in righteousness. Training in righteousness is the same idea as when we raise a child. All children need training and discipline. God says in Hebrews 12:6 that the Lord disciplines (trains) those He loves and punishes (corrects) everyone He accepts as a son. In the verses that follow, He reminds us that we should endure hardship as discipline because God treats us as a son and disciplines us for our good that we may share in His holiness. Though discipline is not pleasant at the time, later it produces righteousness and peace for those who have been trained by it.

The Word of God can do all this: teach, rebuke, correct, and train in righteousness so that the man of God may be thoroughly equipped for every good work. A man of valor stores up God's Word in his heart and walks according to God's Word. (Psalm 119)

A Man of Valor walks according to God's Word.

How to Study the Word

How do we learn to study God's Word? Here's a simple approach to studying the Bible that you can practice yourself, with your family, or with a group of men.

For many men around the world, the first step is very basic. To get into the Word, you have to set time aside to do it. It's not just going to happen; you have to plan it. So first, set aside time to read the Bible—every day.

Second, talk to the Bible's author—pray! Psalm 119:18 reads: "Open my eyes, that I may behold wondrous things out of your law." (ESV) Say to God: "Lord, what is this about? What is this saying? Please help me understand what you want me to understand here."

Ask God for guidance and understanding, and then ask these questions as you read:

1. Teaching: What does this tell me about God? About me? About life?

2. Reproof: Is this passage telling me that there is sin in my life that I need to confess and forsake?

3. Correction: Am I being convicted about something that needs to change in me? Should I be convicted? If not, why not?

4. Training in righteousness: In light of this passage, how will I live?

Give it Time

It will not benefit you if you pick up the Bible, spend two minutes reading, and then go do something else. It takes time to read and understand what the Bible says. Give it time. Be willing to give God your time. Start with at least 10 minutes if you are not in the habit of reading the Bible daily and then, as it becomes a habit, lengthen the time you read. It won't take long to enjoy the time you spend reading and talking to God about what He is saying to you!

You cannot hope to be effective as a man of valor if you are not in the Word. You cannot hope to get through the storms of life without the Bible to guide you. You cannot hope to know the power of God without knowing what He has revealed about Himself and about the path He calls you to.

> **You cannot hope to be effective as a man of valor if you are not in the Word.**

A man of valor reads and studies God's Word on a regular basis, and he lives his life day by day using the principles found in God's Word. Strive above all else to be a man of the Bible, and watch as God transforms you into his likeness—into the man of valor He created you to be.

The Lord is with you, mighty man of valor!

+ + +

Reading the Bible is crucial. But understanding and applying the Word of God is greatly enabled through the application of the next chapter.

Take A Closer Look:

Try This With Philippians 4:6-7

"Have no anxiety about anything, but in everything by prayer and supplication with thanksgiving let your requests be made known to God. And the peace of God, which passes all understanding, will keep your hearts and your minds in Christ Jesus." (RSV)

1. What does this Word of God **teach** me about God? Is there a principle here that I need to apply? I am to 'Have no anxiety about anything' and then God will give me peace.

2. This passage **reproves**. It identifies sin: worry, anxiety. I need to stop worrying!

3. Does this passage help me to **correct** sin? What can I do to stop the sin of worry? 'In everything by prayer and supplication with thanksgiving let your requests be made known to God.'

4. Finally, this passage **trains in righteousness**. How can I be more like God? By trusting Him. By bringing my needs and requests to Him and leaving them there. Then I know peace—which is a fruit of the Spirit. (Galatians 5:22)

Make it Practical

A Bible Study for Men: The Men in the Bible

Try this Bible study with other men. Choose a man in the Bible and find all the verses where he is mentioned. (For example, if you choose Stephen, you will be reading Acts 6 and 7). Read the verses and answer as many of the questions below as you can about each man.

Here are a few to get you started:

Adam (Genesis 1:26-3; 5:1-5)
Gideon (Judges 6-8)
Paul (Acts 9, 13-28)
Gehazi (2nd Kings 4-5, 8:1-6)
Noah (Genesis 6-9)
Titus (2nd Corinthians 6:6-7;
8:6,23; Titus 1:4-6)
Cain (Genesis 4)
Samson (Judges 13-16)
Jonah (Jonah)
Mordechai (Esther)

Nabal (1st Samuel 25:2-42)
Naaman (2nd Kings 5:1-19)
Joseph (Genesis 37-50)
Stephen (Acts 6-7)
Hezekiah (2nd Chronicles 29-32)
Jonathan (1st Samuel 14:1-23;
20:1-17; 23:15-18)
Jacob (Genesis 25:19-34; 27-35)
Elijah (1st Kings 17-19)
Herod (Mark 6:14-28)

1. Who was this man? What kind of work did he do?
2. What can you learn about his character, habits, and attitude?
3. How did he treat others?
4. How did he respond when corrected?
5. Is there anything to admire in this man?
6. Is there anything to dislike about him?
7. How did God see this man? What did God say about this man? (if anything is written)
8. How is this man similar to or different from the ideal man—Jesus?
9. What can you learn from his problems? Do you have any of the problems he had? What did he do about those problems? Should you do anything like what he did?
10. What can you learn from his obedience?
11. What can you learn from his disobedience?
12. What other lessons can you learn from his life?

(Not all questions apply to every biblical account).

Note: You might not be able to study the entire record of a man at one time. For example, for Elijah, read 1st Kings 18:20-40 and talk over how he handled the prophets of Baal. Then the next time you meet, read 1st Kings 19:1-18 about when Elijah was in the wilderness.

Notes & References

---

47 "Lawn Chair Larry" (https://darwinawards.com/stupid/stupid1998-11.html)
48 The authors credit the concepts in this section to Patrick Morley, founder of Man in the Mirror Ministries

Chapter 6

Guy Wilson

A Man After God's Own Heart

"...he went up on the mountain by himself to pray."
Matthew 14:23 (RSV)

Why does a man of valor need to pray? Because prayer is our connection to God. If we do not pray, we will have no friendship with God. The more time we spend talking with the Lord and listening to what He may want to say to us, the closer we will become to God. How close do you feel to your wife and children? If you spend little time talking with them, you cannot have a warm and meaningful relationship. The same is true with God!

> **The more time we spend talking with the Lord and listening to what He may want to say to us, the closer we become to God.**

A Man After God's Own Heart: David

Only one man in the Bible is called "a man after God's own heart": David. (1st Samuel 13:14, Acts 14:22) Why was God so close to David? David spent a lot of time in prayer. Imagine all the time he had to pray when he spent his days and nights out in the fields taking care of his father's sheep.

As a very young man, God gave him the strength to protect the sheep from lions and bears. When he went to the battlefront to check how his older brothers were doing, he volunteered to fight the Philistine giant Goliath. He told King Saul, "The LORD who delivered me from the paw of the lion and from the paw of the bear will deliver me from the hand of this Philistine." (1st Samuel 17:37 ESV) God heard David's prayer and gave him the strength to kill Goliath. After this, Saul took David with him into battle, and soon David was made an officer in Saul's army. David was successful in all that he did because God was with him. (1st Samuel 17:12–18:30)

There are 150 Psalms in the Bible, and David wrote more than half of them. Most of those Psalms are prayers to God; others are songs of praise. In Psalm 32, David wrote, "Let everyone who is godly pray." (Psalm 32:6 NASB) And in Psalm 5:2 he wrote, "Heed the sound of my cry for help, my King and my God, for to You I pray." (NASB) When David prayed, God acted. God never turned His back on David through his years of hiding from King Saul's insanity—Saul wanted to kill David—or through David's forty years as King of Israel.

When David prayed, God acted.

A Man Just Like Us: Elijah

Men of God have always talked with God by praying fervently and often. One of the most godly men of the Old Testament was the prophet Elijah, who listened to the voice of God and always obeyed God's commands.

God directed Elijah to live with a widow during a three-year drought sent to punish the people of Israel for worshipping Baal and to turn them back to Him. She was able to provide food for Elijah, herself, and her son because God never let the food run out, thanks to Elijah's prayers.

Then the widow's son became sick, and after a few days he died. Elijah prayed aloud for his healing. He prayed intensely. He placed the boy on his bed, stretched himself out over the boy three times, and prayed for the Lord to restore the child to life. The Lord answered Elijah's prayer; the boy started breathing and sat up. Then Elijah took him back to his mother. (1st Kings 17:17-24)

The Lord had big plans for Elijah because he listened to God and always obeyed Him. (1st Kings 18:18-46) God had Elijah build an altar and place a bull on it to be a sacrifice. He called together the 450 prophets of Baal, a powerless idol, and challenged them to pray to Baal to send down fire upon the altar and burn up the sacrifice. They prayed aloud to Baal for hours. Nothing happened! Then Elijah prayed aloud to the one true God. The Lord sent fire down upon the altar, and it burned up the sacrifice and the wood and even the stones of the altar. Then, after killing the 450 prophets of Baal, Elijah climbed to the top of Mount Carmel where he bowed down to the ground with his head between his knees and prayed to God. Soon a heavy rain began to fall. A three-year drought ended! In a short time there was grass to feed the animals in the fields. With God's provision of frequent rain, the crops grew and provided food for all the people. Then the people turned away from Baal and worshipped the one true God.

Because Elijah was so faithful to his Lord, God performed many miracles in response to Elijah's prayers. And yet, James describes Elijah as "a man just like us". (James 5:17 BSB) Just think—you and I could be another Elijah!

> **God performed many miracles in response to Elijah's prayers. Yet James describes Elijah as "a man just like us".**

His Prayers Gave Him Strength: Jesus

Jesus was about thirty years old when He began his ministry. From the time He was a young boy, Jesus spent much time in prayer. He was very close to His Heavenly Father.

After Jesus was baptized by John and came up out of the water, Heaven was opened to Him and He saw the Spirit of God coming down like a dove and alight on Him. Then a voice from Heaven said, "This is my beloved Son, with whom I am well pleased." (Matthew 3:17, ESV)

Then the spirit led Jesus into the desert, where He fasted and prayed for forty days and nights. When Jesus was very weak and hungry, Satan tempted Him, but Jesus resisted every one of Satan's tricks to turn Him away from God. (Matthew 4:1-11) His prayers gave Him strength.

Jesus then began His ministry: teaching, preaching, and healing the sick. About prayer, Jesus taught, "But you, when you pray, go into your inner room, close your door and pray to your Father who is in secret, and your Father who sees what is done in secret will reward you." (Matthew 6:6 NASB)

He also urged His followers to pray in ordinary language—like you would talk to a friend. He gave them what we call "The Lord's Prayer" as a guide for prayer: "Our Father who is in Heaven, hallowed be Your name. Your kingdom come. Your will be done on earth as it is in

Heaven. Give us this day our daily bread and forgive us our debts as we also have forgiven our debtors. And do not lead us into temptation, but deliver us from evil." (Matthew 6:9-13 NASB) Jesus also used a parable to teach them that they should always pray and not give up. (Luke 18:1-8)

Jesus said several times that what He did was not of His own choosing, but He did what His Father told Him to do. (John 5:30) Often Jesus would leave His disciples and go off by Himself and spend time in prayer. That is how He knew what His Father wanted Him to do.

That is also true for you and me. The more time we spend alone with God, praying and meditating on His Word, the better we will understand what God wants us to do. And the more we do His will, the more blessed we will be.

> **The more time we spend alone with God, praying and meditating on His Word, the better we will understand what God wants us to do.**

Set aside time each day to go to a place in your home or elsewhere where you can be alone with God. Take your Bible with you. Pray for understanding of His will. Then read a few verses of Scripture and meditate on it. Pray again. If you find it helpful, use the Lord's Prayer as a guide. Give careful thought to every word of the prayer.

If this is new for you, start with ten minutes, and then gradually increase the time you spend with God. Do not neglect to have a regular time alone with God. Soon you will be a new man!

Also, a husband of valor prays with his wife, and a father of valor prays with his children (see Chapters 8, 9, and 10). You may want to hear the children's prayers when you put them to bed. They want to hear you pray, too! They want to understand how you talk to God and what you pray about. They want to know that you are friends with God.

Jesus Prayed for You

Toward the end of His earthly ministry, Jesus said a long prayer for his disciples that they all might really know God, be protected within His will, and know His joy. Then Jesus prayed for all those who would come to believe in Him through hearing the teaching of the disciples. That includes you and me. Jesus prayed that each of us not only believe in Him but be filled with the undeniable love of God the same way

Jesus is. (John 17)

The closer we draw to God in prayer, the more the Holy Spirit will help us live as men of valor. God loves each of us; Jesus died on the cross for us; and God desires a close friendship with us that is possible only through prayer.

> The closer we draw to God in prayer, the more the Holy Spirit will help us live as men of valor.

His Prayers Weren't Perfect: Paul

The Apostle Paul writes a great deal about prayer in his letters. He prays for the believers in Ephesus that "the God of our Lord Jesus Christ, the Father of glory, may give to you a spirit of wisdom and of revelation in the knowledge of Him." (Ephesians 1:17 NASB) And to the Romans, Paul writes, "In the same way the Spirit also helps our weakness; for *we do not know how to pray as we should*, but the Spirit Himself intercedes for us with groaning too deep for words; and He who searches the hearts knows what the mind of the Spirit is, because He intercedes for the saints according to the will of God." (Romans 8:26-27 NASB; *emphasis added*) Again Paul says: "Rejoice always; pray without ceasing; in everything give thanks; for this is God's will for you in Christ Jesus." (1st Thessalonians 5:16-18 NASB)

Keep in mind that our prayers do not have to be "perfect." Our prayers won't be perfect until we are with Jesus face-to-face! Pray what is on your mind and leave the rest to the Holy Spirit who loves you and yearns for that close friendship with you that can only come through regular prayer.

> The Holy Spirit prays with you when you pray.

As you spend more and more time in prayer, you will find yourself yielding your will to the will of God. As your prayers increasingly align with God's will, you will find that God is quicker to give you the answer that you seek. You will also find yourself doing what God wants you to do on a regular basis as David and Elijah did. Then God will recognize you as His faithful servant and continue to make His will known to you.

Praying for Miracles

Do you ever pray for God to perform a miracle? Should you pray for a miracle? David prayed for miracles, as did Elijah, and they came to pass. Jesus prayed for and performed many miracles. The disciples often prayed for miracles after Jesus ascended into heaven. Those that were in line with the Father's will were done; some were not. But does God perform miracles today?

More than a dozen years ago, my former pastor, Kenny Newsome, was diagnosed with Parkinson's disease. That is a disease that gets worse over time and is not curable. Symptoms include tremors of the hands, slurred speech, and difficulty walking. It eventually leads to death.

No one in the congregation knew that Pastor Kenny had the disease until one Sunday when he was serving communion, his hand began to shake badly. After the service, the person who was helping with communion asked Pastor Kenny about the tremors, and he admitted that he had Parkinson's. Some members of the congregation knew about a church that had a regular prayer healing service on Sunday nights, so a few weeks later, two leaders of the church drove Pastor Kenny to the service. All who needed healing went to the altar rail and knelt. Each one was anointed with oil, hands were laid on them, and they were prayed for.

At the end of the service, the pastor invited any to stay who wanted more prayer. It was at that second time of prayer, with the church pastor praying aloud and with many others' hands on him, that Pastor Kenny saw a bright light in the altar area and felt the healing power of the Holy Spirit surge through his body. Pastor Kenny felt that he was healed at that moment, and he has never had a tremor or any other sign of Parkinson's disease since.

James wrote these words about prayer:

> "Is anyone among you suffering? Let him pray. Is anyone cheerful? Let him sing praise. Is anyone among you sick? Let him call for the elders of the church, and let them pray over him, anointing him with oil in the name of the Lord. And the prayer of faith will save the one who is sick, and the Lord will raise him up..." (James 5:13-15 ESV)

A Prayer Warrior: John Wesley

Another faithful man of prayer was John Wesley, the great English evangelist of the eighteenth century, who spent his life on horseback throughout England, Wales, and Ireland, preaching the Gospel of Jesus Christ. Each morning John got up at 4 AM so that he could spend two hours in prayer and Bible study before he began his daily ride. God answered his prayers. Everywhere John went people gave their lives to Jesus or turned back to Him. John Wesley's traveling evangelism grew more and more effective until he was drawing crowds of thousands wherever he preached. The result was that Christianity in Great Britain was totally regenerated, and hundreds of churches grew in the American colonies as well.

It's Not About You

Why pray, man of valor? Because no lasting success happens apart from God's will. It's not your will, it's His will. It's not about you, it's all for Him. David, Elijah, Jesus, Paul, John Wesley, modern-day pastors and ordinary people weren't out for themselves; they prayed God's desires.

Ephesians 1:11 states that God "...works everything in agreement with the counsel and design of His will..." (AMP) The people we just looked at knew that and lived it. They enjoyed a friendship with God. They knew they were in His will and doing His will because *they talked to Him about everything... a lot.* They walked through life knowing and experiencing God. Prayer gives access to that kind of relationship.

Prayer is the recognition that He is the Source for all of our life. A man of valor is a man after God's own heart. A man of valor is connected to God.

The Lord is with you, mighty man of valor!

+ + +

A man of valor becomes a friend of God and follows God because he spends time with Him. In the next chapter, we'll understand that a man of valor's prayers are not just personally strengthening and bring about change, but not to pray is a sin. In fact, if prayer moves God to work in this world's affairs, then prayerlessness excludes God and keeps Him from working. Whoa. You have to read the next chapter to comprehend that!

Make it Practical

1. Why was God so close to David? What difference did prayer make in David's life?

2. Jesus spent many early morning hours talking with His Dad. And Jesus said that He only did and said what His Father told Him. (John 5:19-21, 8:28, 12:49-50, 14:10) Even Jesus would not have known what to do had he not been talking with God. If Jesus needed to do this, don't you? How can you pray more? What changes do you need to make in your schedule?

3. Your prayers do not need to be perfect, whether by yourself, with your wife or children, or with other men. What you pray or how you say it does not matter. Be assured, Jesus knows what you are asking, and He is intently listening; you are talking to God, not to people. Does not knowing how or what to pray prevent you from praying?

4. Elijah, a man "just like us," is someone whose prayers to stop and start rain, to provide flour for the widow, and for fire to come down from heaven were answered. Why were so many of his prayers answered? What do you need to do to see your prayers answered?

5. Take some time now and pray. If you are with a group, do this together. Pray for God to bless you with a desire to pray and talk to him. Pray for yourself—for your daily bread, for your sins to be forgiven. Pray for your marriage, your children, your co-workers, friends, and extended family. Pray for your home church and for the universal church. Pray for your country, its leaders, and its citizens. Pray for the spread of the gospel and that people believe, obey, and apply God's word. Pray for God's Kingdom to come and His will to be done.

Chapter 7

Bruce Campbell[49]

A Man of Valor's Prayers Matter

"Moreover, as for me, far be it from me that I should sin against the LORD by ceasing to pray..."
I Samuel 12:23 (RSV)

My pastor says that we act only on what we believe. Men of valor—men of courage and strength—should pray. If we are going to impact our families, other men, and our cities, villages, and nations, we must be praying men.

A Midnight Call

Luke 11:1-10 tells the account of Jesus' disciples asking Him to teach them to pray. He gives them what we know as The Lord's Prayer and then says,

> "Suppose one of you has a friend, and goes to him at midnight and says to him, 'Friend, lend me three loaves; for a friend of mine has come to me from a journey, and I have nothing to set before him'; and from inside he answers and says, 'Do not bother me; the door has already been shut and my children and I are in bed; I cannot get up and give you anything.' I tell you, even though he will not get up and give him anything because he is his friend, yet because of his persistence, he will get up and give him as much as he needs. So I say to you, ask, and it will be given to you; seek, and you will find; knock, and it will be opened to you. For everyone who asks, receives; and he who seeks, finds; and to him who

knocks, it will be opened." (NASB)

It is interesting to me that the man had to do all three of those things to get the bread for his friend: he had to seek the guy out by going to his home, he had to knock loudly on his friend's door, and he had to ask with explanation and energy in order to get his request met. It was his persistence that resulted in the help he needed.

Prayer takes effort and intention. The point of the story is that one must care about the matter and be passionate about the petition. We have to ask boldly. Prayer is not wishful thinking, a sleepy sort of indifferent request, or distracted repetition. Prayer is bold asking. The intensity of our prayers speaks to God of our real care about something. He tests our sincerity by the effort we put forth.

In the Amplified Bible, James 5:16-17 says, "The heartfelt and persistent prayer of a righteous man (believer) can accomplish much [when put into action and made effective by God—it is dynamic and can have tremendous power]."

Prayer is not wishful thinking
or distracted repetition. Prayer is bold asking.

He Abandoned All Manners

Jesus' story of the friends is interesting because there are very special relationships between these people. There was an understood obligation to one another. The first man, Friend #1, arrived very late, near midnight, at his friend's (#2) house. Friend #2 had nothing to give at the late hour, and yet he knew the need of Friend #1 could not go unmet. Thus the second man felt compelled to go to his good friend (#3) for help. In the middle of night he goes to wake up Friend #3. He is shameless. He has abandoned all manners. He knocks loudly on the door and calls out.

Friend #3 finally gives Friend #2 what he needs, but it is not just because of relationship that he gets up and gives the bread, but rather it is because Friend #2 asks for the bread. We learn from this that relationship alone does not meet the need. Bold asking results in meeting the need. James 4:2 says, "You do not have because you do not ask." (NASB)

The intensity of our prayers speaks to God of our real care
about something.

Now, we are given responsibility, like Friend #2, to care for the people God has brought into our lives. We recognize that God is the One (#3) who is able to meet their needs. We don't have the supply, but we come to God on their behalf, for He has all they need.

After Friend #2 got the loaves, he went from being the petitioner to the provider. He became the means through which the first friend was supplied.

Here's what Jesus is saying. You are important, man of valor, because if you do not pray, the provision is not supplied. Jesus intervenes in our world through us, by us, and in us. In order "to do," God is waiting for us "to ask". So, that means that when we ask, something is going to happen that would not have happened if we had not asked.

> **You are important, man of valor, because if you do not pray, the provision is not supplied.**

Can we Bring About a History That Would Not Have Otherwise Happened?

> "For we do not want you to be unaware, brethren, of our affliction which came to us in Asia, that we were burdened excessively, beyond our strength, so that we despaired even of life... We trust... in Him on whom we have set our hope. And He will yet deliver us, you also joining in helping us through your prayers, so that thanks may be given by many persons on our behalf for the favor bestowed on us through the prayers of many."
> (1st Corinthians 1:8-11 NASB)

Notice that the prayers of the Corinthians were part of God's rescue operation. Likewise, Philippians 1:19 says, "For I know that through your prayers and the help of the Spirit of Jesus Christ this will turn out for my deliverance." (ESV)

Man of valor, realize that whether or not you pray matters!

How prayer can alter history:

✓ Moses prayed that God would not destroy His people. God was determined to destroy Israel after the event of the golden calf, but God's hand of fury was held fast by the interceding of Moses. It was for Moses a long and exhaustive struggle of praying for forty days and forty nights. He did not relent or even eat as he

pleaded on their behalf. In the end, God's mighty wrath was stayed. (Exodus 32, Deuteronomy 9:25)
✓ Elijah prayed for life to return to a dead child. (2nd Kings 4)
✓ King Hezekiah prayed that God would extend his life. (2nd Kings 20)
✓ Peter was freed from prison while his friends were praying. (Acts 12)

There are many, many more examples of the power of prayer in the Bible and elsewhere!

If prayer moves God to work in this world's affairs, then prayerlessness excludes God and declares that His work isn't welcome in your life. Prayerlessness leaves us alone in this world with its tremendous responsibilities and difficult problems and with all of its sorrows, burdens, and afflictions—without a loving God's involvement. Who would want that?

> **If prayer moves God to work in this world's affairs, then prayerlessness excludes God from your life. Who would want that?**

Ask Him to Alter Things That Are Not His Will

Sometimes we don't pray because of defeatism, or because we are too tolerant or comfortable with the evil happening around us. Sometimes we feel unworthy or weak, thinking that others get prayers answered but we don't. We wonder if there is something wrong with us and so we abandon the battle. We just let things happen.

No! We cannot do that! We must hear the beating heart of God and not accept the way things are. Prayer is saying we will not tolerate things that are wrong. Man of valor, you must go into the battle in the name of God Almighty and ask him to alter things that are not His will. That is part of the role of a preservative. It is why Jesus says we are the salt of the earth. (Matthew 5:13) Acts 17:6 says that Paul and Silas turned their world upside down. That's what men of valor do!

> **Sometimes we don't pray because of defeatism, or because we are too tolerant or comfortable with the evil around us.**

David records in Psalm 11 that his advisors are telling him to flee to the mountains to escape the destruction and persecution perpetrated by the ungodly. He responds in verse 3 with, "If the foundations are destroyed, what can the righteous do?" (RSV) 19th century commentator Albert Barnes explains,

> "The word 'foundations'... refers to those things on which society rests, or by which social order is sustained—the great principles of truth and righteousness that uphold society, as the foundations on which an edifice rests uphold the building. This is ... the circumstances referred to in the psalm, when there was no respect paid to truth and justice, and when the righteous, therefore, could find no security. It is under these circumstances the advice is given to flee..."[50]

David then reminds everyone of the Lord's sovereignty, sustainment, and His coming punishment for the wicked (vs. 4-7), David basically says "No way will we run!" Instead, he is determined to "remain and face the evil, and ... endeavor to secure a better state of things."[51]

We're in This Together

Farmers know their partnership with God: they plant and water, but God makes the seed grow. The only way for the farmer to get the plant he wants is for him to initiate burying seed and watering it. But God alone makes the seed grow into a plant. We can wish a plant would grow in the dirt, but nothing will happen until we act. Yet our action alone cannot grow the plant. It takes both us and God.

We are co-laborers. We work together with God to see His will done on earth. A beautiful garden will only grow with the intervention of man. If it is left to itself, it will be filled with weeds. Similarly, when we pray, our will is joined to God's will and we are participants in the means by which His will is accomplished. 1st John 5:14-15 says,

> "This is the confidence which we have before Him that, if we ask anything according to His will, He hears us. And if we know that He hears us in whatever we ask, we know that we have the requests which we have asked from Him." (NASB)

God's Will is Already Set, Right?

Too many times, we think or say, "If God's will is already set, then why should we pray?" It's true that God's "big picture" will is set in stone, for example, regarding the end of the current age and the coming eternal reign of Christ. We cannot influence that. But we can pray regarding day-to-day matters, such as healing for your daughter's sickness, your neighbor's interest in joining you at a Bible study, success in a job search, provision for food, or boldness to share the Gospel with your co-worker.

> **We are co-laborers. We work together with God to see His will done on earth.**

Think about this: would all the miracles of Jesus have happened if He had not been asked to perform them? Mary asked Jesus to intervene when the wine ran out during a wedding feast. (John 2) Bartimaeus shouted out to Jesus to cure his blindness. (Mark 10) The lepers asked Jesus for healing. (Luke 17) The centurion asked for healing for his servant. (Matthew 8) We could cite many more examples.

> **Would all the miracles of Jesus have happened if He had not been asked to perform them?**

Only Men of Prayer Have an Impact

Men of prayer are the only men who have influence with God. Men of skill, men of education, or men of worldly influence are not substitutes for men of prayer, because only men of prayer have an eternal impact. In fact, the apostles made prayer their chief business, and look at the result!

The disciples said "...we will devote ourselves to prayer and to the ministry of the word." (Acts 6:4 NASB) Some versions use the words "devote ourselves steadfastly in prayer." The connotation is to be strongly devoted to it, keep at it with constant care, or to make a business out of it.

The apostles operated under a rule of prayer, which depended upon God to do for them with prayer what He would not do without prayer. They had to be devoted to prayer to make their ministry efficient. The business of preaching is worth very little unless it is in direct partnership with the business of praying.

> **The apostles depended on God to do with prayer what He would not do without prayer.**

Whatever affects the intensity of our praying affects the value of our work. Nothing is done well without prayer for the simple reason that it leaves God out of the picture. It is so easy to focus on the good but neglect the best, such as when we falsely believe that cutting short our praying is fine because we have "important work to do." Satan has effectively disarmed us when he can keep us too busy to pray.

> **Nothing is done well without prayer because God is left out of the picture.**

Show off How Good God Really Is

Let's close this chapter by mentioning one more aspect of prayer. Romans 2:4 says that the goodness of God leads men to repentance. How can your unsaved friends, family, and co-workers learn of the goodness of God? Ask them if there is anything you can pray about for them. From time to time ask if the prayer request has been answered. Many times our Heavenly Father will answer such prayers because it will give you the opportunity to tell them about Him. We cooperate with God to pray His blessing and favor in someone's life so that their heart will be softened to receive the gospel. Pray according to the love of God and His will, and our requests will show forth God's glory—showing off how good He really is.

Pray, Man of Valor!

"For everyone who asks receives, and he who seeks finds, and to him who knocks it will be opened." (Matthew 7:8 NASB)

The Lord is with you, mighty man of valor!

+ + +

Man of valor, your prayers matter—including your prayers for your wife. It's possible that you are the only one praying for her. So pray, men! That's part of your responsibility as a husband: protect your wife through prayer. In the next chapter, we'll learn more about the roles of a husband of valor and how they mimic what Christ does for *His* Bride.

Make it Practical

1. What keeps you from praying?

2. In Luke 11, Jesus' response to the disciples' request to teach them how to pray is the "Lord's Prayer" and the story of the adamant friend. He tells them to seek the Source of the solution to the need; to insistently get the attention of the Source (knock on the door); and to clearly, carefully, and energetically ask the Source for the solution. How serious are you when you have a need?

3. The Revised Standard Version renders Luke 11:8 this way: "I tell you, though he will not get up and give him anything because he is his friend, yet because of his importunity he will rise and give him whatever he needs." It is not because of the friendship these men have, but the "importunity" (the shameless audacity, the urging, and the persistence) that his need is met. Do you pray boldly? Are you insistent, persistent, even audacious? Why or why not?

4. Do you agree with Bruce's statement, "...something is going to happen that would not have happened if we had not asked." What if you do not pray? Would the desired result still happen?

5. Consider these words from prophet Hanani: "For the eyes of the Lord run to and fro throughout the whole earth, to give strong support to [show himself strong on behalf of] those whose heart is whole toward Him." (2nd Chronicles 16:9 ESV) What do you think this means? What does it say about God's desire to answer your prayers?

6. God's natural order ensures that a seed buried at a particular depth, warmed by the earth, watered by showers, and nourished by the sun, will sprout, grow, and flourish. But the seed must first be present. We can't control the soil's temperature, the amount of rain, or the heat/intensity of the sunlight. Only God can do that. But, if you do not plant a seed, will a plant sprout anyway? Maybe... but not the one you want! Do you understand that we must pray to get a desired result?

7. Is there a "secret" to getting prayers answered? (See John 14:13-14, 1st John 5:14-15)

Notes & References

---

[49] Bruce acknowledges significant influence by Edward Bounds on this chapter, particularly the *Complete Works of E.M. Bounds on Prayer*

[50] Albert Barnes, *Notes on the Old Testament* (Baker Book House 1983) 100-101

[51] *Ibid.*

Chapter 8

Brad Smith

The Five Roles of a Husband of Valor

"...so that your prayers will not be hindered."
I Peter 3:7 (NASB)

Most men desire to get married, have children, and leave something that remains of him after he dies. That's a good thing. That's the way God made us. But as husbands of valor, we have a high standard to meet. In Ephesians 5:25-28, we read:

> "Husbands, love your wives as Christ loved the church and gave himself up for her, that he might sanctify her, having cleansed her by the washing of water with the word, so that he might present the church to himself in splendor, without spot or wrinkle or any such thing, that she might be holy and without blemish. In the same way husbands should love their wives as their own bodies. He who loves his wife loves himself." (ESV)

Chapter 5 also says that the wife is to respect her husband. But while the woman is commanded to respect her husband, God lays out for him the kind of man he is to be so that he earns her respect—the respect that every man longs for.

A man is to love his wife—and display his love for her as he fulfills the five roles of a husband of valor: leader, provider, protector, teacher, and friend.

God shows us the kind of man a husband is to be so that he *earns* his wife's respect.

---

1. A Husband of Valor is a Leader

In the book of Malachi, we find a warning to the priests of Israel. Now, you might be thinking, "Priests? What's that got to do with me?"

Biblically speaking, husbands are the "priest" of their homes (Ephesians 5:23, 1st Corinthians 11:3) and the spiritual leader.[52] [53]

> "My covenant with [Levi] was one of life and peace, and I gave them to him. He stood in awe of My Name. True instruction was in his mouth, and no wrong was found on his lips. He walked with Me in peace and uprightness, and he turned many from iniquity. For the lips of a priest should guard knowledge, and people should seek instruction from his mouth, for he is the messenger of the Lord of hosts." (Malachi 2:5-7 ESV)

What do we see here that is applicable to the husband of valor?

He stood in awe of My name. Levi was in awe of God. He feared and respected God. Do you? Do I? The quality of our lives and our ability to be a husband of valor is linked to the depth of our awe—our fear, our respect—of God.

He walked with Me in peace and uprightness. A husband of valor shows integrity in his behavior and conduct. He is an example of integrity. He lives a righteous life. He confronts sin. He deals with sin when He sees it, whether in himself or in a family member. You might also say that a husband of valor "walks" with God. He gets to know God, he spends time with God. And his increasing knowledge of God is lived out before his wife.

He turned many from iniquity. He isn't afraid to confront evil and help others avoid it.

His lips guard knowledge. You and I should know the Word, guarding it in our hearts, and applying it wisely. (Psalm 119:11) Your family and others should be able to depend on you for godly decision-making and guidance. Your wife, your family, other men, should seek instruction from you.

What should a priest of the home look like? There's a great example in 2nd Chronicles 20:14-17:

> And the Spirit of the LORD came upon Jaha'ziel the son of Zechari'ah... in the midst of the assembly. And he said... Thus says the LORD to you, 'Fear not, and be not dismayed at this great multitude; for the battle is not yours but God's. Tomorrow go down against them;

behold... You will not need to fight in this battle; take your position, stand still, and see the victory of the LORD on your behalf...' Fear not, and be not dismayed; tomorrow go out against them, and the LORD will be with you." (RSV)

A priest encourages the people around him not to fear. A priest of the home, a husband of valor, reassures his wife that the Lord is in control. He leads with calmness, confidence, and strength in the Lord.

> **A priest of the home, a husband of valor, reassures his wife that the Lord is in control.**

2. A Husband of Valor is a Provider

I Timothy 5:8 gives husbands a sobering charge: "But if anyone does not provide for his own, and especially for those of his household, he has denied the faith and is worse than an unbeliever." (NASB) A provider earns a living that can meet the household expenses. If he is unable to do that with his primary job, he finds a second job or learns a skill that can earn more money. He may even move to a different location that can offer more options for employment.[54]

A husband of valor is a provider when he:

✓ Works hard to do the very best he can for his family.
✓ Researches wise purchases and doesn't waste money.
✓ Has a good financial understanding. If he doesn't, he talks with and learns from a brother who does. If he seeks to start a new business, he does so in a careful manner that, to the best of his ability, offers the most possible return.
✓ Does not allow his family to go into personal debt. (James 4:14)
✓ Cries to the Lord and seeks His face to do the right thing in every decision. He fully trusts the Lord, and fully uses his resources and the mind God has given him.

I want to be clear: this is not about material gain or pursuing excessive comfort. This is about providing for your wife and family. 1st Thessalonians 4:11-12 states: "Make it your goal to live a quiet life, minding your own business and working with your hands... and you will not need to depend on others." This is your job.

> **Providing for your family is not about pursuing material gain or excessive comfort.**

But include your wife in your decisions about provision. God gave you your wife as a helpmate and you would do well to listen to her counsel and guidance.

One time, earlier in our marriage, I was looking for a job. I had been out of work for many months. I was applying to jobs anywhere I could find one. And one day I received a call from a company asking me to come talk to them. I was excited! I told my wife about the call, told her about the job, told her when the meeting was, everything! She listened and then said, "I don't think you should go talk to them."

I replied, "What? What do you mean don't go talk to them? We need to eat; we need to pay the bills—we need the money! Of course I should go talk them!"

She said, "I don't think that this job is a good fit for you. You aren't the right man for the job."

What would you do?

Well, I went to the interview! And it went very well; in fact they offered me the job right then!

I went home and excitedly told my wife: "They offered me the job! Praise God!"

She said, "I don't think you are the right man for the job. You are not going to be happy, and they will not be happy."

I became angry, and said, "Why aren't you excited about this? God has answered our prayers! Of course I should take the job!

She said "No, I don't think this job is right for you. You are not making the right decision."

Well, what would you do?

I did what I thought a godly Christian man should do—I called several of the elders at our church and asked what they thought. Proverbs 15:22 says there is wisdom in many counselors, so I sought advice from a number of godly men. To a man, they all said, "Yes, you should take the job. You should provide for your family!"

So what did I do next? Yep! I officially accepted the job offer and went to work the next week.

Two weeks after I started, my new boss invited me to lunch. We sat down at the restaurant, and before I even had a chance to look at the menu, she said, "I don't think you are the right person for this job."

!... !!!!

How did my wife know?!

> **Include your wife in decisions about provision. God appointed her as your ally. Listen to her counsel!**

Here's what I learned: God gave her to me as my "helpmate", right? She knows me. She knows me better than anyone apart from God. She understood what the work would be. She knew that it wasn't the right job for me. She knew that I would not be good at it and that I would eventually be very unhappy—in fact, miserable.

That's what God gave her to me for. To provide help, counsel, assistance. In fact, later when I told our pastor this story, he said, "That was a big mistake. Don't ever take anyone else's counsel above your wife's. Hers is the most important advice you should seek."

But because we have a God of grace, He knew full well that He could use this as a significant learning experience where I would come to understand, appreciate, and rely on my wife's insight from that day forward. And, it didn't take long before He gave me a different job, one suited to my skills and training.

God gave you your wife to help you, too, including in your work. Be sure to seek and value her help.

> **"Don't ever take anyone else's counsel above your wife's. Hers is the most important advice you should seek."**

3. A Husband of Valor is a Protector

Protecting our wives from physical, emotional, and financial danger is one of the core tasks that God intended for us to take on.

The fact that most men are taller and stronger than most women says something about them being the physical protector. Generally, one of the things God intended for us as men is to protect our wives and families from physical danger. Why? Because God has built into men the instinct to protect, and we know that "greater love has no one than this, that someone lay down his life for his friends." (John 15:13 ESV)

Joseph, Mary's betrothed husband, is a good example of a protector. When Mary was accused of immorality, he planned to protect her from being stoned to death—even before he was visited by the angel. (Matthew 1)

The Bible provides a couple of bad examples, too: Nabal put his family and household at risk because of his temper. (1st Samuel 25)

Achan caused his entire family's death by stealing. (Joshua 7) That's not being a protector—just the opposite!

We also provide protection for our wives when we pray with and for them. The Bible says in 1st Samuel 12:23: "...the Lord forbid that I should sin ... by no longer praying for you." Indeed, 1st Peter 5:8 warns us to be alert for the ongoing spiritual battle. The verse says, "Be sober-minded; be watchful. Our adversary the devil prowls around like a roaring lion, seeking someone to devour." (ESV) Don't let your family be devoured!

I'll never forget one time when I was unemployed and my wife told me that she felt protected because she knew I was praying. It wasn't about the quality of the prayers, and it didn't matter if I stumbled over the words. It was just the fact that I prayed. I was seeking the help of the Lord who is the ultimate protector. She also feels protected when I pray for her before either of us travels.

> **I'll never forget the time my wife told me that she felt protected because she knew I was praying.**

4. A Husband of Valor is a Teacher

The verses in Malachi also indicate another role—teacher. Malachi 2:6 says, "True instruction was in his mouth."

A husband of valor should be a teacher. But you can't teach if you don't know anything. In order to teach, a man needs to know the Word, studying it daily, just like a priest. He should be able to find or refer to a Scripture that his wife or kids ask about or that applies in a given situation. He must be willing and ready to share thoughts about the Word at any time.

A husband of valor can share with his wife what he has learned from the Scriptures. Perhaps to meet a current need: "Like apples of gold in settings of silver is a word spoken at the proper time." (Proverbs 25:11 NASB) Or perhaps as reassurance, "Do not be afraid..." (Luke 12:7 GNT) And in so doing he "washes" her with God's Word; he "cleanses" her heart and mind, purging her fear and anxiety (Ephesians 5:26)—just like Christ does for His church—with assurance that God is our rock and our redeemer, (Psalm 19:14) our "stronghold in times of trouble," (Psalm 9:9 RSV) and our deliverer in whom we take refuge. (Psalm 18:2)

The husband of valor keeps reminding his wife of the Word: what God says and what He promises. That may not look like "teaching"; it may just be talking together. What it looks like in your marriage is up to you. But you are called to take the initiative. As the man of your home, as the priest of your home, you are to teach.

5. A Husband of Valor is a Friend

1 Peter 3:7 says, "Likewise, husbands, live with your wives in an understanding way, showing honor to the woman as the weaker vessel, since they are heirs with you of the grace of life, so that your prayers may not be hindered." (ESV)

How can you live with your wife in an understanding manner if you are not first her friend? A friend supports, shows loyalty, listens and cares. Friends enjoy one another and spend time together. Friends talk, listen, and share feelings and observations without judgment or criticism. They do things together. They don't expect a "reward" for their friendship activities, and don't expect certain outcomes from the friendship. They simply enjoy one another...and they grow old together.

> **How can you "live with your wife in an understanding manner" if you are not first her friend?**

Now, like every man, I need to pray for God to help me understand my wife. It requires patience for us both to achieve understanding because God made women and men to be very different.

God did that purposely. He did not do this to make our marriages difficult; He did not do this to make us want to give up. Men and women were given their own roles—complementary roles—each with value and worth, each bringing key aspects of the Lord and His character to every situation. Both are perfectly designed to be and do what He has called them to be and do.

Both a man and a woman are shining creations of God's design to fulfill His purposes. To live with your wife in an understanding manner, you need to appreciate your wife for how carefully and beautifully God made her. Men, study your wife. Know her dreams, desires, and concerns.

Finally, note that while 1st Peter 3:7 begins with "...live with your wives in an understanding way...", it ends with "...so that nothing will hinder your prayers." Your tempered, kind, gentle manner with your wife impacts the quality of your communication with God, and may even affect His answers to your prayer requests, or make it difficult to pray at all.

Teach Boys to Become Husbands of Valor

Occasionally I'll hear someone introduce a couple by saying, jokingly, "This man married up!" It's meant to be a compliment to the wife. I used to laugh at that until my daughter shocked me once by saying that most women marry down. She meant that most young women settle for men who are less-than—men who are not as spiritually, socially, or intellectually mature. They settle for guys who haven't proven themselves as leaders, providers, or as wise, sober protectors. In her mind, that was "just the way it is!"

The Washington Times published a column by Janice Crouse entitled "Pop Culture is Producing Male Losers." She wrote, "Immature, ill-educated men who are unprepared to assume the responsibility of forming and supporting a family are not good husband material." She also said that the feminist agenda that has been working very hard to beat men down is backfiring and ultimately hurting women, because they are getting this poor husband material as a result.[55]

So that brings me to this question: Who is teaching boys to be men—men who can lead, protect, provide, teach, and be a friend to their wives as husbands of valor? *You* need to be doing this! If you don't, your boys will learn a false definition of manhood from friends or acquaintances in their neighborhood or school. In those settings they won't be learning the righteous truths and principles of God and the high standard that God calls them to.

The Standard is Purposely High

Several years ago, there was a young man who was interested in one of my daughters. My daughter was away from home at the time to receive advanced education. They came to visit for a few days, which gave us a chance to observe him. On the last day of his visit, I took him to a coffee shop to talk.

I explained the husband's five roles to him. I told him that I saw him as a good friend to my daughter. When she had been going through tough times and facing a lot of criticism while she was in college, he was a friend to her. I commended him for that, and said I saw that he was also probably a good protector. But I told him that he had a long way to go to be a provider, leader, and teacher.

He looked shocked. No one had ever talked to him like that before. But he was interested in my daughter, and you can be quite sure I was going to look out for her and evaluate any man she might one day marry.

> **Men like the challenge of high standards.**

Was I harsh with him? Of course not. He was young and not yet ready for marriage. But I set the bar high, as any father should do for his daughter.

You want your daughter to marry a husband of valor; men like the challenge of high standards. Don't back down! If he wanted to eventually think of marrying my daughter, he needed to meet a high standard. He needed to earn my daughter. Why was this important? Because if he worked hard and if he succeeded, then he would be far more likely to value and cherish her as a prize he had fought to win—as Christ did the church.

How does Christ love His church? He leads it. He protects it. He provides for it. He teaches it. And He is a compassionate friend to His children in the church.

How should we love our wives? As Christ loves the church.

Remember: The Lord is with you, mighty man of valor!

> **How should we love our wives?**
> **As Christ loves the church.**

+ + +

You influence your children more than you can possibly imagine. They are watching you—all the time. In the next chapter, we'll take about three qualities you should seek to develop in your role as a father—a father of valor.

Make it Practical

1. Carefully think through each of the five roles of a husband of valor: leader, provider, protector, teacher, and friend. Prayerfully check yourself: how well are you doing in each of these roles.

> a. As a leader, are you involved with your wife and family, thinking through decisions and talking them through with your wife rather than making the decision and then forcing it on her? Are you willing to receive her helpmate counsel and then proactively make the decision that is in the best interest of the family? (Of course, remember, that you are ultimately accountable for the decisions made in the marriage.)
>
> b. As a provider, are you working hard to provide for her needs?
>
> c. As a protector, are you shielding your wife both physically and through prayer? Are you striving to be a protector solely in your own strength and knowledge—or are you protecting your wife through your dependence on God? Are you praying with her?
>
> d. As a teacher, are you spending time in the Word and sharing your insights with your wife? What does being a teacher look like in your home?
>
> e. As a friend, do you spend time with your wife to just talk, listen, and do things together?

2. Maybe you're a good provider but not a good teacher. Maybe you are leading but you aren't a friend to your wife. In which area do you need to improve the most? What can you do today to begin improving?

3. Embracing and living the five roles of a husband of valor is spiritual leadership. Spiritual leadership must begin with a man's personal walk with God. When was the last time you examined your walk with God? What are the implications of your current spiritual life on your wife's spiritual health?

Notes & References

52 "A husband is to be the family priest. He represents his wife and children to God. He spends time in prayer each day remembering the needs and concerns of his wife. He prays for the salvation of his children. Like Job, he asks the Lord to forgive the sins of his children. He sets the spiritual temperature in the home. He sacrifices his life for theirs. He is a mediator to God for his family."
Patrick Morley, "Exploring a Husband's Role as a Prophet, Priest and King" (Charisma Magazine 2015)
https://www.charismamag.com/life/men/18610-exploring-a-husband-s-role-as-a-prophet-priest-and-king

53 "[I] believe looking at oneself as a priest helps a man view his role in the home in a more other-centered and ministerial way. ...[it puts] male headship in a light that tend[s] to prevent abusive or overbearing exercises of male headship in the home."
Sam Waldren, "A Defense of 'A Man as Priest in His Home' " (The Aquila Report 2013)
https://theaquilareport.com/a-defense-of-a-man-as-priest-in-his-home
See also Waldren's book, *A Man as Priest in His Home* (Reformed Baptist Academic Press 2013)

54 On a few occasions while presenting this teaching, men have asked if the role of provider is "still" the man's role. "Modern times," they've said, "mean that women work and sometimes even earn more money than the man." That's all true. Throughout history, husbands and wives have both contributed to the material provision of their households in various ways. But that doesn't change God's specific commissioning for men. Scholar Owen Strachan says,

> "The fact that Adam's work is cursed in Genesis 3:15 has seemed to many to suggest that in God's economy, men bear the responsibilities of provision. This view is corroborated by texts that touch on the matter either directly or indirectly. [For example] it is the men of Israel who leave the home to provide food for their families (Genesis 37)... [This] fits with the biblical-theological role Christ plays for his church in redeeming her; he is her head, her provision, and she depends upon him to live. (Ephesians 5) In a marriage, men fill this Christic role. We therefore have explicit textual reasons for calling men to be providers for their families..."

Owen Strachan, "Of 'Dad Moms' and 'Man Fails': An Essay on Men and Awesomeness" (*Journal for Biblical Manhood and Womanhood* 2012) 23

55 Janice Crouse, "Pop Culture is Producing Male Losers," *The Washington Times,* 2012

Chapter 9

Brad Smith

A Father of Valor
Turns Hearts

"...the father makes known to the children Your faithfulness."

Isaiah 38:19 (ESV)

There was a long period of public silence following God's messages to the Old Testament prophets. Malachi was the last prophet to convey God's words to the people of Israel, and the Messiah was not born for some 400 years after that. In the last verses of the book of Malachi, God gave closing instructions—His final words before He went publicly silent.

> "Behold, I will send you Elijah the prophet before the great and awesome day of the Lord comes. And he will turn the hearts of fathers to their children and the hearts of children to their fathers, lest I come and strike the land with a decree of utter destruction." (Malachi 4:5-6 ESV)[56]

God could have chosen to talk about the impending birth of Jesus Christ, the problems with Israel's leaders or priests, or the coming Roman takeover of Israel. But no—God chose to talk about dads and their kids. He said that preparation for the arrival of the day of the Lord must involve turning the hearts of fathers to their children and the hearts of children to their fathers.[57]

Four hundred years later, the angel of the Lord appeared to Zechariah to tell him of the coming birth of his son, John the Baptist. In Luke 1:16-17, the angel says of John, "And he will turn many of the children of Israel to the Lord their God, and he will go before him in the spirit and the power of Elijah, to turn the hearts of the fathers to the children, and the disobedient to the wisdom of the just, to make ready for the Lord a people prepared." (ESV)

God said this twice. Clearly, the relationship between fathers and their children is important. The fact that it is stated twice, both in Malachi and in Luke, should get our attention. This matters to God. R. Kent Hughes sums it up plainly: "When a man truly gives his heart to Christ, it is turned toward his children."[58]

Papa God

Why is this so important? God says in Malachi 4 that the restoration of fathers to their children is the starting place to properly prepare for the arrival and reception of Jesus. Could the Lord be saying that a right relationship between a father and his child prepares the child's heart for the work of Jesus in his or her life?

When I was a child, if my dad and I weren't getting along, I had less motivation to succeed. I had more of a desire to rebel, sin, do dumb things, make bad decisions, or simply not care. I needed Dad's approval. I needed to know that he loved me. And if I didn't have his approval, or if I doubted his love for me, I would feel purposeless.[59]

> **Could it be that a right relationship between father and child prepares the child's heart for Jesus' work?**

Author Gary Thomas tells of a time when his youngest daughter, Kelsey, was two years old and was sitting at the supper table. Gary was away from the house that evening. Kelsey was trying out her words and her knowledge of each family member's name. One by one, she pointed to the chairs and said the names of the family member who sat there— Mommy, Allison, Graham, Kelsey. Then she pointed at her dad's empty chair and said, "God". Lisa, Gary's wife, quickly corrected her and said, "That's not where God sits, Kelsey, that's where Papa sits." Kelsey smiled and pointed at the chair and said, "Jesus."

Three days later, Gary was home and they were all at the table. Kelsey again pointed and spoke everyone's names. When she got to Gary, she said, "Jesus."

"I'm not Jesus, Kelsey," Gary said. "I'm Papa."

"You're Papa God," Kelsey replied.

In his book *Sacred Parenting*, Gary said of this incident,

"This opened my eyes as a young dad. And I began to notice that the more time I spent with my kids as they grew, the more open they seemed to God's presence in their lives. The less time I spent with them, the less they seemed to pray... somehow, I help shape their passion and hunger for God."[60]

Papa God. A dad has a big influence on his child, and God stated for us just how important this is. A child's openness to Jesus has a lot to do with his or her relationship with Dad.

Men, you are being watched, and you have a significant role in your child's mental, emotional, and even spiritual development. What do you want your children to see?

"Boys [and girls] watch their dads intently day by day, noting every minor detail of behavior and values. Your sons will imitate much of what you do. If you blow up regularly...at your wife, your boys will be likely to treat their mothers and other females disrespectfully. If you drink to excess, your kids will be at risk for alcohol and substance abuse. If you curse or smoke or fight with your coworkers, your boys will probably follow suit. If you are selfish or mean or angry, you'll see those characteristics...

Fortunately, the converse is also true. If you are honest, trustworthy, caring, loving, self-disciplined, and God-fearing, your boys will be influenced by those traits as they age. If you are deeply committed to Christ and live by biblical teaching, your children will probably follow in your footsteps. So much depends on what they observe in you, for better or worse."[61]

Because of this, there are three qualities every father of valor should seek to develop. Fathers of valor:

1. Take Action
2. Accept Responsibility
3. Look Ahead[62]

1. A Father of Valor Takes Action

It is clear from God's Word that a father is to be actively involved in his family's life and world. Consider these instructions from the book of Numbers:

"If a woman vows to the Lord and binds herself by a pledge, while within her father's house in her youth, and her father hears of her vow and of her pledge by which she has bound herself and says nothing to her, then all her vows shall stand, and every pledge by which she has bound herself shall stand. But if her father opposes her on the day that he hears of it, no vow of hers, no pledge by which she has bound herself shall stand. And the Lord will forgive her, because her father opposed her...but if [he] says nothing to her from day to day, then he establishes all her vows or all her pledges that are upon her. He has established them, because he said nothing to her on the day that he heard of them." (Numbers 30:3-5, 14 ESV)

Note that Dad was to take action to approve or disapprove a vow that his daughter made the day he heard of it. The Lord says in Numbers 30 that men are held to their words, but women and daughters are not, if the dad or the husband steps in. God is saying to these dads, "Be involved, take initiative, be aware of what's going on with your family, and stay on top of it. Take action."

When I was in high school, I helped clean the church my family attended. One of the Sunday school rooms had a decorative poster that stated: "Not to decide is to decide."

Men, realize this: your silence means your approval. What we often don't realize is that by not choosing a direction, we choose a direction. We end up choosing a course of events simply by letting it happen. Many times we do not want to get involved, and we don't want to have to make a decision. I'm guilty of that! But our families expect and need us to take initiative and be involved.

By not choosing a direction, we choose a direction.

Not to decide is to decide.

Have you ever wondered where Adam was when Eve reached for the fruit of the tree of the knowledge of good and evil? Some translations of the Bible make it very clear. In verse 6 of Genesis chapter 3, we read,

"So when the woman saw that the tree was good for food, and that it was a delight to the eyes, and that the tree was to be desired to make one wise, she took of its fruit and ate, and she also gave some to her husband who was with her, and he ate." (ESV, emphasis added)

Where was Adam? He was right there. He was standing right with her. Why didn't he stop her?

We can give Adam some credit—we know he warned Eve about the tree at some point, since she had not been created when God instructed Adam. (Genesis 2:17) Eve told the serpent that God had forbidden them to eat of the tree's fruit. (Genesis 3:3) But in the end Adam didn't stop her. He was right there; he knew what was going on. But he said nothing and did nothing. "Adam ruined paradise by failing to do something."[63]

Why? Why do men still stay silent when there are crucial moments of decision in their homes and they could influence a course of events?[64]

Families cry out for men who will do more than look the other way and tune out when they come home. Kids want dads who are involved, dads who provide spiritual and moral direction, dads who are affirming and life-giving. Women want men who will engage with them, protect them, and listen to them. It is not enough to only be physically present. A dad must also be emotionally present with his family, paying attention to them and actively loving them.

> "Children of highly involved fathers show increased cognitive competence, increased empathy, enhanced school performance, greater motivation to succeed, enhanced social development and self-esteem, less sex-stereotyped beliefs, stronger sexual identity and character, and more intrinsic motivation."[65]

Dads, you have had, you do have, and you will have a big impact on your children—for better or for worse. Again and again, studies have shown the value of a dad in a kid's life. Dads help their kids to become more confident, to be compassionate and kind, to solve problems, to be generous, and to even have higher thinking and reasoning abilities—to be smarter! There is a substantial connection between positive paternal involvement and a child's well-being.[66] [67]

Dads help their kids to become more confident, to be compassionate and kind, and to develop higher thinking and reasoning abilities.

But some time ago, I also came across these disturbing statistics: kids without dads in the United States are:

- ✓ Four times more likely to live in poverty
- ✓ Ten times more likely to abuse chemical substances
- ✓ Two times more likely to commit suicide
- ✓ Nine times more likely to drop out of school

Meanwhile,

- ✓ Seventy percent of men in prison are from fatherless homes
- ✓ 70% of teen pregnancies happen to fatherless girls
- ✓ Ninety percent of homeless and runaway children were from fatherless homes[68]

Not to decide is to decide. Not to act is to act.

2. A Father of Valor Accepts His Responsibility

When our firstborn child, a son, arrived, and I saw him all rolled up like a sausage roll in his little blue cap and blanket, I cried.

I cried because his birth was very difficult, and I was so glad that both he and my wife were okay. And I cried because I was a dad—and I had no idea what that meant or what to do. With tears in my eyes, I prayed for him, I committed him to the Lord, and I cried out for the Lord's help.

We brought him home, and our world changed overnight. Suddenly, everything in our lives was about him. He was tiny when he was born and needed to be fed every two hours, so we couldn't leave our home for long periods of time or get a full night's sleep. His diaper needed changing and often at the worst times. And when I came home from work, I needed to help look after him—I couldn't rest, put my feet up, call my friends, or watch TV, and wait for supper! Within just a few days, I realized for the first time in my life just how selfish I was and the truth of the adage "Men have a natural tendency to avoid responsibility."

> **Men have a natural tendency
> to avoid responsibility.**

I knew that to be a dad, I needed to fight this tendency. "Fathering is at the heart of manliness, of what it means to be a man. Godly fathers put others' needs before their own."[69] A father of valor accepts his responsibility.

The Lord chose to take my dad home to Him when he was eighty-eight years old. Dad had been a hard worker and an honest man. He always provided for his family. He didn't like his job, but he did not have many options, and so for twenty-six years he worked at that same job. He worked long hours and served his employer well because it was the right thing to do for his family. We didn't have much money, but thanks to Dad, our needs were met. He accepted his responsibility.

When I lost my full-time job as a young married man with our first small child, I went out and begged for any work I could find. It was hard to find jobs at that time. Few companies were hiring. None of the few jobs that were available paid well, so at one point I worked three jobs—seven days a week, sometimes fourteen hours a day. That lasted twenty-two months. It was the toughest period of my life.

But it was the right thing to do, and I knew it deep down. I knew what a father does, because that's what my dad did. I had observed from an early age a man who accepted the responsibility God had placed on his shoulders. I imitated my dad.

A Father's Responsibility Extends Beyond Provision

I believe that far too many fathers don't pay enough attention to their sons to help them and to train them to be men. Many times boys don't know what a man is and they don't know when they have achieved manhood—they are just older. I believe a father has to take an active role in his son's development and growth.

When my son turned thirteen, I prayed about and wrote down what I believed should be eight defining characteristics of a man. Inspired by Robert Lewis' excellent book *Raising a Modern-Day Knight*, I asked eight godly men to meet with my son and me one evening and speak to him about these characteristics. We told him that over the next eight to ten years we would all be committed to training him to be a man. Then we laid hands on him and prayed.

That was a central moment in his life. Over those next years, he attended men's teaching, I met with him weekly, and he studied the Bible on his own. Later, I presented to him a written Certificate of Manhood, which I read to him at a special time when we were together. I told him, "You are now a man."

"You are now a man."

To all you men who have daughters, I want to talk about the important relationship you have with the precious little girl the Lord has given you. Pastor James Emery White wrote this about the impact that a father has on his daughter:

> There is a special relationship between a father and a daughter, one set in place by God as part of the very

structure of the family. From a father, a daughter learns what to look for in a man, and an expectation of how she should be treated. From a father, a daughter gains security in her self-esteem and sense of self-worth as a woman. From a father, a daughter is afforded protection, and never has to worry about being vulnerable. From a father, a daughter is given moral guidance and a protected virtue. From a father, a daughter receives affection in ways that fulfill her young, developing heart. In short, from a father, a daughter is provided for, protected and cherished.

But I suppose I should say, "From a good father."

From a disconnected, absentee, derelict father, a daughter accepts almost any treatment from other men; is insecure and seeks to gain her security through the lowering of morals; is subject to the world in all of the worst ways; has no moral compass and often abandons chastity; and seeks affection from men to fill the void. In short, she is not protected, not provided for, and not cherished."[70]

By her father, a daughter is provided for, protected, and cherished.

One of the hardest decisions I've ever made was to give up leading a very active and solid men's ministry at a church. But I did it because my older daughter was beginning to resent that I was always able to spend time with the men in my church but wasn't spending enough time with her. When I became aware of that, my heart sank. The last thing I ever wanted was to have my kids think that my ministry was more important than them. The last thing I wanted was for my daughter to grow up resenting God because her dad was more about ministry than about family or about her. So I quit the men's ministry and doubled my efforts to spend time with her. Much later I received a letter from her in which she thanked me for being not just her dad but also her friend.

For some of you, accepting your responsibility as a father may not be about ministry. You may be placing more importance on your work, sports, hobbies, or time with your friends than your family. Don't lose sight of your priorities and of your calling as a father of valor. We must accept the God-given responsibility the Lord placed on our shoulders when He gave us our children.[71]

3. A Father of Valor Looks Ahead

The history of the United States includes the movement of thousands of people across the mountains, plains, and prairies to settle in the West. In the mid-1800s, families put their belongings into large wagons and traveled for many months through territory occupied by wild animals and hostile Native American tribes. For their safety and protection, these pioneers went together in wagon trains, each of which had a scout. A scout's job was to ride ahead and see what dangers lay further on along the path. He would then return and warn the families, preparing them for what was coming.

A father of valor must do the same. He must look ahead and then prepare himself, his wife, and his family for potential dangers.

The book of Proverbs speaks to this. Consider these verses:

✓ "...the prudent looks where he is going." (Proverbs 14:15 RSV)
✓ "Go to the ant, o sluggard, observe her ways and be wise, which, having no chief, Officer or ruler, prepares her food in the summer, and gathers her provision in the harvest." (Proverbs 6:6-8 NASB)
✓ "Know well the condition of your flocks, and pay attention to your herds." (Proverbs 27:2,3 NASB)

First, Be With Them

Here's your first "Look Ahead" activity: Have dinner with your family. It seems so simple, so basic, we may be tempted to dismiss it or deprioritize it relative to other activities in our busy schedules. But numerous studies have found that children and adolescents who are regularly involved in family meals are less likely to develop eating disorders, fall prey to alcohol or substance use, engage in violence, or develop feelings of depression or thoughts of suicide. Moreover, frequent family meals correlate to increased self-esteem and school success.[72] Routinely eating together gives you a chance to check in, to listen to your children and get a sense for how they're doing and what's going on in their lives. Then, you'll have a better idea of what they need and how to provide for them, lead them, and exhort them.

Next, Prepare Them Spiritually

On New Year's Day, 1996, I took some time to look through the Bible to find the roles of dad and husband. One of these roles was teacher, which I found from verses like Proverbs 1:8: "My son, hear the instruction of thy father," and Deuteronomy, where the fathers are instructed to teach the commandments to their children: "You shall teach them diligently to your children, and shall talk of them when you sit in your house, and when you walk by the way, and when you lie down, and when you rise," (Deuteronomy 6:7 ESV) and in Isaiah, where the prophet wrote, "...the father makes known to the children Your faithfulness." (Isaiah 38:19 ESV)

I realized I had not been actively, purposefully teaching my children, and I decided to make some changes. I was not sure that I could "teach" the Bible or anything else to my kids. But what the Lord showed me was quite simple: I could at least read the Bible to my kids. So that's what we did. I started meeting with my son and older daughter separately each week for one hour, just the two of us. My son was twelve when we started this; my older daughter was eight.

We started reading through the book of Proverbs. I began to explain what I understood the verses to mean. This led me to further study the Bible for myself to make sure I was accurate in what I told my kids. As we continued meeting, we would read a book of the Bible or a book about a biblical character. Sometimes we just talked about current issues and situations. This was how I came to know my kids' hearts, their desires, their challenges, and their dreams.

> **I wasn't sure I could teach the Bible to my kids.**
> **But what the Lord showed me was simple:**
> **I could at least read the Bible with them!**

I am convinced that this decision changed the paths of my kids' lives. If I had not had those intentional times with my children, I don't know if I would have talked to them about important matters of life. I may never have taught them a variety of biblical principles. I may never have taught my son about manhood and about living in an understanding manner with women. (1st Peter 3:7) We may never have gotten into some uncomfortable subjects relating to moral purity—but fortunately, stories like that of Joseph with Potiphar's wife basically forced us into those conversations.

My children are grown now and all live in different cities. All three of them and their spouses live and walk in the ways of the Lord.

Men, make it part of your weekly schedule to read the Bible to your children. It is an activity all fathers of valor should do. It helps your kids learn more about God and helps prepare them for the future. And spending that one hour per week with them also does this: it turns your heart to your children, and it helps turn the hearts of your children to you—just like the Lord said in Malachi.

Read and discuss the Bible with your children.

When my son was nineteen, he surprised me with this note on Father's Day:

> Dear Dad,
> I know we don't see eye-to-eye sometimes, and I know in some ways we're very, very different. But what I want to thank you so much for today is your willingness—your willingness to listen even when I'm wrong, your willingness to let God work in you even when it hurts, and your willingness to do what it takes to provide for my needs, even when it's beneath you. You've set for me a true example of what it means to be a father, a mentor, and a friend. Keep growing so you can keep going, Dad. I love you.

Prepare Their Hearts

Because the relationship between a father and a child prepares the child's heart for the work of Jesus in his or her life, a father of valor must take action, accept his responsibility, and look ahead—recognize and prepare for danger. (Luke 12:54-56) He must spend time with his kids to know their hearts. And, as my son reminded me, a father of valor must never stop growing in Christ.

The Lord is with you, mighty man of valor!

+ + +

A father of valor's role is to turn hearts. Next, we offer some practical guidance on the day-to-day actions of a father of valor, when dad "acts like a man."

Make it Practical

1. The Lord's final statement to the people of Israel before a 400-year period of public silence was about turning the hearts of fathers to their children and the hearts of children to their fathers, highlighting the vital importance of the father-child relationship. Would you describe your heart as inclined towards your children? If not, how can you intentionally focus on your relationship with your kids?

2. Whether we realize it or not, we as dads influence our kids either toward or away from God. Examine the spiritual influence you have on your kids. How do you continually strive to point your kids toward God through your words and actions?

3. When was the last time you initiated a conversation or special event with your children? How would you need to rearrange your schedule in order to plan on a weekly or biweekly time to spend with each of your children one-on-one?

4. Children face more than physical danger—they are also vulnerable to emotional, spiritual, and intellectual dangers. How do you guard your children from each of these dangers? What "looking ahead" are you doing for your family?

5. Look at what Jesus said in Luke 12:54-56. Even Jesus grew a little exasperated with His followers. He's thinking, "How could you *not* know what the signs of the present age are showing you and what that means?" Fathers, how do you *not* know the impact of what your child is doing or experiencing today on what he or she may become? How could you *not* surmise the influence these things may have on their character and behavior in the future?

6. What tends to inhibit you from accepting your responsibility as a father? What do you allow to come before your children? It could be your work, the way you spend your free time, an addiction, or even your ministry. What steps can you take to change that?

Notes & References

56 Several recent versions of the Bible have adopted gender-neutral language, replacing the word 'father' in Malachi 4:6 with 'parents' (and making similar replacements in many other places). However, the Hebrew word here is 'âb and it means the father or grandfather of an individual. It does not mean parent; this prophecy does not apply to the father and the mother. This incorrect rendering may lead a father to minimize the importance of his influence on his children. According to Strong's Concordance, 'âb (father—the male parent) appears in the Bible 1,469 times.

57 "The Hebrew word for curse in this verse is one of the harshest in Scripture, suggesting complete annihilation. That means that only when men stop abdicating their God-mandated role as leaders in their families and communities will we be able to survive and thrive as a nation."
Rick Johnson, "The Difference a Father Can Make" (New Man 2006) 35

58 R. Kent Hughes, *Disciplines of a Godly Man* (Crossway Books 2001) 54

59 Robert Rohr says that a mom's love is "...assumed, taken for granted, relied upon instinctively... But Dad is [the] 'other' in the house, at a greater distance. He does not 'have' to love you. His love is not inherently felt and drawn upon, like Mother love. He must choose to love you!... he picks you out, he notices you among the many. [His love] redeems, liberates, and delights, therefore, in a totally different way... It validates us and affirms us deeply, precisely because it is not [a given]. We need him to like us, to bless us even after our mistakes, to enjoy our company, to tell us that we can succeed."
Robert Rohr, *From Wild Man to Wise Man: Reflections on Male Spirituality*, quoted by Brett and Kate McKay, "Looking for a Daddy in All the Wrong Places", (The Art of Manliness 2021)
https://www.artofmanliness.com/articles/looking-for-a-daddy-in-all-the-wrong-places

60 Gary Thomas, *Sacred Parenting* (Zondervan 2004) 11

61 J. Dobson, "June 2020 Letter" (Dr. James Dobson Family Institute 2020)

62 Brad credits the first two attributes of fathers of valor to Robert Lewis' book *Raising a Modern-Day Knight*. The third attribute comes from Stu Weber's book *Tender Warrior*.

63 Larry Crabb, *The Silence of Adam* (Zondervan 1995) 91

64 "Since Adam, every man has had a natural inclination to remain silent when he should speak. Adam was a silent man, a passive man. Like many men in history, he was physically present but emotionally absent..." *Ibid.*, 12

65 Dr. Stephen Duncan, "The Importance of Fathers" (Montguide 2000)
https://stillwater.msuextension.org/fcsmontguides/TheImportanceof Fathers.pdf

66 "Studies show that children with involved fathers do better in school and are more likely to get A's. Children with 'absent' fathers are more likely to repeat a grade and are twice as likely to drop out of school."
Kim Peterson, "Fathers Play Key role in Healthy Child Development" (Auburn Pub 2012)
http://auburnpub.com/lifestyles/fathers-play-key-role-in-healthy-child-development/article_89ce66bf-9c63-5c90-acc4-b9bd54362a12.html

67 "Children who grow up with involved fathers are more comfortable exploring the world around them and more likely to exhibit self-control and pro-social behavior."

R.D. Parke, "The Importance of Fathers in the Healthy Development of Children" (Childwelfare.gov 2006)
http://www.childwelfare.gov/pubs/usermanuals/fatherhood/
[68] "The Extent of Fatherlessness" (National Center for Fathering 2013)
https://fathers.com/statistics-and-research/the-extent-of-fatherlessness/
See also "Appreciating How Fathers Give Children a Head Start" from the U.S. Department of Health & Human Services:
https://eric.ed.gov/?q=fathers+head+start&id=ED543023
[69] Rick Johnson, "The Difference a Father Can Make" (New Man 2006) 34
[70] James Emery White, "What's Wrong with Lindsay?" (Crosswalk.com 2012)
https://www.crosswalk.com/blogs/dr-james-emery-white/whats-wrong-with-lindsay.html
[71] For more on fathers and their impact, see "The Father Factor" section at https://www.josh.org/resources/apologetics/research/
[72] https://www.ncbi.nlm.nih.gov/pmc/articles/PMC4325878/

Chapter 10

Bruce Campbell[73]

A Father of Valor Acts Like a Man

"Be strong, and show yourself a man."

I Kings 2:2 (RSV)

P aul had some insights about parenting that he wrote in his first letter to the Thessalonians. The passage helps any man or woman of God to understand their value in the life of any person of any age. Paul wrote to the Thessalonians of his love for them, of his special care and concern for their spiritual welfare, and of his desire that they lead a life worthy of God.

The Mothering Aspect of Parenting

When you look at 1st Thessalonians 2:7, we see Paul state in so many words that his team of ministers—Timothy, Silas, and himself—gave them tender care and gentleness. In verse 8 he said, "Having so fond an affection for you, we were well-pleased to impart to you not only the gospel of God but also our own lives, because you had become very dear to us." In verse 9 he says, "For you recall, brethren, our labor and hardship, how working night and day so as not to be a burden to any of you, we proclaimed to you the gospel of God." (NASB)

That is the mothering aspect of parenting. Paul says his team was like a tender, gentle, nursing mother, giving round-the-clock, personal, intimate care to them. That's part of spiritual leadership—providing a haven or place of safety and protection and providing security, peace, affection, kindness, gentleness, mercy, and love.

The Fathering Aspect of Parenting

In addition to the side of Paul that acted like a mother, there was another side of him that acted like a father. Paul continues: "You are witnesses, and God also, how holy and righteous and blameless was our behavior to you believers; for you know how, like a father with his children, we exhorted each one of you and encouraged you and charged you to lead a life worthy of God, who calls you into his own kingdom and glory." (1st Thessalonians 2:10-12 RSV)

The mother side wants to cherish, nurture, love, hold, and affirm. And the father comes along and says that's all wonderful (and means it!), but in the end we want to be sure that our children are living according to God's standards, to walk in a manner worthy of the God who calls them.

In his mentoring, Paul had a tender side and also a strong, courageous side in which he demanded the highest uncompromising life. That's the balance. The mother demonstrates God's kindhearted love, and the father comes alongside her, exhorting children to the conduct God requires, motivating their hearts to respond, and solemnly showing the consequences of failure. And, he lives the life that he demands of his children.

> **We must live the life we demand of our children.**

On the one hand a concern for the person; on the other hand a concern for the process. On the one hand a concern for kindness; on the other hand a concern for discipline. On the one hand a concern for affection; on the other hand a concern for authority and respect. On the one hand embracing; on the other hand exhorting. On the one hand cherishing; on the other hand challenging.

Sometimes our kids need a mom; sometimes a dad. But sometimes our child wants a mother to coddle and comfort him when maybe what he really needs is a father to hold him to his commitments and responsibilities, and to keep him accountable.[74] So let's look more at what the fathering aspect of parenting teaches.[75] [76]

Act Like Men

What is the most basic fundamental virtue of manliness—the one or two distinct qualities that make a man a man? 1st Corinthians 16:13 says, "Be on the alert, stand firm in the faith, act like men, be strong." (NASB)

Act like men. How do men act? In our society in the United States they act any way they want. Some of them are lazy; some of them are passive doormats or pushovers; others are angry, proud, and self-centered; still others are manipulative, controlling, or even violent. Even men who have been in the church all their lives do not understand the strength and sacrifice of Jesus and how that sets a manly example to them of what they should be for their wives, for their families, and for the church.

But Paul says here to conduct yourself in a courageous way with strength. That means to have staying power, stamina, and determination. It means to have strength of conviction and the courage to stand on it. That's how men are supposed to act.

> **Strength of conviction and the courage to stand on it: That's how men are supposed to act.**

But notice verse 14: "Let all that you do be done in love." Men seek accomplishment. They want to face life with courage and stand on their beliefs. They want and should make the hard decisions—at minimum they will be held responsible for the decisions their family makes (see Genesis 3:17)—but they need to do all this with caring and love.

Show Yourself a Man

In Deuteronomy 31, Moses is advising Joshua as Joshua is about to take over. Moses was forthright but encouraging. Verse 6 says, "Be strong and courageous, do not be afraid or tremble..., for the LORD your God is the one who goes with you. He will not fail you or forsake you." Then the Lord speaks directly to Joshua in v.23: "Then He commissioned Joshua the son of Nun, and said, 'Be strong and courageous, for you shall bring the sons of Israel into the land which I swore to them, and I will be with you.' " (NASB)

Now look how Joab, David's battle commander, motivated his men in 2nd Samuel 10:12: "Be strong, and let us show ourselves courageous for the sake of our people and for the cities of our God; and may the LORD do what is good in His sight."[77] (NASB)

And finally, look at David's charge to Solomon as Solomon takes over the leadership of Israel. 1st Kings 2:2 says, "I am going the way of all the earth. Be strong, therefore, and show yourself a man." (NASB)

What Kind of a Man Are We to Be?

Based on the advice given to these Old Testament leaders on how to conduct themselves:

What kind of men are we to be?

What kind of men do we want our sons to be?

What kind of men do we want our daughters to marry?

Those who are strong and courageous!

Strong in their faith; strong in the things of God; strong in their understanding; and possessing discretion and wisdom so that the courage of their convictions causes them to live boldly, like the prophet Daniel and his companions in exile in Babylon. (Daniel 1-6)

Our society often rewards compromisers and resists the courageous. So how do we find the strength and courage to deal with difficulty, face challenges, meet the enemy, face problems and obstacles, bear pain, and press on to a difficult goal? By remembering God's words. He told Joshua,

> "Only be strong and very courageous; be careful to do according to all the law which Moses My servant commanded you; do not turn from it to the right or to the left, so that you may have success wherever you go. This book of the law shall not depart from your mouth, but you shall meditate on it day and night, so that you may be careful to do according to all that is written in it; for then you will make your way prosperous, and then you will have success. Have I not commanded you? Be strong and courageous! Do not tremble or be dismayed, for the LORD your God is with you wherever you go." (Joshua 1:7-9 NASB)

The first thing that gives you courage in fatherly leadership is knowledge that you have the presence of God. He will never leave you; He is with you wherever you go. The second thing is knowledge of whether or not your cause is just and right. You gain that by meditating on His Word and obeying it. Then the sovereign God will give you success, man of valor.

Set the Standard

Back to 1st Thessalonians 2, where we see that Paul and his team "parented" through modeling, instructing, and motivating the Thessalonians when they were with them.

Modeling is demonstrated in verse 10: "You are witnesses, and God also, how piously and justly and blamelessly we behaved ourselves among you that believe." (AKJV) A father's responsibility is to set the standard of integrity in the family. One of the most helpful contributions to our children turning out to love the Lord is to model the virtues of Christ—the fruit of the Spirit. That's what Paul also said to the Philippian church. In Philippians 4:9 Paul told them, "The things you have learned and received and heard and seen in me, practice these things, and the God of peace will be with you." (NASB)

> **A father's responsibility is to set the standard for integrity in the family.**

One of the most difficult things for us to do in our homes is to model what we believe. We can teach, exhort, and motivate, but modeling is the hardest part. The best way to keep on track with modeling that I know of is to have "courageous conversations" with our family. Ask them questions like, "On a scale of one to ten, with ten being the worst, how would you rate my anger or spirit of anger?" or "Do I have your heart? What would I need to do to win it?" They will almost always tell you. Even if some of what they say they want you to do is selfish, there will be other things woven in that you know you need to act on. You might need to ask forgiveness for behaviors you have been modeling that are not what you want or should be doing.

Instruction is discussed in 1st Thessalonians 2:11. Teaching should come right along with modeling: "... we exhorted and comforted and charged every one of you, as a father does his children." (AKJV) The word 'exhort' has a specific meaning in the New Testament:

> To exhort is to develop relationships with other believers for the purpose of encouraging them in their spiritual growth. Exhorters are among the first to find believers who are floundering in their faith. Exhorters... come alongside the weaker ones to encourage, confront, if necessary, and model victorious living. People with the gift of exhortation do not merely proclaim truth, as prophets often do. They develop relationships, often taking time to do those little extras that make the difference when someone is struggling. Rather than say, "You should begin reading the Psalms every day," an exhorter might say, "Let's start a Bible study together on Psalms. How about coffee Tuesday morning?" [78]

A father gets alongside his children and moves them in a specific direction, exhorting them in the path of conduct that is Scriptural and that he believes is right for them. Sometimes discipline is involved. It is essential that discipline should not be done in anger but calmly—

after finding out all the correct facts and clarifying the offense.

> **A father gets alongside his children and moves them in a specific direction.**

And then there's motivation—an encouragement that says, "I know it's tough, but keep going." We declare that we are a personal witness to the fact that if the child keeps obeying the principles we have taught them and stays on the path laid out for them, they will follow in our footsteps as we follow Christ. (1st Corinthians 11:1)

Express Gratefulness

A father should express genuine gratitude to those in his own family for the efforts they make to live a life of faith; otherwise they will cease to make the effort.

Your family will learn to express their gratefulness as they see you do it. Consider the example of the apostle Paul. In nearly every letter he wrote, he thanks the Christians and frequently names specific people for something. Romans 1:8: "First, I thank my God through Jesus Christ for all of you that your faith is spoken of throughout the whole world." (KJV) Colossians 1:3-4 says, "We always thank God... when we pray for you, since we heard of your faith in Christ Jesus and of the love that you have for all the saints." (ESV)

A basic foundation of gratitude is a spirit of contentment. Philippians 4:11 says,

> "Not that I speak from need, for I have learned to be content in whatever circumstances I am. I know how to get along with humble means, and I also know how to live in prosperity; in any and every circumstance I have learned the secret of being filled and going hungry, both of having abundance and suffering need." (NASB)

For fathers, this means stopping and enjoying the accomplishments of the family. If you constantly urge your family on to more achievement without pausing to enjoy and praise what they have done, they will get discouraged and want to give up trying. They will feel they can never do enough to please you.

> **If you constantly urge your family on to more achievement without pausing to enjoy and praise what they have done, they will get discouraged and give up.**

Maintain a Genuine Spirit of Humility

Philippians 2:3-8 tells us that our Lord Jesus humbled himself—and we should take on that same way of thinking. 1st Peter 5:5-6 says, "...be clothed with humility: for God resists the proud and gives grace to the humble. Humble yourselves therefore under the mighty hand of God, that he may exalt you in due time." (NKJV)

Your wife and each child need to be told that they are needed and loved. They need to hear that you need their prayers and help in order to be the spiritual leader that God intends you to be.

Admit when you are wrong. If we don't admit obvious faults and sins, they will translate this as pride and react to it. James 5:16 says to confess your faults one to another and pray one for another.

All members of a family will fail each other sometimes—this cannot be avoided. Fathers should lead the reconciliation process. 2nd Corinthians 5:18 tells us that God reconciled us to himself through Jesus, and now He has given to us the ministry of reconciliation with each other. Ephesians 4:32 says, "Be kind to one another, tenderhearted, forgiving one another, even as God for Christ's sake has forgiven you." (NKJV)

Fathers should lead the reconciliation process.

Do not demand to be heard. Earn the privilege by developing a relationship with each person in the family. Display good manners. It demonstrates to others what we really think of our wife and children. It shows we value them as people. A lack of manners by a father will infect the family. His sons will develop disrespect for their mother and sister; his wife and daughters will tend to withdraw. The very essence of good manners involves sacrifice and yielding rights as Christ did. (Philippians 2:3-8)

**Fathers earn the privilege of being heard
by demonstrating good manners.**

Control Your Tongue and Emotions

James warns us in chapter 3 that the tongue is an unruly evil, full of deadly poison. Harsh words and thoughtless statements cut deeply within the heart of a family member and are not easily healed. Proverbs 15:1 states, "A soft answer turns away wrath but a harsh word stirs up anger." (ESV) Proverbs 12:18 and 18:21 tell us that careless words stab like a sword, and that life and death are in the power of the tongue.

Consistency in emotions is very important, too. It is a terrible drain on the family if the father's emotions are way up one day and way down the next. He should not be frequently depressed or complaining. Our children need emotional stability, reassurance, and encouragement from us.

Our children need emotional stability from us.

Accept Each Child at His Own Rate of Development

Fathers should seek to balance supervision and the freedom to fail. Too much freedom will be interpreted by children as rejection. Too much supervision will be interpreted as a lack of trust. Ephesians 6:4 says, "Fathers, do not provoke [exasperate or frustrate] your children to anger, but bring them up in the discipline and instruction of the Lord." (NASB) Express appreciation for what your children are now, rather than just what they might be in the future.

Our children need reassurance that we love them and—whether they are right or wrong—we always will love them. They may break our heart by doing evil, but they must know that we will never disown them just as the father did not disown his prodigal son. (Luke 15:11-32)

Our children need reassurance that we love them and that we always will love them.

Recognize Individual Worth and Potential

Your children are different from each other and will mature physically and spiritually on their own unique schedules. Paul warned the Corinthians against comparing themselves to one another. (2nd Corinthians 10:12) Never compare anyone in the family with another with a greater ability or achievement. God gifts and equips each person uniquely.

They Want to be Like You

So, how does a father of valor encourage his children? The father of valor models, teaches, and motivates them. He accepts who they are, now, not what they might become in the future. He is consistent in discipline and emotions; he controls his tongues, admits mistakes, and is grateful.

Is there anyone else in the world that your kids look up to like they look up to you? They want to be like you! Proverbs 17:6 says "the glory of sons is their fathers." (RSV) So you need to live like Christ and be the man of valor he has called you to be, be the man that you want your sons to be, and an example of the kind that you want your daughters to marry. Father of valor, walk in a manner worthy of the God who calls you.

The Lord is with you, mighty man of valor!

While you are required to take care of the physical needs of your family, that's not more important than spending time and gaining their hearts, as we have just been reading. Work is *not* your first, second, or even third priority! But in the next chapter, we'll turn our attention to work and talk about what a man of valor does and doesn't do at work, and also what God provides to help you in your work.

Make it Practical

1. What examples can you think of in the Bible of men who proved to be fathers of valor? Why? What qualities do you see?

2. Re-read 1st Corinthians 16:13-14. Would you describe yourself as strong? As standing firm in the faith?

3. Would you describe yourself as alert? Alert to what? What could that encompass? (Reference Job 1:7; 1st Peter 5:8; Luke 21:34; Proverbs 4:23, 7, 12:1 & 5, et al.)

4. This chapter could have simply stated "do all fathering in love." But most men want specifics. ("Don't just tell me to do something, show me how!") Bruce suggests six ways to show love to your children (listed below). Which of these do you do well in? Which do you need to improve?

> a. Set the standard of conduct in your home
> b. Express gratefulness
> c. Maintain a genuine spirit of humility
> d. Control your tongue and emotions
> e. Accept each child at his own rate of development
> f. Recognize individual worth and potential

5. In the MOV Conferences, we do a hands-on illustration with two volunteers from the audience. In front of the room, the volunteers compete to see how fast they can rip leaves off a tree branch. Then we hand out cellophane tape and tell them to tape the leaves back on their respective branches, "just as it looked before." Obviously, the second contest takes much longer than the first; many times, the men simply give up because it is impossible to do!

Sometimes, men, we say something to our child that comes out quick. It may be harsh and hurtful; it doesn't build up, it tears down. Sometimes we realize it—though many times we don't—and then we quickly try to say "I'm sorry, I didn't mean it!" And we try to take it back... or soften it by saying, "What I meant to say was..." But it is very, very difficult to remove the hurt, to erase the pain that those quick, harsh, thoughtless words caused. Relationships and feelings that are torn, even destroyed by careless words or actions, take a lot of time or may be impossible to make right.

Read Proverbs 12:18, 15:1 and 18:21. These verses are challenging! A father can either strengthen or shred their child's heart. Describe a recent time when you blurted hurtful words to your child. Talk about what you did to apologize. If you haven't apologized yet, make a commitment to do so.

6. Bruce writes, "A father of valor lives the life that he demands of his children." That's a tall order. What can you do to ensure that you are living that life?

Notes & References

---

[73] Bruce acknowledges significant influence from Dr. John MacArthur on this chapter, derived from various messages broadcast on the *Grace to You* radio program, especially "Parental Pictures of Spiritual Leadership," available at:
https://www.gty.org/library/sermons-library/52-5/Parental-Pictures-of-Spiritual-Leadership-Part-1 & https://www.gty.org/library/sermons-library/52-6/Parental-Pictures-of-Spiritual-Leadership-Part-2

[74] This in no way is to suggest that a mother does not nor cannot hold children to their commitments and responsibilities or keep them accountable! Like any good teacher, Paul is providing an easily-perceived illustration for his readers: a general picture of a father's vs. a mother's approach to raising children. He clearly reinforces that both are needed, both are vital. We are especially grateful that Paul helps men to understand their role here. If he didn't, men might say "she's got this" and avoid their role as dads. In fact, Paul seems to suggest that the father's behavior toward his children ought to be "holy and righteous and blameless"! (1st Thessalonians 2:10)

[75] See also Ephesians 6:4.

"The fact that [Paul] speaks to fathers and not mothers [in Ephesians 6] emphasizes the man's leadership within the home, and perhaps also his tendency to ignore his responsibilities and defer child-raising to his wife. Yet God lays the responsibility on the father to be gentle with his children, to treat them with dignity, and to take responsibility for their spiritual growth."
Tim Challies, "Accept Your Leadership" (Challies.com 2017)
https://www.challies.com/ articles/lead/

[76] For more on the fathering aspect of parenting, see Glenn Stanton's articles "The Involved Father" in *Focus on the Family* and "Why Dads Matter—And Moms Don't Toss Babies" in *Plough*:

"Go to any playground and listen to the parents. Who is encouraging kids to swing or climb just a little higher, ride their bike just a little faster, throw just a little harder? Who is encouraging kids to be careful? Mothers protect and dads encourage kids to push the limits. Either of these parenting styles by themselves can be unhealthy. One can tend toward encouraging risk without consideration of consequences. The other tends to avoid risk, which can fail to build independence and confidence. Together, they help children remain safe while expanding their experiences and increasing their confidence."
https://www.focusonthefamily.com/parenting/the-involved-father/
https://www.plough.com/en/topics/community/education/why-dads-matter

[77] In place of "let us show ourselves courageous," the RSV translates the key phrase in this verse as, "let us play the man"!

[78] https://www.gotquestions.org/definition-exhortation.html

Chapter 11

Mark Seager, Brad Smith, Jesse Taylor

A Man of Valor
at Work

"Not slothful in business; fervent in spirit; serving the Lord."
Romans 12:11 (KJV)

We often view work[79] as one of those "necessary evils" in life, and it takes up a major part of our time. So when we don't enjoy it, or when we'd rather be doing something else, we resent it. Yet, often we use it to define us—we mistakenly think "we are what we do."

Well, what is the biblical view of work? Does the Bible actually speak to how we should be working, or does it limit itself to our behavior on Sundays and at home? How does a man of valor's faith make a difference to how he thinks and acts during the work week?

Why Work?

Why should we work? Because we were made for it. In fact, this is one of the very first things God modeled for us in the Bible. We see in Genesis 1 that in the beginning, God worked six days as he created and organized the world, and then He rested from His work on the seventh day. God is a creator—and He has placed a reflection of Himself in each and every one of us. His same creative spirit resides in us. We were designed to create and to work just like our Father in Heaven.

We can think of many examples of creating and of bringing order to disorder: farming, landscaping, construction, medicine. We do it intuitively. That's why we paint a house or repair something that is broken. It's why we clean or invent or teach. There is great satisfaction in seeing what we worked on look much better afterwards!

Have you noticed that God made Adam and then put him in the

garden to take care of it? (Genesis 2:15) God didn't say "come on in, Adam! Sit down here in the lawn chair and smell the roses. Your drinks are on the way!"

No, God gave Adam a purpose and a responsibility by assigning him work. Also note that it was before the curse that God placed Adam in the garden to work. Work is not a result of the curse. It was only after the curse that work became conflict-filled, frustrating, and sometimes unfruitful. (Genesis 3:17-19)

Work is hardwired in us as men. Deep down, it feels right to earn an honest living from honest labor. We were designed to do something, to accomplish things, to have an impact, to make a difference. We get a good feeling when we do a good job. It's built into us. It is the way men are. We are made to provide for our families. We are made to earn a living so we can bless others. Deep down we know that we are made to work.

> **Work is hardwired in men. Deep down, it feels right to earn an honest living from honest labor.**

But some days... it's rough. Very rough.

I (Brad) don't know how things go for you at work, but I've had days, week, months, even years, when work was a nightmare. The politics, backbiting, jockeying for position all around me... you know, meeting after meeting, prioritizing after prioritizing, one step forward, two steps back... Maybe you've had times like that.

On the worst days, when I'm emotionally spent—I close myself off and get grumpy. I get discouraged, frustrated... which may turn into intense navel-gazing and self-isolation—stewing over questions like, "why am I here??"

And then when I've gone home, I resist interacting with my family. I shut down conversation at the family dinner table. I answer questions from my kids with a grunt or only one or two words. After the meal, I feel dog tired, I watch a little of some program or movie with my wife and then start heading toward bed.

But just before I close my bedroom door, one of my children stops me. She gives me a kiss and says goodnight. She says she loves me and gives me a hug.

Then as I close the door, tears come to my eyes. The Lord speaks to me. Why do I work? Why do I work at that job? For her. For them. For my families' care.

Your Life Is Not a Set of Boxes

Through the Scriptures, we see that God wants all of our lives—not just the "religious" parts. Deuteronomy 6:4 says, "Hear, O Israel, the Lord our God, the Lord is one." (ESV) God is unlike idols and other "gods" that the ancients worshipped (and some still worship). Some worship multiple deities who each handle a particular responsibility: a "goddess of fertility", a "god of war", a "god of commerce," and so on. But our God is not like that; He is the God of the universe. Christianity sees the one God as the Source and everything else as a resource. Resources can change: food, shelter, clothing, money, job, etc. We ask the Source to provide the resources, but the resources are not our focus of attention—God is. (Matthew 6:31-33) He is God over all aspects of His creation and over all aspects of our lives. This means that He is Lord of our work, too.

God is the Source. Everything else is a resource.

"Whether, then, you eat or drink or whatever you do, do all to the glory of God." (1st Corinthians 10:31, NASB) There is no spiritual / secular divide in biblical thought. We are to do everything that we do "as unto the Lord." Thus, God is relevant to—and Lord over—every area of our lives. As men, we like to put things in "boxes." We have a box for family, a box for sports, a box for work, and a box for church. But God doesn't work that way and neither should we.

God is over all aspects of His creation and over all aspects of life. He is Lord of your work, too.

Before I (Mark) began pastoring, I was a civil engineer. Much of my work involved dealing with sewage and garbage. (About as unspiritual as you can get!) I remember being absolutely stumped trying to solve a technical issue for a landfill gas project in a country closed to conventional missionaries. My colleague was as bewildered as I, but he asked our business hosts if we could have a few hours to pray and ask God for wisdom. I was surprised and a little uncomfortable with his openness, given the situation, but I followed him back to the guesthouse where we spread out the plans on a table and prayed. Within thirty minutes, we discovered a solution to our problem.

I learned that day that God knows everything—including technical matters. He wants us to involve Him in our work life. Working for the glory of God and worshipping through it all means that we are consciously aware of God's presence and power in the day-to-day routine of our work.

God wants to be involved in our work life.

The account of Joseph in the Bible tells us that God does not see a separation between our work and our spiritual lives.

Joseph had the gift of administration. When he was sold into slavery by his brothers, he was bought by a man who valued his help to keep his home running in an organized manner. When the man's wife wanted Joseph to have sex with her, he refused. He told her, "...how could I do such a great evil and sin against God?" (Genesis 39:9 BSB) Joseph understood that his work and his faith could not be taken apart. They are tied together; they are essential to a unified, undivided mind and life.

You may know what happened next. Potiphar's wife lied about Joseph. She said that Joseph had tried to rape her. His boss sent him to prison. But Joseph did not give up. He offered to organize things in the prison, and the prison guard liked him because everything Joseph worked on went well. And Joseph rose to be the leader of the prisoners. Eventually, because Joseph's wisdom, reputation, and integrity were so strong, Pharaoh put Joseph second in command in all of the country of Egypt. God honored Joseph's hard work and honesty and his refusal to do things that went against God's laws.

God does not want us to think or act differently when we are at work than we do at church.

With these truths in mind, how should men of valor view our work?

Recognize Your Ultimate Authority

We should work as if God is our boss—because He is!

> Slaves, obey those who are your human masters in everything, not with eye-service, as people-pleasers, but with sincerity of heart, fearing the Lord. Whatever you do, do your work heartily, as for the Lord and not for people. (Colossians 3:22-23 NASB)

Yes, we all have supervisors and managers, but we are really serving a higher authority. Knowing that God is our boss is comforting and freeing. Sometimes we work very hard—maybe even too hard—for the praise of men or in hope for a promotion or a raise in salary. When we don't get one, it's easy to grow frustrated and angry with our employer. That attitude impacts our work. But when we remember that it is God who gives promotions and raises—for it is He alone who can advance us in work or keep us where we are—then we're free to simply do our best, knowing that we are right where God wants us. And He will see to it that we get our reward. "...from the Lord you will receive the reward... It is the Lord Christ whom you serve." (Colossians 3:24 NASB)

View Your Work as Worship

Believe it or not, the words "work" and "worship" in Hebrew actually come from the same root word, *avodah*. It is used 289 times in the Old Testament , sometimes translated as work or service, and sometimes translated as worship.[80]

> "This is a powerful image to think that the word for working in the fields is the same word used for worshiping the God of Abraham, Isaac and Jacob. *Avodah* is a picture of an integrated faith. A life where work and worship come from the same root. The same foundation."[81]

Martin Luther, one of the catalysts of the Protestant Reformation, strongly avowed that any vocation can be done for the glory of God and that one didn't need to be a member of the clergy to glorify God.[82] That means you can milk cows to the glory of God, or clean toilets to the glory of God. No matter what you do—whether it's pastoring a church, building a skyscraper, preparing a meal, digging a ditch, engineering a complicated system, making a delivery, or coding software—do it as if you're doing it for God. It then becomes an act of worship.

If you are in a secular job that doesn't violate Scripture, your work or vocation is just as important to God as that of a pastor or full-time missionary. God calls each of us to our own work. It is in that work or vocation where He desires to use us for His kingdom. You can worship God as you work: if you say, "God, I'm doing this for You," then He is given glory.

Think of how this would look in your work. If you began to perform every task as though you were working for the Lord and not just for people, how would the way you work change? For instance, let's say your job is to dig ditches to lay cable. If you think, "I'm doing this as if Jesus were going to walk in this ditch," then you are probably going to dig the ditch with more care and attention to detail.

In 1981 the movie *Chariots of Fire*, about missionary and 1924 Olympic runner Eric Liddell, hit the big screen. Eric had been called to be a missionary to China. But he was also good at running and qualified to race for Great Britain in the upcoming Olympic Games. While he was training, Eric's sister challenged him as to why he was doing this comparatively unimportant running, delaying serving God in China. Eric answered, "I believe God made me for a purpose, but he also made me fast. And when I run I feel His pleasure."[83]

Men of valor, like Mr. Liddell, let's pursue God's pleasure in doing our work—doing what God has gifted us in—as an act of worship and obedience to our divine design!

Ultimately, our attitude toward work is really a matter of the heart. With the right focus, the daily grind can become daily worship as we devote all our efforts to His glory.

View Your Work as God's Training Ground

I (Brad) have often struggled with viewing my day-to-day work as unimportant or without spiritual significance. I've asked myself at times how it can be enough for the Kingdom. But God has shown me that right now, what I am doing today is for the Kingdom, and my work is what God wants me to be doing.

> **What am I doing for the Kingdom? Everything.**

As God takes us through life, He allows us to develop specific skills and talents for His purposes. Many of us have the greatest opportunity to display these gifts when we work. The workplace is oftentimes our training ground. A good friend's favorite saying is "God is always preparing us for the next job."

As you recall, David was only a small shepherd boy when he went up against Goliath. (1st Samuel 17) Rather than using King Saul's armor and weapons, David took a sling and stones, and used the skills he had developed as a shepherd. He called on the great courage and fighting skills he had honed out in the fields, caring for his family's sheep. When facing Goliath, David used the talents God had trained him to use. The shepherd fields were David's training ground. There he learned to fight lions and protect his sheep; now, he would protect God's sheep—the people of Israel. (Psalm 78:70-72)

Not all of us will have to fight ten-foot-tall giants, but we will have other challenges. God uses our training, like David's training as a shepherd, to prepare us for future battles and future experiences that

He will use for His purposes in our lives, and for His Kingdom. The workplace is a training ground for us.

In college, I (Brad) majored in both Bible and Psychology and minored in Communications. I chose these subjects simply because they sounded interesting. In my first job after college, I worked in marketing. I learned how to persuade organizations to hear a presentation about our services and to offer our products for sale. I wrote letters and proposals. (Psychology and Communications)

My next job was as a writer. I wrote marketing materials, press releases, and magazine articles. (Communications)

In my next several jobs, I learned how to conduct improvement projects for my company and our government. I helped them conduct work efficiently. This involved making speeches and giving presentations, training and coaching leaders, and understanding how people think and what motivates them to work. I also wrote reports and proposals. (Psychology and Communications)

I applied my understanding of the Bible in my work and also the churches I attended when I started doing men's ministry, led men's Bible studies, and led teams of men to reach and build other men. (Bible and Communications)

Today, for Men of Valor International, I write articles, papers, and proposals; I apply psychology in understanding how to minister to and through men; and I make speeches and teach the Bible to men all over the world. (Bible, Psychology, and Communications)

None of this was something I orchestrated. I didn't select my college courses because I knew what jobs I'd be doing. I did not arrange ahead of time to learn skills that I could use in the next job. In fact, prior to starting most of the jobs, I did not fully understand all I would be doing in the job. I had no idea that these jobs would prepare me for the next job or three jobs later. But God did.

The workplace is a training ground for us.

God trained me in each job. I was faithful to do each task well, no matter how big or how small, interesting, or mundane. In Luke 16:10, Jesus says, "He who is faithful in a very little thing is faithful also in much..." (NASB) So, even though you may be in a "small" or "less important" job, how well or how poorly you do the small things tells others how well or how poorly you will do big things. A boss may look at you and think, "If this man doesn't do the little tasks well that I give him, why should I give him bigger responsibilities?"

Little Things Matter

Many years ago, a young man named Abraham worked in a store as a clerk. The owner of the store knew that he could trust Abraham to run the store because he was honorable and honest. One day a woman came to the store and bought sugar, coffee, spices, and flour from Abraham. That night, as Abraham was closing up the shop, he found that he had a small amount of money left over. Adding up the sales for the day, he discovered that the change belonged to the woman who had bought the sugar, coffee, spices, and flour. He had not given her the correct change!

After closing the shop, Abraham walked the three miles to the woman's house and handed her the money. The woman looked at the money and said, "You mean that you came all the way here in the dark to bring me six cents?" [84]

The Bible says in Proverbs 22:29, "Do you see a man skillful in his work? He will stand before kings..." (ESV) Well, in this case, he became the king—or rather, the leader of the United States. President Abraham Lincoln, a Christian, led our nation through its civil war in the 1860s. The Lord prepared him for leadership amid crisis through his integrity and obedience in small things... many years earlier.

> **"Do you see a man skillful in his work? He will stand before kings..." (Proverbs 22:29)**

If you do your work for God, He will help you in your work. He is interested in all we do, and so even our work is important to Him. He will give you what you need in order for you to do it well for His glory. In Exodus 31:3-5 we see that God gave Bezalel special skills as a craftsman:

> "I have filled him with the Spirit of God in wisdom, in understanding, in knowledge, and in craftsmanship, to make artistic designs for work in gold, in silver, and in bronze, and in the cutting of stones for settings and in the carving of wood that he may work all kinds of craftsmanship..." (NASB)

This skill set was provided for building the new tabernacle. [85] But I'm pretty sure Bezalel used those skills as well to earn income apart from that and put some food on the table!

Both Joseph and Daniel prayed and asked God to help them interpret dreams—for them, this became a part of their job! God answered those prayers. He'll answer your requests for His help. He understands you and your job, and He will give you what you need to do it well for His glory.

God gives us the talents we need in order to achieve the things He wants us to achieve so that we can serve others and benefit the kingdom of God. He wants us to use our talents, abilities, and opportunities He has given us for His greater glory in this world. Our work is where we deal with everyday challenges of life, and it is also where God wants to reveal His glory "...so that all the peoples of the earth may know that the LORD is God..."[86] (1st Kings 8:60 NASB)

**God gives us the talents we need
to achieve what He wants us to achieve.**

We can find comfort in the knowledge that there is no higher calling than to be where God calls us—regardless of the nature of the work. He gives us purpose in every kind of work that He sets our hands to do, and He will not fail in using our work to train us for what He wants us to do.

View Your Work as Necessary

We all wish money grew on trees, or that someone would just give it to us. All of us have felt this way at times. We see someone who is better off with more money and possessions, and we think how nice it would be if they would just give us some of that.

But in God's promises to take care of us, He never promises that He will just lay His provision at our resting feet. It is our work that is most often God's way of providing for us. "Whoever works his land will have plenty of bread, but he who follows worthless pursuits will have plenty of poverty." (Proverbs 28:19 ESV)

Work is a Commandment, Not an Option

Laziness is an unbiblical attitude. To be lazy is to deny what God made us for. God did not create Adam and drop him onto a beach with a ready supply of food; He put him in a garden and told him to work for what he needed. Scripture is not kind to the man who tries to get out of working: "If anyone is not willing to work, let him not eat." (2nd Thessalonians 3:10 ESV)[87]

Laziness is idleness. It's been said that empty hands and an idle mind are the devil's playground. When boys or men have nothing to do, they end up getting in trouble. In 2nd Samuel 11, instead of being at work commanding the army, David slacked off and stayed home, which led to him looking at what he shouldn't have been looking at (Bathsheba), which led to adultery and later to murder. It all started because David avoided his work.

> **God did not create Adam and drop him into a tropical paradise with a ready supply of food; He put him in a garden and told him to work for what he needed.**

1st Thessalonians 4:11-12 states,

> Make it your ambition to lead a quiet life and attend to your own business and work with your hands, just as we instructed you, so that you will behave properly toward outsiders and not be in any need. (NASB)

It is good and biblical to provide for yourself and your family. We recognize that some may be unable to do so because of difficult health or other reasons, but the expectation is that a man provides for himself and his family. The Bible promises that the man who works diligently and honestly will have what he needs: "The one who works his land will have plenty of food, but whoever chases fantasies lacks judgment." (Proverbs 12:11 BSB)

> **The Bible promises that the man who works diligently and honestly will have what he needs.**

View Your Work as a Mission Field

Your work is a mission field full of opportunities to share Christ with others. How you conduct yourself in the daily routine should draw positive attention to Christ. If you're an employee, your boss should be able to trust you. If you're a boss, your workers should know that you'll treat them well and pay them fairly. And your coworkers should see that there's something different about you.

However, also remember that your boss is not paying you to witness. You need to be wise in how and when you talk to others at work about the gospel. Maybe at a lunch break or an after-work conversation with a coworker. Don't squander your testimony by annoying people at inappropriate times or by talking about God when you are expected to be producing results for your company.

Conduct Yourself in a Manner Worthy of Christ

Titus 1:2 tells us that God cannot lie—and neither should His men of valor. Proverbs 11:1 notes that, "A false balance and dishonest business practices are extremely offensive to the Lord, but an accurate scale is His delight." (AMP) Honesty and integrity in our work are essential as we strive to reflect the character of Christ in everything we do.

In Zachariah, the Lord records for us what every man of valor should do in his work:

> "...Speak the truth to one another, render... judgments that are true and make for peace, do not devise evil in your hearts against one another, and love no false oath, for all these things I hate, says the Lord." (Zachariah 8:16-17 ESV)

Based on this Scripture, here's how we glorify God in our work:

1. Speak truth always.

2. Make decisions that are fair and bring peace.

3. Do not say or do anything to hurt or damage another business or a person you work with. Do not say or do things that make you look better than others.

4. Make no false promise. Instead, as the saying goes, "under promise and over deliver."

King Hezekiah was not a perfect man; he did many things wrong. But he also did a few things right. In 2nd Chronicles 31:20-21, it says, "Thus Hezekiah... did what was good and right and faithful before the LORD his God. And every work that he undertook... seeking his God, he did with all his heart, and prospered." (ESV)

Will God say that about you? About us? Will He say, "Thus [your name] did what was good and right and faithful before the Lord his God, with all his heart?"

Would God say that you do what is good and right and faithful before Him?

Your Work is Important

Work matters. It's not just something you do to pay the bills. It's not "unspiritual," separated from your faith. It matters to God, and it should matter to you, too. You were made for it. Work is part of your worship, and it's often God's training ground for you.

Work in such a way that you are not dependent on others, and do not be lazy. Recognize that hard work is generally God's means of provision for you and your family. And remember that it is a mission field for you, so in God's strength, conduct yourself in a manner worthy of Christ at work, with honesty and integrity.

Man of valor, work as if God is your boss—because He is!

The Lord is with you, mighty man of valor!

+ + +

We've described how you are to perform work as a man of valor. We said that a man of valor who seeks God and does what is good and right and faithful before the LORD his God, with all his heart, in all he undertakes, will prosper. But we all have some fundamental choices to make daily. Choices to make *before* you head to your place of work—before you go *anywhere*.

Make it Practical

1. God holds an interest in everything you do—including your work. He cares about and desires to be involved in each of your daily activities. How does this change your view of God? How does this change your view of your work?

2. If you began to perform every task as though you were working for God and not just people, how would the way you work change?

3. Work and worship come from the same Hebrew root word, *avodah*. Have you ever been aware of worshipping at work, or worshipping through work? What caused it?

4. We are called to worship through work, but we have to make the choice to do so. Frequently, this requires taking a moment to intentionally refocus on God in the midst of work. What are some practical ways for you to do that?

5. Think back over each job that you've had. What have you learned from them? How have you seen God's leading and equipping through the work He's given you? Can you see how God has trained you for each succeeding promotion or job? How did the lessons, experiences, and training help you in other areas of life?

6. Even if you feel that the tasks you do at work hold no particular spiritual significance of their own, your work is an opportunity to develop friendships with people you might otherwise never have met. How can you be salt and light in your workplace?

7. Think of some of the most important qualities an employer generally looks for in potential candidates during the hiring process. For example, your list may include trustworthiness, honesty, preparedness, reliability, loyalty, motivation, a willingness to learn and a strong worth ethic. How can you grow in each of these qualities in order to reflect Christ through the way you work? How can you teach other men about these qualities?

8. We are called to worship *through* work and while *at* work, but not to worship work. For many men, work consumes their entire life— all that they focus on and all their identity is wound up in their work. How is this true or not true for you?

Notes & References

[79] **Pastors**: Replace "work" with "ministry". **Men**: Your ministry service for your church or Christian organization is Priority #5; it comes after all other priorities, including work.

[80] Darrow Miller, "Work and Worship Blend in One Hebrew Word" (Darrow Miller and Friends 2018)
http://darrowmillerandfriends.com/2018/07/23/work-worship-go-together

[81] Austin Burkhart, " 'Avodah': What It Means to Live a Seamless Life of Work, Worship, and Service" (Institute for Faith, Work, and Economics 2015)
https://tifwe.org/avodah-a-life-of-work-worship-and-service/

[82] "Therefore I advise no one to enter any religious order or the priesthood, indeed, I advise everyone against it—unless he… understands that the works of monks and priests, however holy and arduous they may be, do not differ one whit in the sight of God from the works of the rustic laborer in the field or the woman going about her household tasks, but that all works are measured before God by faith alone."
Martin Luther, *The Babylonian Captivity of the Church* (1520)

[83] *Chariots of Fire*, directed by Hugh Hudson (20th Century Fox 1981)

[84] The authors credit The Institute in Basic Life Principles for this story.

[85] When Solomon was building the permanent Temple, he recruited the help of Hiram, who also "was full of wisdom, understanding, and skill, for making any work in bronze." (1st Kings 7:14 RSV)
"God gave Hiram special skills. God gives skills to all of us… they are to help us do our calling."
John G. Butler, *Solomon: King of Splendor* (Scripture Truth 2007) 173

[86] For many of us today, "all the peoples of the earth" are in our workplaces!

[87] See also Proverbs 10:4, 14:23, 18:9, 21:17, and 28:19

PART III: A Man of Valor's Practices

Practices describe how a man of valor lives. They infuse every area of his life. They reinforce a man of valor's position. They keep him focused on his priorities—even protect them.

Chapter 12

Mark Seager & Brad Smith

The Daily Choices
of a Man of Valor

"And he said to them, "Follow me..."

Matthew 4:19 (ESV)

A man of valor lives intentionally and makes wise choices that count for eternity.

Before the Game Begins

Are you familiar with the game of Monopoly? When you play, you move around the board and have the option to buy properties you land on. Once you own that property, anyone else who lands on it has to pay you rent. If you buy a series of similar properties, you have the option to develop the properties with houses and hotels, which makes the rent much more expensive to someone else who lands on it.

Some things in the game happen to you by your decision and some by "Chance" cards. A "Chance" card may say that you might have to pay hospital bills, pay double the rent, collect a bank dividend or—a favorite funny one—win second place in a beauty contest and collect $10!

The goal of the game is to accumulate the most property and money and eventually force your opponents to go bankrupt. This is the surface or what-we-see level of the game.

But while we're playing on the what-we-see level, we are also operating on another level. It is not on the board or in the roll of the dice; it is what is in our hearts as we play the game. Monopoly is very competitive, so, what are our attitudes and actions during the game? How badly do you want to win, and what are you willing to do to get there? Greed, anger, manipulation, maybe even meanness or cheating—Monopoly can really bring those out. How we play games can reflect our character.

> **How we play games reflects our character.**

In a way, our lives are like a game. Games involve both skill (making wise decisions) and happenstance or coincidence (what some call "luck") because of the cards we draw or how the dice rolls. In life, we know there is no such thing as luck, but things do happen to us without an obvious reason and sometimes without warning. To respond to those "chance" events well, in addition to the things that are in our control, we need to make good decisions, knowing that any decision made today could have long-term consequences well beyond tomorrow.

We tend to focus on the events in our lives like we do to the events in a game. But God is more concerned about our attitudes as we figure out our path—how we *respond* to the things that happen to us that are not of our choosing, as well as to the deliberate decisions we make.

So, how do you play the "game" of life? A man of valor must think about this and make a choice. When he's playing the game of life—the everyday events; the challenges; the decisions he has to make; dealing with issues in his family, with his church, with other men—he needs to decide what will guide him. What choice must he make to honor the Lord and reap the blessings of obedience?

A man of valor must make this choice now—before the game begins, before life events suddenly come upon him—and then recommit to it every day.

> **This choice must be made ahead of time
> and carried out daily.**

Choose For Yourself This Day

A man of valor must choose the direction he wants his life to go. Our natural manner is to slide into just doing whatever feels good at the moment. It may be for quick pleasure or it may be a way we try to escape from the many pains of life. If we don't make wise choices, we will end up doing the wrong thing, leading to:

✓ disappointment for what could have been...or

✓ serious negative consequences, such as the loss of a job or a divorce... or worse

✓ death—yours or a family member's.

There's a story in the Old Testament when God's people were confronted with such a choice. It was a decision that all men must make because it determines how we live from here on out. God's people were confronted on this matter after they'd gotten into the Promised Land. They were feeling sorry for themselves and wanted to go back to the old way of living...the old gods...the immoral lifestyles. It was tempting! They knew what it was like, and because it was familiar and what they were used to... well, why not? They had one foot in the Promised Land and one foot in the cursed land.

After over forty years witnessing the people's cycle of trust and fear, of obedience and sin, their leader Joshua had had it. He said to the Hebrews: "And if it seems evil to you to serve the Lord, choose for yourselves this day whom you will serve.... But as for me and my house, we will serve the Lord." (Joshua 24:15 NKJV)

He declared, "I will follow God. What about you? Are you with me, or against me? Make a choice. Right now. And let's move on."

> ### Make a choice. Now.

The Lord does nothing randomly. The Lord does everything "according to the purpose of his will." (Ephesians 1:11 RSV) A man of valor should strive to do the same; make the right choices today that are in line with the scriptures and God's will. And live by them.

There are obvious right and wrong things men can do. For example, if a man wants to marry a godly woman, he shouldn't hope to find a worthy mate in a bar; he should look in a church!

A man of valor does not sit on the fence trying to decide whether he will climb over or climb back down. Right now, choose Christ, and choose long-term contentment. We want to challenge you to make two decisions right here, right now. Then make those same two decisions again tomorrow and the next day:

> ### A man of valor doesn't sit on the fence,
> ### trying to decide whether to climb over
> ### or climb back down.

1. Choose To Follow Jesus Christ Wholeheartedly

In many places around the world, pastors struggle to acquire Bible knowledge. Some receive good training, but many do not. As a result, not knowing the Word clearly, they might receive and mix teaching from Mormons, Jehovah Witnesses, Muslims, and they may even mix a little Animism and culture in with the pure Gospel of Christ. Not surprisingly, the men under their teaching and leadership do the same.

Men, Jesus is God. He surpasses any other idols or religions; He told his disciples that "all authority in heaven and earth has been given to me." (Matthew 28:18, RSV)

Choose Christ, men.

Jesus offers you forgiveness—no idol can do that. No other religion grants you a full pardon without having to earn it.

I (Brad) majored in Bible in college. While I learned a lot, my professors also taught about how various people and religions argued about important texts in the Bible and had very differing views. That confused me and weakened my faith. It wasn't until about five years after graduation when I was attending a solid, Bible-teaching church that I realized that I had to make a choice: would I continue questioning what I was reading? Would I be skeptical of a particular passage's meaning because some other man doubted it? Or would I choose instead to believe exactly what the Bible said? Would I allow the Bible to stand for itself, as a complete, whole, integrated revelation of God throughout the ages?

It was really the same issue: Who would I follow? Who would I serve?

I decided that day that the Bible as stated is the Truth—and that I will trust its infallibility, reliability, and promises for the rest of my life. That decision changed my life, and it formed the basis for every decision since. Because God fulfills His promises in His Word over and over in all aspects of my life.

Second Choice... or Was It?

A little over a year after the birth of our first child, I lost my job. My wife and I were living in San Francisco—a very expensive area, and I really needed work. I applied to another company not far from there and I had a very good interview. After much prayer, we became convinced it was the right job.

But after some time when I hadn't heard from them, I called the company to get what I thought would be the good news... and learned that I had become their second choice—not because I didn't qualify, but because the other guy offered an extra skill that wasn't even on the job description! What?! Second choice is not bad, but not good enough when you are out of work. Second place meant I lose!

But we had been so convinced the job was mine. How could God allow the company to make a "mistake" like that?

Two months later, I was offered a position with another company. A position that had us move across the United States and set up a new home.

Four months after the move, after we were settled in, the first company called me again. They said they had made a mistake hiring the other guy; could I come now and take the job?

Wow. We really had been right in the first place. But now what? At this point it didn't seem right to abandon the company I had committed to in Washington, D.C., so we turned it down.

Then, just six months later, the company I had been faithful to stay with—the one for which I moved 3,000 miles—laid off all their employees for lack of funds!

Once again, I had to look for a job. The whole experience was like a real-life worst-case Monopoly game! It's not easy at a time like that to trust in the Lord with all your heart. I had really wanted that first job, and had felt certain that it was right!

Not a Fun Decision, But the Right Decision

It made me evaluate: had I made a good decision to move to the new home so far away? Yes, because I did what was right to meet the needs of my family. They were my responsibility. I had no way of predicting that the first company would change their minds and come back to me with the offer; I needed to move to where a job was.

Had I made a good decision to honor my commitment to the company in Washington, DC? Yes! Proverbs 3:3 exhorts, "Let not loyalty and faithfulness forsake you; bind them about your neck, write them on the tablet of your heart." (RSV) It was the kind thing and the right thing to do for a fledgling organization. I had no way of predicting that it would struggle financially.

But it was definitely not an enjoyable time for us. We struggled to pay the bills and put food on the table before the next opportunity came along. Our circumstances were not what we wanted, but God was operating on a higher plane. He was interested in the attitude of my heart and the perspective with which I faced life: would we still follow Him wholeheartedly even in our confusion and disappointment?

But what's really important to note here is that that period of unemployment (22 months!) was one of the most spiritually fulfilling, fruitful seasons of growth I've ever known before or since. It had impact in my spiritual development, in my marriage, in how and what I taught my children—and even now with Men of Valor International. Because it was during that time that I first started getting involved with men's ministry. In fact, it likely didn't matter that I ended up in Virginia with a different job—maybe He would have eventually moved me to Virginia anyway, and I just got there a little faster (that first company eventually moved to Virginia, too)! God's purposes were not foiled when the company hired someone else by mistake; God just re-wrote the story and got me here another way.

During this time, I learned that I could trust the promises in the Bible; I could trust God's character; I could trust the Holy Spirit's leading. All because I had chosen whom I would serve.

Choose to follow Jesus with a whole heart, men. He will not let you down.

> **Choose to follow Jesus with a whole heart, men. He will not let you down.**

2. Choose Contentment Over Quick Pleasure

Guess what: sin is often fun. We are all born preferring sin and self-centered behavior at the core of our being. Our desires are a result of our sinful character. (Isaiah 53:6) We think we are going to be happy, but we are actually making choices that will make us unhappy in the end. Sin is fun! But it is not wise. Sometimes it is even deadly.

Even Moses enjoyed the pleasures of sin for a while—but he changed his mind.

> By faith Moses, when he was grown up, refused to be called the son of Pharaoh's daughter, choosing rather to share ill-treatment with the people of God than to enjoy the fleeting pleasures of sin. He considered abuse suffered for the Christ greater wealth than the treasures of Egypt, for he looked to the reward. (Hebrews 11:24-26 RSV)

Instead of taking the path to fulfillment, significance, and joy, we try to take the "Happiness Shortcut," and by so doing we squander our chance for contentment by choosing a quick rush of happiness. But as Moses learned, contentment is far better than fun or any fleeting happiness, and it comes when we trust that God's purposes are far beyond anything we can understand. We were made for lasting contentment—fulfillment, significance, and joy. Romans 6:21 says, "What return did you get from the things of which you are now ashamed?" (RSV)

Doing what's right doesn't always lead to quick happiness. While happiness is good, happiness depends on the "happenings" in your life going the way you want. Happiness is a distant second compared to contentment!

Men, if you build your life around pursuing happiness, you will end up miserable. A man's tendency is to take shortcuts and look for the easy path, but the Lord says to us in Proverbs 3:5-6: "Trust in the Lord with all your heart and lean not on your own understanding. In all your ways acknowledge Him and He will make your paths straight." (NKJV)

> **If you build your life around pursuing happiness, you will end up miserable.**

Let's look at an example, written in Proverbs 7:6-23 (NASB)

> For at the window of my house I looked out through my lattice, and I saw among the naive, and discerned among the youths a young man lacking sense...

This young man was in the wrong place at the wrong time... by choice. He was looking for some quick pleasure.

> Passing through the street near her corner; and he walks along the way to her house, in the twilight, in the evening, in the middle of the night and the darkness.

The Bible tells us to "...make no provision for the flesh, to gratify its desires." (Romans 13:14, RSV) The fool allows himself to be in places he can sin easily; the fool skates as close to the edge as he can. It says that he was strolling down the path by her house. Why? What was he doing there? This young man was clearly not going to a Bible study! He was taking a dangerous chance.

> And behold, a woman comes to meet him, dressed as a prostitute and cunning of heart. She is boisterous and rebellious, her feet do not remain at home; she is now in the streets, now in the public squares, and lurks by every corner. So she seizes him and kisses him, and with a brazen face she says to him: "I was due to offer peace

offerings; today I have paid my vows. Therefore I have come out to meet you, to seek your presence diligently, and I have found you.

Yeah, right. "I came to find you—you especially—because I wanted just you." By slyly and seductively lying, she makes him foolishly and naively think that he is special. Not the truth at all. But he's so blind, he can't see it. She goes on:

I have spread my couch with coverings, with colored linens of Egypt. I have sprinkled my bed with myrrh, aloes, and cinnamon. Come, let's drink our fill of love until morning; let's delight ourselves with caresses. For my husband is not at home; he has gone on a long journey.

"Come on in, honey! No one's going to find out!"

With her many persuasions she entices him; with her flattering lips she seduces him. Suddenly he follows her as an ox goes to the slaughter, or as one walks in ankle bracelets to the discipline of a fool, until an arrow pierces through his liver; as a bird hurries to the snare, so he does not know that it will cost him his life.

At this point, men often blame God for allowing consequences to happen. But God is not obligated to stop consequences from happening. He does forgive, but we still suffer when we sin... starting from the precise moment we choose to take the wrong path.

> **God is not obligated
> to stop consequences from happening.**

The father concludes the story in Proverbs by saying:

So listen to me, my sons, and pay attention to my words. Don't let your hearts stray away toward her. Don't wander down her wayward path. For she has been the ruin of many; many men have been her victims. Her house is the road to the grave. Her bedroom is the den of death.

That young man wasn't smarter than his behavior showed, but he was foolish and made bad choices... with terrible consequences.

On the Edge of Death

Victoria Falls, on the border of Zimbabwe and Zambia, is a major tourist attraction. In the rainy season its 5,600-foot-wide wall of cascading water is absolutely spectacular. The roar of the water rushing over the cliff every minute and crashing onto the rocks below is deafening. Due to the noise and resulting mist, it is called the "Smoke That Thunders". But in dry season, less water runs over the falls. So much less that the "Devil's Pool" forms on the edge of the falls. It is created when low water levels allow rock to appear right on the edge of the cliff. Some visitors then take a dangerous chance: they stroll along the rim to peer 350 feet down into the chasm. They literally walk on the edge of death; there's no rock wall, no railing. Just one misstep...!

The Tiger Did What Tigers Do

I read a news story about some teenage boys who were walking by the tiger den at a zoo. One young man dared another to climb into the fenced pen. We don't know if the boy was on drugs or just plain stupid, but he did it. He climbed up the twenty-foot wire fence and slowly made his way down the other side. All the while being taunted and dared by his friends.

He wasn't wise enough to ignore his friends' challenges. He may have thought: "This is great—I'll show my friends that I'm a brave man and I can do this—my parents will never know!"

Or maybe he thought the tiger was tame and wouldn't bother him. Maybe he thought that the need to show off to his friends was worth the risk of whatever might happen inside the tiger's cage. Who knows what he thought.

And, guess what! He reached the ground on the other side of the cage and turned back to look at his friends—and nothing happened. He was the man! He did it!

Nothing happened... at first.

But then his friends were horrified to see the tiger start walking toward him. They started yelling, and this alerted the zoo staff. The young man inside the fenced compound jumped to the fence to climb back out, but the tiger did what tigers do. It leaped on him. The staff jumped in and tried to get the tiger's attention away from the boy, but it was too late.

Maybe you know some men who have walked too close to tigers, too close to the edge of the cliff, or too close to the neighborhood of sin. They say, "Nothing will happen...no one will find out...the tiger won't attack me... I won't fall...."

Why do smart people make dumb choices? Because we let pride or selfish desires direct us. But the Happiness Shortcut won't get us to contentment—or even to happiness in the end. Perhaps it will seem that way at first, but: "There is a way that seems right to a man, but its end is the way of death. " (Proverbs 14:12 NKJV)

A man of valor remembers that you don't see the benefits or the consequences of your decision right away. It may be days, weeks, months, even years before you know the results. But there are some choices you can make right away.

Make Two Choices Today

Men, we urge you to make wise choices. No matter what life brings your way, live your life with your eyes on the goal. Make two choices today that will impact all your decisions in the future.

1. Choose Christ.

2. Choose long-term, godly contentment over temporary happiness.

Don't walk along the edge of the cliff. Don't get close to the tiger because you think nothing will happen. Look at life from an eternal perspective, God's perspective, and not the momentary perception of whatever feels good for the moment. Choose you this day—and every day—whom you will serve, and stick to it. That's what a man of valor does. "Listen to counsel and receive instruction, that you may be wise in your latter days." (Proverbs 19:20 NKJV)

The Lord is with you, mighty man of valor!

+ + +

Choose Christ and choose long-term contentment: can it be that simple? Yes! These correct decisions are critical to everything, including handling money properly. What are you to do with what you've earned? Keep reading.

Make it Practical

1. Read Deuteronomy 28:1-14. What strikes you about the blessings God promises? What might they look like today?

2. Now read Deuteronomy 28:15-68. My *Study Bible* calls this section "The Curses of Disobedience." It is much longer than "The Blessings of Obedience" section, isn't it? Study it. What might the curses look like today? Thank the Lord for Christ's death on the cross that removes the eternal punishment for our sins! Suffering the earthly consequences of sin is already more than we can handle.

3. Why is making the decision to serve the Lord so fundamental to all future decisions and actions?

4. Do you agree or disagree with the two reasons stated for why happiness is not enough (it won't last and our desires tend to be selfish)? Cite Bible verses to support your position.

5. Proverbs 7 says that following the seductress into her home would cost the young man his life. How?

6. Review and discuss these Proverbs: 1:23, 4:13, 8:33, 10:17, 11:14, 12:15, 13:18, 14:18, 15:5, 15:22, 15:31-32, 19:20, and 29:1.

7. Will you choose this day whom you will serve?

Chapter 13

Mark Seager

A Man of Valor
and ~~His~~ Money

And He told them a parable, saying, "the land of a rich man was very productive. And [the rich man] began reasoning to himself, saying, 'What shall I do, since I have no place to store my crops?' Then he said, 'This is what I will do: I will tear down my barns and build larger ones, and there I will store all my grain and my goods. And I will say to my soul, Soul, you have many goods laid up for many years to come; take your ease, eat, drink and be merry.' But God said to him, 'You fool! This very night your soul is required of you; and now who will own what you have prepared?' So is the man who stores up treasure for himself, and is not rich toward God."

Luke 12:16-21 (NASB)

The most important thing about money is how you answer this question: "Whose money is it?"

"...you are to remember the LORD your God, for it is He
who is giving you power to make wealth..."
(Deuteronomy 8:18 NASB)
"The earth is the Lord's and all it contains."
(Psalm 24:1 NASB)

Since God blessed you with the ability to earn money, and since it is God's money, you are only a steward (manager) of His property. You do not own it; He does. You are provided the privilege and responsibility to manage some of His money.

> **The most important thing about money is how you**
> **answer this question: "Whose money is it?"**

We will have to give account to God for what we do with His money. Here on earth we are managing His money, and we therefore need to think of money management as looking out for His interests. God's values should determine what we do with His money.

We men focus a lot on money. We often misguidedly think that if a person has a lot of wealth that he is either really important or God must favor him. This is a normal human reaction, but it isn't right. [88] We need to reject this worldly thinking and transform our minds to accept these two truths:

1. Money does not determine your worth. Your worth is not determined by how rich you are; your worth was determined at the Cross. 1st Peter 1:18-19 says, "...you were not redeemed with perishable things like silver or gold from your futile way of life ... but with the ... blood of Christ." (NASB)

2. What you do with money is a mirror into your soul. Your money habits are a reflection of your heart. Jesus said that our heart goes where our treasure is. (Matthew 6:19-21) Don't say you love God and others when you are stingy. (James 2:15-16)

So in light of these truths, it's important that we aren't disorganized with money. We need to be good stewards with God's money so that we'll enjoy giving an account to Him someday.

> **Your worth is not about how rich you are.**
> **Your worth was determined at the Cross**

Budget His Money

We are not in control—God is—but we should create a budget faithfully, recognizing that our circumstances may change, and that God will give us what we need to make the necessary changes. Now, if you don't get a steady paycheck on a reliable schedule, you may wonder how you can budget, or even find it discouraging. However, inconsistent cashflow is all the more reason to plan!

Your budget should include giving, saving, and spending.

1. Give

All Christians are called to give first to God before doing anything else. This is an act of worship and faith. And he promises blessing as a result:

> "Honor the LORD from your wealth, and from the first of all your produce; then your barns will be filled with plenty, and your vats will overflow with new wine."
> (Proverbs 3:9-10 NASB)
> "One gives freely, yet grows all the richer; another withholds what he should give, and only suffers want."
> (Proverbs 10:24 ESV)

Men of valor acknowledge God above all else, and by giving to Him first, we are recognizing that He is more important than all else.

So how much should we give to God? And what does it mean to give to God?

Start with giving a minimum of ten percent of your total earnings directly to God and His work. Giving a tenth of our earnings has its roots in the Old Testament, appearing initially in Genesis 14:18-20, where Abram gives a "tenth of everything" to Melchizedek, the "priest of the Most High". There is no explanation in this passage of why Abram gave 10% versus 5 % or 50%. The Old Testament later speaks of tithes and offerings, as the Hebrews added additional amounts for various purposes, but ten percent is a good place for us to start. These instructions provide guidance for what a man of valor does with God's money.

Tithing is also implied in the New Testament:

> "Do you not know that those who perform sacred services eat the food of the temple, and those who attend regularly to the altar have their share from the altar? So also the Lord directed those who proclaim the gospel to get their living from the gospel."
> (1st Corinthians 9:13-14 NASB)

Although ten percent is not directly commanded in the New Testament, the Bible assumes it is obvious that we should be giving.

Why isn't tithing clearly commanded in the New Testament? Because if a percentage or amount was commanded, we would not give a penny more! We are prone to give as little as possible, and if we knew a certain amount was the requirement, we would stop there.

Ten percent is painless for a rich man. The richer you are, the less sacrificial it is to give ten percent. God calls us to give sacrificially (2nd Samuel 24:24), so don't focus on the percent; focus on the sacrifice!

> All Christians are called to give first to God before doing anything else.

How Should We Give to God's Work?

Consider developing three "Giving Buckets": your church, other Christian organizations, and the needy.

1. Give to Your Church. This is the "storehouse" that receives the first tithe. (Malachi 3:10) Just as you have regular living expenses, so does the church. What does the church need the money for? Church buildings have regular utility bills and need to be maintained; church workers need to be paid so they can provide for themselves and their families; teaching resources need to be purchased; missionaries need to be supported, etc. Since the church has regular scheduled expenses, it makes sense that God's people would give regularly—not erratically—to their local church

2. Give to Other Christian Organizations. Give to missionaries and other ministries, but not as a substitute for giving to your local church. These gifts should be above and beyond what you give to the local church.

3. Give to the Needy. Give to those in need, just like the Jerusalem Church did in 1st Corinthians 16. "Give to the poor and you will never be in need." (Proverbs 28:27 GNT)

Giving Attitudes

Give Cheerfully. "Each one must do just as he has purposed in his heart, not grudgingly or under compulsion, for God loves a cheerful giver." (2nd Corinthians 9:7 NASB)

Give Regularly. "Now concerning the collection for the saints... On the first day of every week, each of you is to put something aside and store it up, as he may prosper." (1st Corinthians 16:1-2 ESV)

Don't Give to Impress Others.

> "Take heed that you do not do your charitable deeds before men, to be seen by them. Otherwise you have no reward from your Father in heaven. Therefore, when you do a charitable deed, do not sound a trumpet... do not let your left hand know what your right hand is doing, that your charitable deed may be in secret; and your Father who sees in secret will Himself reward you openly." (Matthew 6:1-4 NKJV)

166

Pastor Greg Laurie put it like this:

"Every believer should be giving a portion of his or her finances to the Lord on a regular basis, but it should not be done in an ostentatious way or in a manner that would draw unnecessary attention. When people want to be noticed because of their giving, they want others to think they are more spiritual than they really are. This is hypocrisy."[89]

2. Save

After giving, set aside some money for unforeseen emergencies. We don't know what tomorrow holds, but we should be prepared. God revealed the wisdom of saving to Joseph in Genesis 41, and Proverbs 27:23-27 tells us:

"Know well the condition of your flocks, and pay attention to your herds; for riches are not forever, nor does a crown endure to all generations. When the grass disappears, the new growth is seen, and the herbs of the mountains are gathered in, the lambs will be for your clothing, and the goats will bring the price of a field, and there will be enough goats' milk for your food, for the food of your household, and sustenance for your attendants." (NASB)

In other words, be aware of your economic condition; stay on top of the financial details. (Remember the budget?) Save for the future, and wisely prepare for potential needs. (Proverbs 6:6-8)

Also set aside some funds for things you can't afford now. While Scripture does not forbid going into debt, it is clear that the wise man limits his debt for a reason: "The rich rules over the poor and the borrower becomes the lender's slave." (Proverbs 22:7 NASB)

A recommended practice for a healthy budget is saving a minimum of between ten and twenty percent of your income. That is impossible for many people (as it was for Brad for many years), but it is a good target when your income permits.

The world encourages us to "get whatever you want, whenever you want it, and if you can't afford it, so what!" Reject this idea. If you can't afford it now, ask yourself whether you really need it now. Remember Proverbs 21:20: "Precious treasure and oil are in a wise man's dwelling, but a foolish man devours it." (ESV)

You might wonder how this lines up with what Jesus said: "Do not lay up for yourselves treasures on earth, where moth and rust destroy and where thieves break in and steal; but lay up for yourselves treasures in heaven..." (Matthew 6:19-20 NKJV)

Greg Laurie explains,

> "This verse isn't saying that it is wrong to save or invest your money. What it is saying is that it is wrong to accumulate possessions for the sake of accumulating them and, more specifically, for the purpose of impressing others."[90]

**If you can't afford it now, ask yourself,
"Do I really need it now?"**

---

3. Spend

Be faithful to God as you spend money. 1st Corinthians 4:2 says, "It is required of stewards that they be found trustworthy." (RSV)

First, spend for what you need, such as food, rent, utilities, etc. If you spend money on yourself when your family does not have enough food to eat, God will hold you accountable for that. He has made you—the man—the provider and leader of your home and you will be held responsible. Honor God and your family by thinking of other's needs first. (Philippians 2:3-4)

Second, settle obligations promptly. Proverbs 3:27-28 says, "Do not withhold good from those to whom it is due, when it is in your power to do it. Do not say to your neighbor, 'Go, and come again, tomorrow I will give it'—when you have it with you." (ESV) These verses have broad application—there are many situations in which the principle of "prompt payment" applies, such as apologizing right away for a harsh word spoken or meeting a need that a missionary has when you have the ability to do so. But certainly it applies to borrowed money. A man of valor pays back his debts as soon as he can, if not immediately!

Man of valor, you are there to see that your family has its financial needs met.

Third, buy things that you want. There's no sin in buying what you want, unless buying those things means neglecting your family's needs, neglecting your giving to the Lord, neglecting to save for emergencies, or neglecting your financial obligations, such as paying off debts. Man of valor, you are there to see that the family eats and survives and has all its needs met. That is one reason God made you. So spending money for fun things or unnecessary items is not necessarily a sin, but we need to be careful not to take from what God has entrusted us with to spend on our own pleasure.

He is the Boss

Everything we have is God's; we are simply stewards. The best way to be a steward is to be a planner. Plan to give; plan to save; and plan to spend wisely, carefully, and fearfully—all the while acknowledging that it is God's money. He is the boss, and as a man of valor, you serve and honor Him. Remember, "The Lord makes poor and makes rich; he brings low, he also exalts." (1st Samuel 2:7 RSV)

The Lord is with you, mighty man of valor!

One of the many temptations that a man faces is attempting to succeed—alone. Yes, you read the Bible, love your wife, have your kids' hearts, serve Him at work, and manage His money well... but we all know that that's *really* hard. "Sometimes it seems no matter how hard I try / With all the pressures in life, I just can't get it all right."[91] That's very true—you can't get it all right, especially by yourself. In the next chapter, we'll talk about the key to maintaining a man of valor's fruitful walk in Christ.

Make it Practical

1. How do you feel about the money you have earned actually being God's money? How does knowing that change the way you view money? The way you manage money?

2. "Money does not determine your worth." Very important to know... but do you really believe it? Will you ask God to help you embrace this truth?

3. Read 1st Timothy 6:9-10, and Proverbs 8:10-11, 11:18, 15:16 & 27, 18:11, 28:2 27:20, 23:4-5, and 30:8-9. The Bible clearly cautions against the pursuit of wealth. How are you doing in this area? Do you struggle with wanting "just a little more"?

4. Pray: "Let me be neither rich nor poor; give me only as much as I need. If I have more, I might say I do not need You. But if I am poor, I might steal and bring disgrace on my God." (Proverbs 30:8-9 GNT)

5. It's been said that your priorities can be clearly determined via how you spend money. Where does the majority of your money go?

6. Do you tithe? Why or why not?

7. Do you give cheerfully?

8. Some have enough money to save and extra to invest in additional money-making ventures. There's no sin in that, but do you also give some of your investment earnings away to your church, other Christian ministries, and those in need?

9. The Bible strongly recommends avoiding debt. (Romans 13:8, Proverbs 22:7) However, sometimes we get carried away with impulse spending and suddenly debt becomes an ever-tightening noose around our necks. If that's true for you, what's your plan to get out of debt?

10. Sometimes an emergency leads to unavoidable debt, such as a major medical event for a family member, or a storm that damages your home. In those situations, James reminds us to ask for help. (James 4:2) Do you ask your church and/or brothers in Christ for help when you need it? Why or why not?

11. Money management and stewardship is important! But remember what Jesus also said in Matthew 6:28-34 and Luke 10:38-41. Let's be careful with how we manage His money, but not to the point of obsessive concern. On a scale of 1-10 with 10 being "intensely concerned", what is your stress level concerning money? Why? If your stress level is high, please talk to a brother whose stress level is low for guidance and prayer. If low, please talk to a brother whose stress level

is high to provide encouragement and assistance.

Notes & References

---

[88] The Bible strongly cautions against the pursuit of wealth. See 1st Timothy 6:9-10, and Proverbs 8:10-11, 11:18, 15:16 & 27, 18:11, 23:4-5, 28:2, 27:20

[89] Greg Laurie, "Money and Motives" (One Place 2020)
https://www.oneplace.com/ministries/a-new-beginning/read/articles/money-and-motives-9220.html

[90] *Ibid.*

[91] "I Want to Be Just Like You", Philips, Craig and Dean, *Lifeline* (Star Song Music 1994)

Chapter 14

Brad Smith

Men of Valor
Stand Together

*"Only let your manner of life be worthy of the gospel of Christ,
so that... I may hear of you that you are standing firm in one
spirit, with one mind striving side by side..."*
                                    Philippians 1:27 (RSV)

One of my favorite biblical accounts is recorded in 1st Samuel 13-14. These chapters recount Saul's first skirmish with the Philistines as king of Israel. Some 30,000 Philistine chariots and troops had encamped at a place called Michmash. All of Israel's army was camped nearby, trembling.

Saul's son, Jonathon, decides to enter the Philistine camp. He was alone but for his unnamed armor-bearer.

> Jonathan said to the young man, "Let's cross over to the camp of those heathen Philistines. Maybe the LORD will help us; if he does, nothing can keep him from giving us the victory, no matter how few of us there are." (1st Samuel 14:6 GNT)

In verse 7, his armor-bearer replies, "Do all that your mind inclines to. I am with you; as is your mind, so is mine." (RSV)[92]

As is Your Mind, So is Mine!

Does this statement ring in your soul like it does in mine? Every man wants to hear that. Every man wants to have a man like that at his side—someone who tells you, "Whatever you want to do, even if it endangers our lives, I'll do it with you. Let's go!"

Every man needs a friend in conflict, a friend who's with you through all of life's challenges, joys, and sorrows, a friend who knows your mind and even knows what you would do in a given situation—a friend who is closer than a brother.

Let's get back to the story. God honored the bravery of Jonathan and his armor-bearer. They kill twenty Philistine soldiers, causing the others to panic and run. Inspired by their bravery, Israel's full army attacks the scattering Philistine troops and are victorious. All due to two men of valor.

We are not told anything more about Jonathon's armor-bearer; perhaps he was killed at some later time. But God cared about Jonathan, and He brought another solid friend into Jonathan's life. Remember the story of David and Goliath? Jonathan had watched all that David had done through that act of faith, and he was amazed at David's bravery. He was struck by his determination, his initiative, and his leadership.

The Friendship of Jonathan and David

1st Samuel 18:1-4 says, "When he had finished speaking to Saul, the soul of Jonathan was knit to the soul of David, and Jonathan loved him as his own soul. Then Jonathan made a covenant with David..." (NASB)

Every man wants a man that he can look up to, someone we can follow—maybe a hero. Someone that we can be like. Jonathan is just like you and me. And he decides, "I want be with this guy!"

You can follow this close friendship in 1st Samuel chapters 18-23. The Lord used this friendship to keep David alive when Jonathan saved him several times from Saul. Through all of it, Jonathan encouraged David. For example, in 1st Samuel 23:15-16, Jonathan went to David when he was running from Saul, and "strengthened his hand in God." That's even more amazing when you remember that Jonathan was the rightful heir to the throne! Saul was his dad; in the world's way of thinking, Jonathon should have been next in line to be king. Yet he chose to support his friend David anyway.

Note that Jonathan didn't just come up to David, slap him on his back, and ask how he was doing. When he saw what the situation was, Jonathan didn't say, "Come on, act like a man. You can do it. Buck up!" Or, "Keep your chin up, buddy—you'll get through this!"

No, Jonathan reminded David of the prophecy that God had spoken over him: David would someday be king. Jonathan reminded him of the truth of God's Word and the hope that could be found in Him.

Jonathan reminded David of his destiny.

Jonathan "strengthened David's hand in God."

Don't breeze through passages like this and miss the details. God could have spoken to David directly, just like He'd done while David was alone in the wilderness all those years tending Jesse's sheep, but He didn't. God used Jonathan to deliver His message to David. Jonathan was the human flesh and blood through which God acted to accomplish His work.

What Every Man Needs

Men, we all need a brother at our side. We need a flesh-and-blood arm on our shoulder to encourage us. We need a man who looks in our eyes and speaks words of assurance, hope, respect, and admiration. We need someone who will stand with us in times of trouble. We need someone we can look up to, follow, and imitate. Someone who will "strengthen our hand in God." A man who will direct us to God, reminding us of the truth of His Word and of His purposes for us. We need a brother in our lives! God knows that, and He gave one to David.

To have success in the daily battles of life, we need reliable support from our brothers. "Going it alone" is a foolish and dangerous choice. Every man needs a friendship with another man that is deep, direct, and dedicated.[93]

✓ **Deep**. Your friendship goes to the heart. A friend who is closer than a brother helps you to get through the issues at the core of your soul. This is a man you can trust with your life. He is there for you when you need to be picked up, and you can be there for him when he stumbles or falls. Ecclesiastes 4:9-10 says, "Two are better than one, because they have a good reward for their toil. For if they fall, one will lift up his fellow; but woe to him who is alone when he falls and has not another to lift him up." (ESV)

✓ **Direct**. He's very clear when he speaks. He does not ignore the issues in your life that need attention. He speaks to your heart. He gets in your face if necessary. Proverbs 27:6 tells us that "Faithful are the wounds of a friend..." (KJV) This friend is honest, yet uplifting through his directness. He will tell it like it is and will not hide the truth. As Proverbs 27:17 says, "Iron sharpens iron, and one man sharpens another"—one builds the character of another.

✓ **Dedicated**. He cares enough to be there when you need him. He is not only loyal to you, but you are a priority in his life, just as he is in yours. He's dedicated to you. Proverbs 18:24 tells us that "...there is a friend who sticks closer than a brother." (ESV) That's the kind of friend we need.

A Divine Appointment

Some time ago, a brother asked me to meet with him. At the time, I was going through a difficult period at work. I was working many hours and finding it hard to keep up with everything my boss was asking me to do. The stress was bad, and it was affecting my relationship with my wife and children. As the meeting drew closer, I really wondered if I should take the time to do it because I was under so much pressure and had so many things to get done.

(Almost every man tries to work things out alone. When facing challenging times, the average man doesn't reach out—he closes in).

But I kept my appointment with John, and it turned out to be an amazing conversation. We didn't talk about sports, the weather, or the latest news; we immediately went *deep*. We talked about things that mattered. Turned out that like me, he was going through tough days at work. Like me, he was feeling the strain in his marriage and family. And he also told me how bad his attitude was about it all. That also sounded familiar! You know what I heard when he said that? I heard, *"I am like you. I have similar problems."*

> ### When he described his situation, I heard:
> ### "I am like you. I have similar problems."

And then John got *direct* with me. He asked me if I was praying about my situation. And he quickly confessed, "Because I'm not!"

His clear, blunt words broke through my tension and frustration and avoidance. John's directness pointed out the obvious: I wasn't praying. I wasn't praying to the God who offers His help in time of need. I wasn't praying and asking God to provide His power to get me through the situation.

And then I realized that my reaction to the pressure and the tension and the deadlines was just like any other man at work. I was being just like anyone else in the office, saved or not. I wasn't seeking the Lord for His help. I wasn't being a man of valor. John's question helped me see that.

Because I took the time to meet with a brother, I understood what was wrong in my life. And I was ashamed of myself. Sometimes what we really need is a good, swift kick in the pants. My brother was direct, but he was also *dedicated* to my success in my Christian walk. My friend's desire to go deep, coupled with his directness and his dedication—his caring for me—changed me. It changed the way I saw my work and the way I talked with God. It increased my dependence on Him and made me ask for His help more. And it improved my attitude.

> **Sometimes what we need is a good swift kick.**

That morning, my brother and I committed to changing our habits and seeking the Lord for His help. We committed to praying daily, and we agreed to check up on one another to see how things were going.

Six months later during my annual performance review at work, my boss commented on an attitude change that he had noticed in me, one that had begun a few months back. I thought about it and realized that my change in attitude had begun at about the time of that meeting with John—the meeting I almost skipped.

Into the Light

It's hard for men to be open with one another. I definitely get that. It's difficult to talk about what's inside—our fears and failures, the bad things that happen, what we're going through—without trying to hide something. But it is vital to our Christian life. The only way to overcome the tendency to hide is through close, trusting, and invested friendships. Friends who are deep, direct, and dedicated.

I John 1:7 says, "But if we walk in the light as He is in the light, we have fellowship with one another, and the blood of Jesus Christ His Son cleanses us from all sin." (ESV) When we bring our issues, our struggles, our pressures into the light and talk about them with one another, it draws us together because we realize that we are not alone. We see that others have similar problems, and that releases us from the darkening and isolation of sin.

As my daughter put it once, a lack of transparency—not saying what needs to be said and not telling the truth—leads to things that drag on and on without ever getting addressed. Problems don't get fixed, and sin doesn't get healed. Without close friendships, we develop warped perspectives on life. When we are alone, we often cannot see clearly what we are doing wrong. We can deceive ourselves very easily.

The Bible warns us about this very thing. In Proverbs 18:1, the Lord tells us, "Whoever isolates himself seeks his own desire; he breaks out against all sound judgment." (ESV) Men, being alone can lead you to do evil. Evil takes root when we decide to stay in our own private, isolated, little secret world that we work so hard to create—even in the midst of our family, our work, and church. I need more than two eyes; I need four, six, and eight. I need someone who will say to me, "Can't you see what you are doing?"

**Without close friendships,
we develop warped perspectives on life.**

Fierce Dependence

Why is it so hard for men to share our weaknesses or hidden struggles with a trusted Christian brother? Unfortunately, it's our nature. When it comes to building friendships with other men, most of us prefer to tough it out ourselves. If we do share a weakness, we're afraid they'll tell someone else or think less of us. So we conclude, "I can get through this; I can fix this myself. I don't need anyone." Cultures all around the world have lied to us about this, telling us that independence is manly and friendship indicates weakness. Mark Greene, senior editor at The Good Men Project, explains that "to ask for friendship suggests vulnerability... or even willingness to admit need. All values which are roundly condemned in men."[94]

Where do you find that in the Bible? You don't! Men's tendency of fierce independence is not of God. What you do find in the Bible are passages such as these:

- ✓ "...encourage one another day after day, as long as it is still called "today", so that none of you will be hardened by the deceitfulness of sin." (Hebrews 3:12-13 NASB)
- ✓ "...and let us consider how to stimulate one another to love and good deeds, not forsaking our own assembling together..." (Hebrews 10:24-25 NASB)
- ✓ "Confess your sins to one another and pray for one another..." (James 5:16 NASB)
- ✓ "Though a man might prevail against one who is alone, two will withstand him. A threefold cord is not quickly broken." (Ecclesiastes 4:12 ESV)

Without men in our lives who love and care for us, we are destined for destruction. Without regular contact with our brothers in the battle, we are on a solo mission that is quickly defeated by weariness and the pain of the wounds inflicted by the enemy. But connected men—men striving side by side—can achieve victory against overwhelming odds.

> **Connected men achieve victory
> against overwhelming odds.**

Let's Cheer For One Another

When I was in high school, the cross-country running coach challenged me to join the new long-distance running team he was starting.

What did I say? A man I respected and liked asked me to spend time with him and help him in a project that required physical challenge and skill? He's asking me?! "Yes!"

Well, I was a fool, because I knew nothing about the sport. Every tournament consisted of one race—for 5 kilometers, or 3.1 miles. And what do you have to do to practice for these races? Run. A lot. Every day we ran 10, 15, sometimes 20 miles (32 kilometers)! It was grueling. It was very difficult. What a fool I was!

Then one day, a few weeks after we started, the coach handed out team uniforms. He told us to put them on and to follow him. He halted at the doors to the gymnasium. We didn't know what we were doing or why we were there.

For some reason I was first in line. The gym doors were opened and my teammate behind me pushed me forward into the gym. Someone in the center of the gym motioned me to come to him. I jogged into the room—and saw that every space in the bleachers was filled with standing, cheering classmates. Everyone in my school—over 1,200 students—was in that room! They were screaming and throwing confetti. They were cheering, for me! And then over all that noise, I heard over the sound system, echoing around me, my name: "BRAD SMITH! BRAD SMITH! BRAD SMITH!"

What were they doing? It was a pep rally, where the whole school comes out to encourage and cheer their sports teams on to victory.

Hearing my name echo around the gym made me feel like I could do *anything*. I felt like I could outrun a cheetah, jump over a skyscraper, or even fly! Being cheered for made me feel that I could conquer the world!

When was the last time someone cheered for you? When did a brother say to you words like:

✓ "Great, Mark! That was the right way to handle your son!"
✓ "Francisco, right on! You avoided that alluring woman."
✓ "Jose, you remembered and acted on the promises of God rather than giving into hopelessness."
✓ "Excellent, David! You did the right thing in standing by your co-worker when he was falsely accused."

We need cheers when we pursue and do what's right. Let's start cheering for one another!

**When was the last time
someone cheered for you?**

You Don't Need to Be Alone

Brother, do you have one or two men who will cheer you on to the finish line?

Find a man who will be that friend who is "closer than a brother." You can ask a guy to meet with you weekly and study the Bible together. Build a friendship that's deep, direct, and dedicated.

Will you commit to doing that today?

Stand Together

"Only let your manner of life be worthy of the gospel of Christ, so that whether I come and see you or am absent, I may hear of you that you are standing firm in one spirit, with one mind striving side by side for the faith of the gospel, and not frightened in anything by your opponents." (Philippians 1:27-28 ESV)

God's men of valor strive side by side for the gospel and for godly living. They stand firm in one Spirit with hearts that are joined. They are not frightened by problems and discouragement because they have the Lord, and they have one another.

You cannot live a successful Christian life without close brothers at your side. Do you have a friend about whom you can say, "As is your mind, so is mine"? Can you boast of a friendship with a man that is a "soul mate" as Jonathan was with David?

"Though a man might prevail against one who is alone, two will withstand him. A threefold cord is not quickly broken." (Ecclesiastes 4:12, ESV) One man striving alone against Satan will not stand. But two or three brothers fighting Satan together can. Find a man with whom you can stand.

The Lord is with you, mighty man of valor!

+ + +

We need a brother to help us face the battles of life. With God's strength, power, and Spirit, a close brother at your side, standing with you, can help you do the right thing every day – as long as you make the right decisions! And now, everything we've written leads to the next chapter. God wants to use you now, but He also wants to use you later on. *Much* later on.

Make it Practical

1. Each man needs friendships with other men that are deep, direct, and dedicated. Do you have at least one or two friends with whom you share this kind of brotherhood? If not, with which of your friends could you strengthen your friendship until it looks like this?

2. Like Jonathan for David, God often chooses to speak to us through the words of the people He places in our lives. Who has He used to speak truth, hope, and life to you? To whom has He spoken through you?

3. Think of a time when a brother in Christ challenged you or asked you tough questions. How did you respond? Did thinking over his words change your mindset or your actions? Have you ever been similarly challenging to a brother? If not, what holds you back?

4. Probably there is a sin or struggle that you are currently dealing with. Have you brought it into the light with a trusted brother in Christ?

5. Who cheers for you? Can your brothers in Christ count on you to cheer for them?

Notes & References

[92] I also like how the ESV renders verse 1st Samuel 14:7: "Do all that is in your heart. Do as you wish. Behold, I am with you heart and soul."

[93] Thanks to pastor Robert Lewis, author of *Raising a Modern-Day Knight*, for this description of a close friend (given at a 2002 men's conference).

[94] Mark Greene, "Why men have so much trouble making friends" (Salon 2014) https://www.salon.com/2014/04/12/why_do_mens_friendships_feel_so_hollow_partner/

Chapter 15

The Legacy of
A Man of Valor

"The memory of the righteous is a blessing."
Proverbs 10:7 (ESV)

Washington, D.C., the capital city of the United States, is filled with monuments and statues. One of the largest statues is that of Thomas Jefferson, the man who wrote our Declaration of Independence and many other important documents that helped to establish our nation some 250 years ago. His statue is twenty-five feet tall—almost eight meters! In the rotunda surrounding his statue, a few of the statements from his writings are engraved in stone. Those engravings help us to know something of the man—his heart and his passion. His character is reflected in those words. In that sense, the legacy of this man lives forever. He died 200 years ago, but his legacy lives on.

I don't know if he was aware that this statue would be built. I don't know if he considered it likely that his efforts to establish our country would be remembered and his words would be read, that his heart could be understood, and the things he believed in would be quoted word-for-word over 200 years later.

The legacy of this man lives forever.

But if he had known this, he surely would have been pleased. Like most men, Jefferson wished to leave a legacy. Every man wants to know that who he is and what he does makes a difference, that he will be remembered by those he leaves behind here on earth, and that he will continue to have an impact on the world even after he dies. He

183

yearns to believe that the principles he stood for, the character he had, and maybe even some of the things he did are not only remembered, but will influence the coming generations long after his last breath.

A Man Who Gave Everything to Serving God

My father-in-law, John Snavely, was an extraordinary man who served for many years as a missionary bush pilot in South Africa. He grew up a little wild because he had divorced parents and an alcoholic mother. But with purpose and determination, he turned his life around and eventually relocated his family to Africa. His small life became a huge life, full of meaning and eternal consequences, until he died of a sudden heart attack at the age of sixty-two. [95]

At the time, my wife and I were living in San Francisco. I picked up the phone when the call came to give us the news. After listening, I handed the phone to my wife, went to take a shower, and began to sob. I was crying because John Snavely had left a challenging example for me: he was a committed, godly man who had served the Lord consistently for thirty-seven years without wavering. He was a man who had given everything he had to serve his God. He had left a legacy that stirred me deeply. No one else in my life had set such an example.

> **He left a legacy that stirred me deeply.**

A Legacy of Valor

We've talked about a man's position. We've said that if a man has accepted Jesus as his Savior, he is a new creation in Christ, and the Lord is with him. He is a man of valor—before doing anything, before he's assigned any task. We've argued how vital it is that he understands why he is important in God's eyes, and how this perspective gives him the ability to have a big impact on his wife, his family, his community, the church, and on God's kingdom, as an ambassador, as a servant leader, and as a real man enabled to live and act on who he is by the Holy Spirit.

A man's position directs his priorities. He keeps God first; he is a man of the Word and a man in constant, bold communication with God. He strives to love his wife as Christ loves the church, serving as a leader, protector, provider, teacher, and friend to his bride. As a dad, the father of valor takes action in the affairs of his family; he accepts his responsibility and looks ahead for the good of his family. As a father of valor, he also helps his children walk in a manner worthy of the God who calls them. A man of valor works as unto the Lord, to whom he is ultimately responsible. He is not lazy; he is not dependent on others; and he worships the Lord through his godly work habits.

A man's position orders his priorities and determines his practices. He has a plan to give, save, and spend as a steward of God's money. He regularly joins with other men because men of valor stand together. He chooses Christ and he chooses contentment over short-term happiness.

Lastly, a man of valor imparts a legacy. What will that be for you? One way or another, you will leave a legacy. I want to challenge you to consider now how people will remember you after you die. What do you have to do leave a legacy? Who do you have to be?

> **A man of valor imparts a legacy.**

"Dad, I want you to find me a warrior."

Over the years, men have repeatedly asked for a succinct definition of a man of valor. While I would like to have a nice short quote to hang on a wall, there's a reason we developed the Men of Valor International teachings! (One man in India told me, "We never knew the definition of a godly man until you came.") A t-shirt-size slogan may be memorable, but is it adequate?[96]

My daughter surprised me a few years back when she texted me, "Dad, I want you to find me a warrior." She was in college at the time. We talked about it, and later she sent the following. She said she wanted me to find her a warrior who was:

1. Spiritually, physically, and emotionally strong. He gets that strength from God.

2. A protector and a provider. His wife and children feel safe and cared for.

3. Disciplined, humble, and self-controlled.

4. Dedicated. He stands up for what he believes in. He has a vision and mission that is bigger than him. His passion is so strong that he works every day to see it through. He does not give up.

5. A leader and a follower. And he understands when to do both.

6. A man of integrity. He always does what's right—no matter what.

7. Confident.

8. Respectable, respectful, and loyal.

9. Tender and compassionate toward his wife and his children,

earning their love and respect.

What father wouldn't want her daughter to marry a man like that?? (I'm pleased to report that she married this kind of man!)

A Man of Valor Has Nothing to do with Evil

Well, here's where a good *biblical* definition starts: Psalm 101. In this Psalm, David wrote out a statement of commitment that he was making before the Lord. He committed that he would sing of God's love and justice, that he would walk carefully, that he would hate the deeds of faithless men, that he would stop others from slandering, and that he would not spend time with those who lie or deceive. And in verse 4 he wrote, "A perverse heart will be far from me. I will have nothing to do with evil." (WEB)

If you want to leave a legacy, men, if you want to be remembered with fondness and respect, you must say that, too. You must commit to it. For the man of valor, this is where it starts. This is the heart of everything we must be. A man of valor has nothing to do with evil.

A man of valor doesn't lie. A man of valor does not steal. A man of valor does not get drunk. A man of valor says:

- ✓ I will have nothing to do with laziness.
- ✓ I will have nothing to do with pornography.
- ✓ I will have nothing to do with prostitutes.
- ✓ I will have nothing to do with physically or verbally abusing my wife.
- ✓ I will have nothing to do with selling products or services of poor quality.
- ✓ I will have nothing to do with charging more for my products than they are worth.
- ✓ I will have nothing to do with bribery.
- ✓ I will have nothing to do with unkind words or a destructive temper.
- ✓ I will have nothing to do with killing babies before or after they are born.
- ✓ *I will have nothing to do with evil!*

That's the start for a man who wants to leave a legacy. That's the beginning of what God wants for His mighty men of valor. It is the starting place for everything we are and do.

God Defines a Man of Valor in His Word

The Word of God further defines a man of valor and describes his legacy in Psalm 112:1-9.

> Praise the Lord! How blessed is the man who fears the Lord, who greatly delights in His commandments. His descendants will be mighty on earth; the generation of the upright will be blessed. Wealth and riches are in his house, and his righteousness endures forever. Light arises in the darkness for the upright; he is gracious and compassionate and righteous. It is well with the man who is gracious and lends; he will maintain his cause in judgment. For he will never be shaken; the righteous will be remembered forever. He will not fear evil tidings; his heart is steadfast, trusting in the Lord. His heart is established, he will not fear, until he looks with triumph on his adversaries. He has given freely to the poor, his righteousness endures forever; his horn will be exalted in honor. (NASB)

I see at least nine characteristics of a man of valor here. He:
1. Fears the Lord (v1);
2. Delights in His commandments (v1);
3. Is gracious, compassionate, and righteous (v4);
4. Lends generously (v5);
5. Deals justly (v5);
6. Trusts in the Lord (v7);
7. Is not afraid (v8);
8. Has a firm and steady heart (v8);
9. Gives freely to the poor (v9).

Now that's a man of valor!

The Power of a Decision

We all have a decision to make. Let's look again at the previous chapter's big decision—"choose today whom you will serve." It's a decision that will change the path of your life and maybe the path of the generations to follow.

A few years ago, I was listening to a man named Stephen talk about his father and grandfather. Stephen's grandfather was a lazy drunk who led others around him to live worthless lives of drunkenness and sin. As a result, Stephen's father had no good example in his life of what a godly man should be. But someone shared the gospel with him, and he accepted Jesus. He didn't know what it meant to be a godly man or a godly husband and father. Stephen described how, time and again, he and his brother would find their dad on his knees, crying out for God's help to understand how to be a man of God.

> **Time and time again, he cried out for God's help to understand how to be a man of God.**

God answered that prayer, and his father learned—but it was a struggle for him. He worked hard for his family, and little by little the example of his life influenced his sons, Stephen and Alex. Eventually, they became Christians, too. Then the brothers went to Bible school. Then they became pastors. Today, Stephen and Alex Kendrick also write books and make movies that are impacting not only their communities, but their country. And because these resources are being translated into other languages and sent around the globe, they are now impacting our entire world.[97] And it's all because one man—their father—decided to follow a different trail than what his own father had done. His decision changed everything.

My story goes differently. My grandfather did not respond to the gospel, nor did my dad in his younger years. Until I was maybe twelve years old, it was very common for our extended family of Dad's seven brothers and sisters and all their children to get together for family gatherings that were flooded with beer and liquor. I can clearly remember seeing my drunken uncles stumble around at these parties. Even my very young cousins got drunk because no one kept the beer from them. One really sad result of all this was that several of my relatives became alcoholics and died from liver trouble. Others committed suicide.

Thank God my story didn't end there. A decision was made that changed the course of my life. When I was thirteen, someone invited my mom to a woman's Bible study. After several months of experiencing the love, warmth, and support that comes when Christian sisters reach out, my mom accepted Jesus as her Savior. Then she shared the Bible with me and the rest of my family. She took us to a church that taught the Bible. Mom tuned the TV to Billy Graham crusades, and we were not allowed to change the channel! I watched many of these crusades and, through their influence, I became a Christian when I was fourteen. Eventually, my dad accepted Christ also.

> **Her decision changed everything.**

I went on to attend a Christian college where I met my wife.

Together, we founded a Christian home. Although I had much to learn about being a godly husband and dad, the Lord has blessed our lives. More than thirty years ago, I began serving in the men's ministry in church. Then, in 2004, the Lord opened my eyes to the needs of men in other countries. I do what I do now because my mother gave her heart to Jesus and obeyed Him. I can write this today because one woman made a decision. That one decision changed not only her path, but my path, the path of my marriage, and the paths of our children—now all married to godly spouses—and, Lord willing, generations beyond that. Her decision and faithfulness changed everything. Through her family's work and the Lord's blessing, her decision is still changing lives today—including yours.

You too can make a decision like that. A decision that will change everything.

You can make a decision that changes everything.

Change Starts Here

The truth is we all have a decision to make. Not one single decision is made in isolation. Every decision affects not only us but those around us. Just one decision—for good or bad—can change the path of our own lives as well as the path of generations to follow.

Leaving a legacy begins with a commitment, a decision.

Change starts here—with you.

Men of Valor International believes that if we can reach the man, we can reach his wife. If we can reach the man, we can reach his family. If we can reach the man, we can reach his church. If we can reach the man, we can reach his community. If we can reach the man, we can reach his country. If we can reach the man, we can reach the world.

The evidence is clear. God is calling His men of valor to set the example. Men, change begins here and now, with you. A man of valor can change his world when he stands together with other men to grow strong in Christ, when he acts on who he is in Christ, when he leads his community and his church, when he realizes his worth and value before God, and when he looks in the mirror every day and recognizes that he is a mighty man of valor because the Lord is with him.

You Can Make a Difference

Can you make a difference? *Yes!* If you act on the truth that you now know, man of valor, according to Psalm 112:

✓ Your descendants will be mighty (v2);
✓ Your generation will be blessed because of your influence (v2);
✓ Your righteousness will endure forever (v3);
✓ You will have influence and honor (v9); and
✓ You will be remembered forever (v6)!

What Will Your Statue Look Like?

After you go on to be with the Lord, what memories of you will be engraved on the hearts and minds of your wife, your children, neighbors, and friends? What will *your* "statue"—your legacy—look like? What words would be written in stone?[98]

Today is the Day

Today is the day to make a decision to embrace your identity and your calling as a mighty man of valor. Change starts here. Change starts now. Make the decision to follow Christ with your whole heart, *today*. Start today to leave a legacy that will be remembered *forever*.

The world is desperate for its men of valor to rise up. We live in the midst of a spiritual and psychological battle that is intensifying day by day, with consequences enduring for generations—so let's live like it. Let's fight like it. Brothers, it is never too late to start doing what's right.

The world is desperate for men of valor to rise up.

The Lord is with you, mighty man of valor!

Make it Practical

1. Think back over your life and your spiritual heritage. Was there a major spiritual decision made by one of your family members that had a direct impact on you? How have your decisions impacted your family and sphere of influence?

2. Carefully and prayerfully think over this statement: A man of valor has nothing to do with evil. If you strived to live this way, what specific habits, practices, or activities would you need to abandon in God's strength? What in your life would need to change? How can you find accountability with another man to help you stay on target as you strive to have nothing to do with any form of evil?

3. Does your life have a driving purpose and a mission? Are you living for a cause that's bigger than yourself? How does your passion for that mission affect your daily goals and priorities? How does it build the Kingdom of God?

4. How do you want to be remembered? What are the most important things you'd want someone to say about you at your memorial service? How are you cultivating those qualities?

5. Do you believe that change begins with you? How can you begin leaving a rich and unforgettable legacy, not only for future generations, but for the people all around you even now? How can you begin to be the change that is desperately needed in your family, your church, your workplace, and your community?

6. If you are a men's leader, ask each member of your group to write down several words that they would want said at their memorial service. Look over the qualities they've written. Are you teaching them about those characteristics? Are you giving them opportunities to develop those qualities through activities, service, and leadership?

Notes & References

---

[95] Dad died in 1985. Many years later, at a Men of Valor Conference in nearby Eswatini (Swaziland), we met a pastor who as a boy had suffered a serious illness and remembered that Dad flew him to the hospital where my wife's family was stationed—saving his life!
You can read John Snavely's story in the memoir *Wings Over Zululand*.

[96] In a seminar, Gary Thomas offered this definition: "The biblical model of a godly man is a passionately engaged man empowered by God to influence the world." I like that!

[97] The Kendrick Brothers wrote and directed the movies *Flywheel, Facing the Giants, Fireproof, Courageous, War Room, Overcomer,* and *Show Me The Father*.

[98] "A friend of mine wrote recently, 'If we died tomorrow, the company that we are working for could easily replace us in a matter of days. But the family left behind would feel the loss for the rest of their lives. Why then do we invest so much in our work and so little in our children's lives?' We need to make time for our children and trust that the Lord will provide for all of our physical needs. Children, whether our own or those we disciple, are our lasting legacy—an investment we'll never regret."
David Roper, "Stand Strong" (Our Daily Bread Publishing, 2018)

Man of Valor,
The Lord is With You!

"Those who hope in Me will not be disappointed."
Isaiah 49:23 (ESV)

For Leaders of Men of Valor

This bonus section is written with pastors and church leaders in mind, though anyone will certainly benefit.

"Why Men Don't Go to Church" helps leaders understand what the church must do differently to secure its future. God is in control of the future, but men are appointed caretakers of His bride. Without men living for Him and doing His work, marriages crumble, families disintegrate, and communities decay. God appointed His Church to teach men how to live as men of valor. Given the dwindling numbers of men attending church worldwide, something is wrong. The chapter is valuable for everyone, but it's designed to give pastors and church leaders some things to think about and hopefully change how they "do" church.

"Three Things Every Man Wants" describes three areas of activities—all biblical—that men not only want, but need, to help them live out who they are as men of valor.

Why Men Don't Go
to Church

Brad Smith

"[so] that He might present to Himself the church in all her glory, having no spot or wrinkle or any such thing; but that she would be holy and blameless."

Ephesians 5:27 (ESV)

The church is in crisis: men have been dropping out. Because men aren't attending, they aren't growing as Christians. Because they aren't growing as Christians, they aren't living or leading in a godly manner. Because they aren't living or leading in a godly manner, their families aren't following. And marriages, families, churches, communities, and nations are paying the price.

What's going on? Why don't men go to the very place that offers solutions for their lives?

Uncomfortable and Awkward

Several years ago, I was attending a gathering of American missionaries who were serving in a foreign country. I was asked to teach a small group of the male missionaries about reaching men. Serving in this country is particularly challenging, and this team worked closely with one another to reach the people they'd come to serve.

Before the class I was told the number of men to expect, so I tried an experiment. I set up twelve chairs in a tight half-circle facing the podium.

At ten minutes before the start, the first missionary came in the meeting room. He looked at the group of chairs and then sat on one end. A minute or so later, the second man came in. He looked around and then sat at the other end of the group of chairs—in the chair farthest from the first man.

A third man came in the room. He looked at the men sitting on the opposite ends of the row of chairs and walked around into the space between the chairs and the podium. Instead of sitting next to or even near one of his teammates, he sat in the exact middle of the row of chairs—as far as one could get from the other men.

Two men came next, and they each sat exactly in between the man in the middle of the row of chairs and the men on either end, apart from one another. Then other men came in and sat down filling up all the remaining seats except one.

It was time to start the session, so I welcomed everyone and began. After a couple of minutes, the last man came in. He approached the remaining empty chair from the back, pulled it out of the half-circle of chairs and sat down. And he did not slide it back in with the other men! He stayed separated from his team members.

Look Through New Eyes

Does anything like this happen when you get men together? Do men keep distance—even if they know each other? Depending on your culture and if the men are very close friends and have been coming to men's events for years, they may not have trouble with cramped/close seating, but generally this reluctance is common, everywhere.

Your desire is to have new men join your gatherings, right? So, try to think like a man who maybe hasn't been to a gathering like this, ever. Imagine the mindset of the man who lives near you or works with you. Would he go to an event with men that he doesn't know and sit close enough to touch shoulders? Most wouldn't. Actually, let's be honest: even if they do know one another, they might not want to sit close. These missionaries didn't!

What Are We Doing Wrong?

We are trying to reach men from the neighborhood and community. Are there things we do in church that repels them? That causes them to not want to come again? That makes them feel that church isn't a place for them? That provides them nothing to do, no role to play, and nothing that's practically applicable in their lives?

If we want to know why men don't go to church, we need to understand some differences between men and women. What about men is different? What is it about the church that is not attractive to men? What are we doing wrong?

What follows is a collection of observations from various books,[99] studies, and discussions on the reasons why men don't go to church. Some of these may be culturally specific, so consider carefully which of these may apply to your particular church. As you are reading, think about the men you want to reach. Would any of these things matter to them? Could any of this be a reason why few men go to your church?

The Church Feels Like a Place for Women

What might an average man experience when he walks into a church?

- ✓ The greeting team is mostly women.
- ✓ The way the chairs are configured forces him to sit uncomfortably close to his neighbors. His arms touch those of the person sitting next to him.
- ✓ He looks around and notices that there are few men and those that are there are clearly elderly.
- ✓ As he stands for the singing, he notices it is led by women and the musicians are women. They sway and close their eyes and raise their hands as they sing. He also notices that song after song contains phrases like, "Hold me in Your arms," "Draw me closer," "I love You, Lord," "Nobody fills my heart like You do; nobody thrills me like You do."
- ✓ The director of the women's ministry gives the announcements. She mentions the need for volunteers to provide snacks for the children's ministry, the upcoming women's craft night, and the children's musical that evening. There are no announcements concerning men.
- ✓ Following the sermon, the pastor calls for people to share "what is on their heart" and what the Lord is doing in their lives. Several women stand to give lengthy personal testimonies and prayer requests; some of them have tears streaming down their faces.

What do these not-too-unusual aspects of a worship service have in common? They are geared toward emotions and toward women's and children's activities. Most men visiting a typical worship service these days will conclude, "This place is all about women!" David Murrow urges, "Examine everything your church does through the eyes of a man, and ask, "Would this intrigue/encourage/interest a guy?"[100]

When men feel that a service is not directed toward them, and they don't see men participating, they may shut down. The perceived feminine focus distracts them, and those distractions stop the message from reaching them. While women are generally willing to tolerate a masculine focus in the main service, men do not want a feminine focus.

When a man visits a church where these distractions are present, he may not be able to put his finger on what he didn't like, but he will probably say, "I'm not sure what it is, but that place just doesn't do it for me."

> **"That place just doesn't do it for me."**

This is not to say that the Holy Spirit cannot break through and work in spite of distractions, but if you are already struggling to get men to come to church, why not do everything you can to ensure that they want to stay? Men are smart. It doesn't take them long to figure out whether the church cares about men. Think about it: if all the announcements are about women's activities, and if all or many of the people in public roles are women, and if the elements of the service are designed—intentionally or not—to speak to women's hearts, then what will men think? "Gotta go!"

Murrow observes,

> Unfortunately for the church, many men see churchgoing as womanly behavior... This is one reason many Christian men hide their faith from other men. They're not ashamed of Christ; they're ashamed of feminization.[101]

To be clear, we are not saying that this is a good or a true attitude on the part of men. It's not! But it is a real obstacle we have to overcome in order to reach, not just today's men, but the next generation. LifeWay Research found that seventy percent of kids who were brought to church by their mom dropped out of church in adulthood when they were young adults, but kids whose fathers attended church regularly were more likely to stay in church during adulthood.[102] It seems clear that you cannot feminize a church and keep the men, and if a church does not keep the men, it won't keep the next generation.

Why Men Don't Go To Church

Church Feels Like a Place for Women
- ✓ Does the seating make men sit close to one another?
- ✓ Do the songs talk about falling in love with another man?
- ✓ Do the services include lots of emotional content, like crying?
- ✓ Are the announcements only about activities for women and children?
- ✓ Are only women serving in most of the visible roles?

We Teach to the Women
- ✓ If your flock is mostly women, you will teach to the women.
- ✓ "Preach to the men and the women will listen. Preach to the women and the men will leave."
- ✓ Preach using Jesus' words about sacrifice, mission, hardship, commitment, reward ... what men want.

Men Don't Feel Needed
- ✓ 85% of Christian men are not spiritually challenged.
- ✓ Help men understand who they are in Christ and God's high calling for men.
- ✓ Call them to the great mission of delivering God's justice, standing against evil, and sacrificing for the greater good—like the men in the Bible.

Men Don't Follow Women
- ✓ 70% of the sons brought to church by mom drop out; the opposite happens when Dad brings them.
- ✓ "When women lead, men leave."

Men Follow Men
- ✓ Men want to follow strong, motivated, courageous, manly leaders.
- ✓ Visionary boldness attracts men.
- ✓ Men follow leaders, not dictators or controllers.
- ✓ Pastors: Be humble, authentic, and encouraging; be a man's man.

Adapted from *Why Men Hate Going to Church*
www.churchformen.com

Talking to Women is Easier

At the missionary gathering I mentioned at the start of this chapter, after I had finished my session, an older missionary came up to me and said, "I like everything you said, but I just find that talking to women is easier."

He's right! Talking and reaching out to women is easier. Although most pastors are male, women often make up the majority of regular churchgoers and volunteers who keep church ministries going. Pastors naturally focus on those who show up. Women come. Women respond. Women get involved. And women love being with one another, sitting and talking and praying. Women love the safety, friendliness, and warmth of church.

When I asked a group of pastors in Tanzania what they do to attract men to their church, one seasoned pastor stood and said, "We open our doors on Sunday morning, brother!" So I asked how many men he had in his church, and he said, "A few."

The days of just ringing the church bell to call men to come are long gone. Women will come, though! That doesn't mean their husbands will. Most won't. And the problems in the marriage, in the home, in the community, just continue. The church suffers, too. Without intentional effort on the part of the church leaders, men might visit, but usually won't stick around—so the church struggles with a lack of male leadership and the absence of the spiritual gifts and other contributions those men have to offer.

Man It Up

So how can we ensure that our churches are places that attract and keep men? We have to "man up" our services. Doing this doesn't seem to turn away the women, so you won't lose them; you'll just gain men.[103]

What do we mean by "man up the service"? Though this certainly varies by culture, generally men do not want to hold hands when they pray. They do not want to cry in public. They are not excited about the idea of falling deeply in love with another man—even if His name is Jesus.

Consider the following:

1. Seating: Does the seating arrangement in the church force men to sit close to one another?

✓ Move the chairs. Men need space between them.

2. Lyrics: Do the lyrics in all or most of your church's worship songs speak of love, relationship, safety, being held, or other ideas and desires that are typically considered more feminine?[104]

✓ Include songs that speak of the battle, challenge, and adventure of following Christ. Choose songs that convey respect and honor for God—not only love and devotion.

3. Emotional emphasis: Do your services include emotional responses such as crying and "sharing what is on your heart?"

✓ Most men will not be interested in this. Public crying is a form of weakness to many men. Sharing long personal testimonies is okay in the ladies' Bible study, but not in the church service.

4. Announcements: Do the announcements only consist of activities for women and children?

✓ Include announcements every week for men. And remember that men are wired to look for risk, challenge, and adventure— so title the men's Bible study something like "A Dangerous Man." (More on this in the next chapter).

Most men are not excited about falling in love with another man—even if His name is Jesus.

Preach to the Men

Men want to be spoken to directly in a message. They want to hear from the pastor what the teaching means for them. They want to hear from the pastor, "Men, this is what this means for us..."

Here are a couple ideas to get a man's attention:

1. Stop in the middle of the Sunday message and call out the men—"Men, look at me a minute—what this says to you is _____."

2. At the end of your service, occasionally call all the men up to meet with you for three minutes. Concisely recap the main points of your message and offer one or two applications in their life, in their marriage, in their family, workplace, or with their friends. (On the way home or at the dinner table, the men's wives or kids will ask, "What did he say?")

Preach to the men and women will listen. Preach to the women and men will leave. Most women don't mind at all that you speak to the men, either directly or in your general teaching. They want their men to listen!

Attracting Men to Your Church
❏ What do men see other men doing in your church, or when they read your bulletin or hear your announcements? ✓ Men want to see strong men up front; they are attracted to good teaching, service opportunities, and varied and active men's activities.
❏ Identify the activities that men in your community like to do together. Is it sports? Games? Pool? ✓ Get your men from the church into those places to meet men; provide those activities in or through your church.
❏ Look at your song lyrics. Are they all about adoration and love? ✓ Balance these with songs that have strong lyrics—about faith, power, the Christian fight.
❏ Consider the content of your messages. Are they mostly about love, relationships, peace, and safety? ✓ Preach using Jesus' words about sacrifice, mission, hardship, commitment, reward, etc.–the masculine side of Jesus. This is what men understand and desire.

Change Your Image

If the majority of the people in your church are women, then your programs, your words, your stories, the tone you use, everything about everything you do will naturally direct itself to ministering to women. They are your flock, so of course you do that. But if you keep doing that, they will always be your only flock.

Many pastors are accustomed to using feminine descriptions and images. But we must stop offering men a personal relationship with the "Lover of their soul" who will provide them with peace and security. That's not what God designed men to want! We must follow Jesus' example when He taught men. He told them to leave everything and follow Him. Join the mission. Join the adventure. It won't be easy, the laborers are few, and you might even give your life for the cause. But it is all worth it. He made it clear that His church, His kingdom, is not for the fainthearted.[105]

Jesus knows men.

Jesus made it clear that He needs men who:
- ✓ **Sacrifice**: take up their cross and follow Him (Luke 9:23)
- ✓ **Commit**: won't look back (Luke 9:62)
- ✓ **Work**: strive to enter through the narrow door (Luke 13:24)
- ✓ **Focus**: give up all they have to follow Him (Luke 18:22)
- ✓ **Endure**: abide to the end (Matthew 10:22)
- ✓ **Stand Tall**: are prepared to be hated by all for His name's sake (Matthew 10:22)
- ✓ **Serve Others**: lose their lives for His sake in order to truly find their life (Matthew 16:25)

In other words, Jesus attracted men by telling them that only a few good men are worthy of His mission. Oh, and those that stay true to the end will be rewarded handsomely.[106] He asks, "Are you up to this? Are you man enough?" To attract men, Jesus challenges. He doesn't beg, and he doesn't make it sound easy. He knew that if he did, few or no men would respond.

Follow Jesus' example when He taught men: **He told them to leave everything and follow.**

That's a far cry from what we often hear in church.[107] Jesus knows men. He made them to be brave, heroic, generous, and sacrificial. He made them that way!

Though it is true that God is love, we must also preach the masculine side of Jesus' message. Jesus Christ was strong. He turned over tables in righteous anger. He called the Pharisees out for their hypocrisy and spoke severely to them when He needed to—see for example Matthew 23:13-26. He fasted in the wilderness for forty days. He stayed up all night to pray. He made a difference in people's lives. He spoke boldly in public—see John 7. He *led* people.

Murrow delivers this challenge:

> Grab a cheap paperback [New Testament]. Take a pink highlighter and mark all the passages where Jesus is tender, loving, and kind. Then take a blue highlighter and mark the verses where he's tough, challenging... You'll be shocked at how much blue you find.[108]

Men want marching orders, so call them to ongoing growth and discipleship. Call them to sacrifice, responsibility, meaning, and mission. Challenge them! Use manly illustrations and stories, ideas that speak to battle (e.g., David and Goliath, the Battle at Michmash), survival against all odds (e.g., Elijah and the confrontation with the prophets of Baal, Samson's destruction of the Philistine Temple), and adventure (e.g., Abraham's journey to Canaan, Israel's journey through the wilderness, Paul's missionary journeys). Show them that the noble Christian life—the life of a man of valor—promises to be the greatest and most challenging adventure a man can embark on.

Wednesday Talk vs. Sunday Talk

A former pastor of mine taught a men's Bible study every Wednesday night. Many men attended the study. I did, too, and just like the other men, I loved hearing our pastor's honesty. His stories about the mistakes he made. His stories about how he and his wife did not always get along. He talked loudly sometimes. He used hard words. Sometimes he spoke with anger and passion. He taught the Word of God in a way that spoke to men. And they loved to be under his teaching... on Wednesday nights.[109]

But Sunday was a different story. He preached gently. He used a quiet voice, he did not tell stories about mistakes he made, and he did not talk with anger and passion. Why? Because women were present.

Some of the men actually said that they found other things to do on Sunday so they could avoid the church service. They just didn't like the way he teaches on Sunday. On Wednesdays he taught the men. But on Sundays, he taught the women.

> **Men loved to be under my pastor's teaching—**
> **on Wednesday nights. Sunday was different.**

Michael Zigarelli studied churches that are intentional about reaching men, learning that men-friendly churches:

> Build messages with men in mind and make them intensely practical. One church's marriage series, 'In the Ring', used boxing imagery. Another titled a series on generosity, 'G Force', and to teach Philippians, another pitched the series 'Batter Up.'[110]

> **Pastors: Men will respect you—they will model you—if they**
> **see that you are like them.**

Men Follow Men, Not Women

It seems generally true that women will follow a man, but few men will follow a woman.[111] The same holds for leadership in the church. Pastor Dan Jarrell commented: "When women lead, men leave."[112] Statistics indicate that denominations that have female leadership are generally declining in membership.[113]

It's true for boys, too. Murrow writes of a church who hired a female leader for their youth program, and within six months, seventy-five percent of the boys had disappeared.[114]

Men follow bold men who lead strongly and biblically. They want manly leaders with energy, who speak well, who know where they are going, and who have a plan to get there. They want a man's man for a pastor. Men look for a man to follow. Every man needs another man to look up to and strive to be like.

> **Men follow bold men who lead strongly and biblically.**

When Peter knew he had found someone worth following—someone with whom he could change the world—he told Jesus that he would be willing to go to prison and death with him. (Luke 22:33) Jesus was able to inspire men to follow Him, no matter the cost. Maybe even because of the cost.

How to Be a Leader Men Will Follow

Pastors and leaders, remember that you represent Jesus to the men in your congregation. Don't allow Satan to puff you up with that, but realize that men want to look up to another man. When they see you, they think, "If the man up front acts like this, I guess Jesus would act like this."

In *Pastoring Men*, Patrick Morley writes:

> The senior pastor is the key to everything. [In highly effective, outreach-driven, discipleship-centered churches, the senior pastor has]... [a] vision to disciple every man in the church... the determination to succeed... and a sustainable strategy to make disciples.
> Pastors are the logical choice. [Applying God's grace, they can] ...see men not so much for what they are, but for what they can become in Christ. Pastors are the ones whom God called to instruct, encourage, correct, challenge, inspire, and call men to "act like a man."[115]

Murrow agrees:

> Men don't follow religions. Men don't follow philosophies. Men don't follow ideas. Men follow men. Every man is, at his core, a hero worshipper. And you [pastor] are his God-hero. A man walks into church searching for a leader he can look up to and respect. He wants a father who will instruct, encourage, and guide him. He seeks a man who is strong enough to confront him with the truth—in love. [116]

Here are a few suggestions for representing the strength, grit, and purpose of Christ from the pulpit and any position of leadership:

- ✓ *Be a man's man.* Men respect a masculine man. If you like sports and other "typical" men's activities, refer to it from the pulpit. Find out what men do in your community and join in. If you were or are employed in a field other than ministry, be sure to talk about it. Men respect a man with non-church, working-man, real-world experience.
- ✓ *Be enthusiastic and visionary.*
- ✓ *Be gracious but uncompromising.*
- ✓ *Express conviction.* Convince men you believe what you say.
- ✓ *Live like you say you do* and men will respect your message.
- ✓ *Talk and pray like a regular guy.* Talk to men like a man. Speak to God like you would to another man. Don't use "holy words" or keep repeating phrases. Men are listening to how you talk to your heavenly Dad.
- ✓ *Be real.* Men will respect you more and want to model you more if you are like one of them and not like one of the "holy clergy". Don't try to be somebody you're not. A leader who speaks openly of his struggles, failings, and challenges will win points with men.
- ✓ *Don't set yourself above others.* Don't insist on being called "Doctor," "Bishop," "Reverend," or "Pastor." People should call you by your first name just like you call them by their first names—and I don't mean "Pastor Paul'; I mean simply "Paul". Men prefer to be led by straight-talking, normal, down-to-earth men.
- ✓ *Focus on building strengths*, not on reminding men of weaknesses. Focus on who your men are in Christ and what they can be, not what they have been in the past or have failed to be. They get enough of that everywhere else!

✓ *Let your men lead.* Maybe they'll be in charge of smaller things at first, but give them space and permission to learn, fail, develop, and grow.

Men Follow Men on a Mission

Men want to believe that God is doing something through your church. They want to be a part of a church that is going somewhere, a church that is impacting and helping the community. So, church leaders, be an example of a man of valor. Be a warrior that men can follow. Follow in the footsteps of the men of the Bible. Strive to be like Moses, Elijah, David, Daniel, Peter, Paul. Look at the lives of the "great cloud of witnesses" described in Hebrews 11 and 12. These men were not lambs; they were lions. They took charge and risked everything in service to God. They fought boldly and spoke their minds. They were leaders, tough guys respected by the community. Strive to become like the man—Jesus Christ. His strong leadership, blunt honesty, and courageous actions attract men.

"The Lion of Judah is like canned spinach," Murrow writes. "He's sometimes slimy, unpleasant, and hard to swallow, but he builds muscle—especially in men. His insane courage, bold truth telling, and severe absolutism ignites a flame in my heart. I love the Lamb of God, but I'm intimidated by the Lion of Judah. That creates the tension that makes Jesus so fascinating to men."[117]

Let Men Be Lions

Men follow strong male leaders. But here is something that's really important: men follow leaders—not dictators. I want to tell you about two Bible-teaching churches I know. One was a church that had its beginning in the late 1990s. It began to grow and thrive, but then after a few years, the people started to leave, and eventually it closed its doors. The second church has been around more than a century, but it has few men, and is generally declining today. I'd heard about the problems in the first church, and I recently worked with the pastor of the second church. I learned that they both had the same issue: both pastors wanted to do church only in their way—they were controlling of the church and of the people who attended.

A controlling leader drives men away.

In many churches, the pastor controls everything. But that will turn men away. Men want to contribute. If you want men in your church, and if you want to expand the kingdom, you can't be controlling. Men need strong pastoral leadership, but they need the right kind. They don't need a controlling dictator. Church leaders should want a team rather than a one-man show so that the men we get will be lions and not lambs.[118] I learned this the hard way.

I Held Them Back

Early on as a men's ministry leader, I wanted lions.

Or so I said.

I wanted men to lead and own the activities in the men's ministry. The Lord was blessing the ministry—so much so that men started approaching me about joining my leadership team. They were driven, competent men, and they wanted to do things in ways I wasn't used to. They wanted to move in directions I wasn't sure about. I felt like they were beginners in men's ministry and didn't really know what they were doing. For the longest time, I resisted them. I kept holding them back and telling them they were wrong. I was guilty of being controlling and dominating. It had gotten to the point that I was in danger of driving them away.

God spoke to me about this. I was reading through the book of Philippians at the time, and when I came to chapter 2, I had some trouble getting through it. I kept returning to the start of the chapter and reading verses 1-16 over and over again. It took a while for me to understand what the problem was, and when I did, I didn't like it.

Verse 2 calls us to be "in full accord and of one mind." (RSV) What was that saying to me, in my situation? That no matter the circumstances, no matter how many mistakes others make, no matter how "messed up" everything is or may become, we are to be of one mind. That's what leadership must strive for—one mind.

In verse 3, we are urged to do nothing from selfishness or conceit, rivalry, or competition, but instead to count others better than ourselves. That's a hard truth for leaders to swallow. We want to be in charge, to be superior. But the Word is pretty clear here that leaders are required to show the characteristics of Christ. We are told that He emptied Himself and became a servant (2:7). He humbled Himself unto obedience, even unto death (2:8). He looked to the interests of others (2:4). That is our model.

But wait, there's more:

> Do all things without grumbling or questioning, that you
> may be blameless and innocent, children of God without

blemish in the midst of a crooked and perverse generation, among whom you shine as lights in the world, holding fast the word of life, so that in the day of Christ I may be proud that I did not run in vain or labor in vain. (14-16 RSV)

"Okay, okay!" I told the Lord that I was definitely guilty of grumbling and questioning. But how did that relate to my leadership style or the way I interacted with the men? What is wrong with healthy disagreement?

Grumbling, questioning, murmuring, and disputing—especially if they are ongoing—are symptoms of sin and self-centeredness. People quickly grow tired of our criticism and our accusations because, let's face it, we don't know the full story. The Lord wishes for us to shine as lights in the world, and our goal is the bigger picture. In other words, the specific project, activity, or ministry doesn't matter as much as do the men involved, the overall message or impression that is conveyed, the lasting effect, the long-term impact of our attitude and behavior. Today, the project or ministry activity might seem hugely important. But next year, next month or maybe even next week, all that may remain of that "very important" ministry is the bad impression we left as a Christian and as Christ's representative—the image burned into people's minds of our actions or demeanor.

> **Tomorrow, all that remains of that "very important" project might be the bad impression we made.**

As leaders, we have to say to ourselves: "I am God's light. I am holding fast the Word of Life. I am Christ's ambassador. I am His message and image bearer. I demonstrate the Word." This applies to the way we run our ministries, too. Are we controlling? Too "all-knowing"? Too secretive?

I got it. I stopped trying to control everything. I loosened my grasp and give up my need to manage every detail. And God honored this change. Within eight months, we grew from a leadership team of four to twenty-four. More men became involved in the ministry; it eventually grew to 400 active men!

What happened? God transformed me from a controlling manager to an encouraging leader and facilitator.

This is not what just *my* men needed. It's what *all* men need.

The only way we can attract lions to our churches is by letting them be lions. Isn't that what Jesus did? He trained seventy lions and then sent them out with all of his authority. (Luke 10) As leaders of men, we should do the same thing. 1st Corinthians 12:7 says that each believer in Christ is given a gift by God for the common good. We need to give men room to use those gifts.

When you get a reputation as an equipping church, lions will come. God's pattern and purpose for men in the church is to be leading and supporting the vision of the leader God has selected. So as pastors and leaders, we need to give men more opportunities. We need to give them the freedom to grow. You are the key to successfully reaching, building, and keeping men in your church. Let them be the men they were created to be. Because we need them!

> **When you get the reputation of being an equipping church, lions will come.**

"We Need You!"

At a men's conference, a pastor told this story:

> A lady in my church came to me and said that she could tell her husband was going through some tough days. He was struggling. He was upset and discouraged. She did not know why because he would not talk to her. So she asked me to talk with him. Maybe her husband, Joe, would talk to me, she said.
>
> I saw Joe at the church the next Sunday. I went to him and asked how he was doing. Maybe he guessed that his wife said something to me, because he turned away. And he actually left the church building. Whatever it was that was troubling him must have been very serious, because that same day he left his wife and family, too.
>
> No one heard from him for months.
>
> Then one day, I was in town and I stopped to get gas for my car. I happened to look across the street and at that moment, Joe came out of a store. It was a liquor store, and he was carrying a brown paper bag.
>
> He was walking down the sidewalk; I yelled across the street, "JOE! WHERE HAVE YOU BEEN?" Joe stopped and looked around and saw me. He raised the bag to his lips as if to say, "This is where I've been." Then he continued walking. I yelled again and said, "JOE! WHERE HAVE YOU BEEN? I NEED YOU!!" That made

Joe stop... but just for a moment, and then he walked away.

I thought that was that and I wouldn't see him again. But, that weekend, he returned to his family.

A week later, he showed up at church. A few weeks after that, he started helping with setting up for the services. A few months later, he started helping with the youth ministry.

When I finally had a chance to talk with Joe, I asked him what brought him back. Joe looked at me and said, "You did. No one ever told me they needed me."

> ## "No one ever told me they needed me."

Kenny Luck, founder of Every Man Ministries, writes:

> Men have skills, but have never been told directly that they are specifically needed at church by anyone. In most churches around the world, there is no intentional effort to meet, get to know, help, and call for men to be on the team. [119]

Most people assume that men are less religious than women. I disagree. Jesus pulled men to Him, and other religions have little trouble attracting men. Today, many men are dying for Allah, while few are living for Christ. Why?

Our churches are not effectively helping men understand who they are, their value before God, and their purpose. Our churches are not teaching men the positive impact they can have on their wives, families, the church, and the community. If you ask around, you'll find that many men are not spiritually challenged, or feel that there is no role for them in the church. [120] They don't understand their great mission in the kingdom of God. And pursuing a shared, urgent mission draws men.

Even more confusing is the fact that the Bible is full of stories of great men who delivered God's justice, stood against evil, and sacrificed for the greater good. Today's churches ask men to mow the lawn, take out the garbage, or fill backpacks to give to needy children, which only speaks to men with the gifts of helps or service. Evangelists, prophets, givers, skilled craftsmen, administrators, leaders, and others need to be actively engaged as well!

Each man of God has a life and leadership calling from God. The church must intentionally provide an environment to develop what God has already placed in every man. Men will take their place in church when they feel needed and affirmed there.[121] We need to give them something to do, something that matters, something that makes a difference—something big. We need to challenge them to more than an ordinary life.

We *need* them.

> **Men will take their place in church**
> **when they feel needed and affirmed there.**

Sharpen Your Vision

I'll close with this quote from Kenny Luck: "If male involvement in the local church is weak, it is because our vision in the church for them is weak."[122]

We must present men with sufficient challenge. Let's sharpen our vision for our communities, and achieve it—with God's blessing—*through men*. Who knows what the church could accomplish if the men were all-in?

+ + +

There's hope! We don't want to leave you thinking only about everything you need to correct. Next, we'll discuss three simple things every man wants. Recognizing these will help you envision and put in place an effective ministry to and through men. These principles are being applied around the world, because they work! If you do these three things, they will help you reach and keep men. Are you ready? Are you serious? Let's do this!

Make it Practical

1. When the church focuses on attracting women (intentionally or not), it hinders itself from fulfilling its own mission; it doesn't have the full spectrum of biblical leadership, gifts, and perspectives it needs. What is stopping men from coming to your church?

2. Do a little observational research next Sunday:

   a) Are there more women than men?

   b) Is it men or women who seem to be more involved and engaged in the service? (such as singing) Is it men or women leading worship, ushering, or giving announcements?

   c) Do the elements (songs, décor, announcements, and seating) seem to be geared more toward men or towards women? How do you think these elements affect the gender involvement you noticed?

   d) What changes could be made that may help in attracting men to be involved and to participate?

3. What is your church doing well in reaching out to men?

4. Reflect on these statements: "...many men are dying for Allah while few are living for Christ" and "few men are spiritually challenged." How do you see the truth of these statements in the lives of the men around you? What would it look like for you and other men to be spiritually challenged?

5. What kind of difference do you think it would make in your community if every man who goes to your church knows that he is needed?

6. Whether you are a leader in your church or "just an ordinary guy" who influences men through your daily activities, realize that you are an ambassador for Christ. Men will likely look up to you and consider your words, conduct, and character as a representation of who Christ is. How seriously are you taking this responsibility?

7. Pastor: Are you a bold leader that could attract men to follow you into the community and the world? Are you giving the men you lead the space and encouragement they need to become lions?

Notes & References

---

[99] Recommended further reading on this subject includes *Why Men Hate Going to Church* by David Morrow and *The Man-Friendly Church* by Michael Zigarelli. For a complete list, see Appendix D.

[100] Murrow, *Why Men Hate Going to Church*, 210

[101] *Ibid.*, 40-41

[102] *Ibid.*, 185, 236

[103] "Pastor Ross Sawyers (121 Community Church, Grapevine, TX) said, 'Women love that I'm talking to their husbands and dads, challenging them to be the spiritual leaders in their home, because our women long for that.' Pastor Chad Stafford (Coastal Church, Daphne, AL) agreed, 'No lady has ever said we're too masculine. But I've had dozens of them come to me with tears in their eyes, saying 'I've been trying to get my husband to go to church for 20 years and this is the only church he will ever go to.' Jim White (Mecklenburg Community Church, Charlotte, NC) echoed, 'I've heard it a thousand times: 'I can't believe my husband actually wants to go to church. Even when I don't go, he goes and takes the kids!' Women love it when I talk to their husbands and they love what this is doing for their family." Zigarelli, *The Man-Friendly Church* 27

[104] "Much modern worship music uses romantic and sometimes even erotic language to describe the relationship between man and God." Julia DeCelles-Zwerneman, "Where Are All the Men? Exploring the Gender Gap in Church" (Capterra 2016) https://blog.capterra.com/where-are-all-the-men-exploring-the-gender-gap-in-church/

[105] "When Christ called disciples, he did not say, 'Come, have a personal relationship with me.' No, he simply said, 'Follow me.' Hear the difference? 'Follow me' suggests a mission. A goal. But a personal relationship with Jesus suggests we are headed to [the coffee shop] for some couple time." Murrow, *Why Men Hate Going to Church*, 165

[106] "Be faithful unto death, and I will give you the crown of life." (Revelation 2:10 RSV)

[107] "Following Christ includes adventure, risk, and purpose… Any church that turns the gospel into a soft, congenial message minimizes the cost of discipleship or imputes weakness to Christ does its people a disservice. Charles Spurgeon decried such a watered-down message in his day: 'There has got abroad a notion, somehow, that if you become a Christian you must sink your manliness and turn milksop.' " GotQuestions.org, "Why Are There So Few Men In The Church?" https://www.gotquestions.org/men-in-the-church.html

[108] Murrow, *Why Men Hate Going to Church*, 48

[109] "Men appreciate forthrightness and honesty. They respect a teacher who tells it like it is and doesn't beat around the bush. Teach as Jesus did. Be direct—and get to the point." *Ibid.*, 158

[110] Zigarelli, *The Man-Friendly Church*, 20-21

[111] "Maybe this is one reason the Scriptures presuppose male leadership in the church. Perhaps these commands rise not from first-century sexism but from the realization that both genders respond well to competent male leadership." Murrow, *Why Men Hate Going to Church*, 157

[112] *Ibid.*, 157

[113] *Ibid.*, 178-179, 235

[114] *Ibid.*, 189

[115] Morley, *Pastoring Men*, 21, 27, 28

[116] Murrow, *Why Men Hate Going to Church*, 45

[117] *Ibid.*, 51

[118] Murrow writes that pastors like the image of Christ as a Lamb "because he's such a good role model to the parishioners. Lambs are much easier to control than lions. They're docile and easy to lead. What pastor would want a church full of lions, overturning the missions bake sale table and warning the new members' class of impending doom?" *Ibid.*, 39

[119] Kenny Luck, *Sleeping Giant* (B&H Publishing Group 2012) 19

[120] "Laying aside the biblical assumption of male leadership for a moment, look at the practical side. If men see men in leadership, they think, *This is something I could get involved with. My gifts are needed.* If they see women in leadership, they tend to think the opposite." Murrow, 156

[121] "Whenever possible, put men in leadership positions. It's good for your church. Men's natural bent toward risk taking and challenge can change the atmosphere in your church, making it more attractive to men." *Ibid.*

[122] Luck, 16

Three Things
Every Man Wants

Brad Smith

"[Christ gave gifts] for the work of ministry, for building up the body of Christ, until we all attain to the unity of the faith and of the knowledge of the Son of God, to mature manhood, to the measure of the stature of the fullness of Christ."
Ephesians 4:11-13 (ESV)

What can we do to help men come to Christ, to become discipled, and lead their homes, influence the workplace, the community, and grow the church?

I believe that there are three things that every man wants. These three things will not only gain men's attention, but will also help to build men of valor who stay in the church, become your future leaders, and change their worlds.

It's simple, actually. What every man wants is to be connected, to grow, and to serve. No matter what he may say or imply, every man wants friends; every man wants to improve; and every man wants to make a difference, have an impact, and do things that really matter.

Connection (fellowship), growth (sanctification), and service (pursuing the great commission) is the definition of a disciple. A disciple is connected with other believers, he knows the Lord and is pursuing spiritual growth and godliness, and he's serving the Kingdom.

Connect, Grow, Serve (CGS). Pretty straightforward. Not the coolest terms. Not new and different. Really quite basic. But think about it; does your church offer specific, consistent opportunities for men in each of these areas? Most don't. Will yours?

Men Will Not Come to You

Don't expect that any man will walk into your church lobby asking for these three things. We need to go after them. We cannot expect them to come to us.

This chapter is designed to inspire pastors and church leaders to start down that path. Our prayer is that with these basic suggestions and guidelines, you will be able to develop ideas that could help you attract men, build a ministry to men, and minister through men.

However, this is not a guaranteed, step-by-step formula that will automatically bring great results. It may take a long time to see fruit, but the results for your church, and the men and their families are worth the work![123]

1. Connect

Go Where They Are

On a night of unusual openness, a non-Christian coworker, who was separated from his wife at the time, told me that he had no friends outside of work and wanted some; that he wanted to grow, improve, and become a better man; and that he wanted to make a difference. I've learned that all men—believers and unbelievers—want these same things.

But men aren't likely to go to a church to get what they want. There's something about church that can turn men off. Most men rarely sing in groups, they don't naturally have emotional outbursts or hang around others who do, and they don't tend to sit for an hour (unless their job requires it) listening to someone speak about something they do not understand and appears to offer no practical value to their life!

Walking into a church building is often a cultural earthquake for men. So in order to reach men, you have to go where they are. You have to do the things men want to do. You have to reach out to men in the environments that they're in—not where you wish they were.

> **Walking into a church building is often a cultural earthquake for a man.**

In Good Company

I used to live quite a distance from the church we attended. I was missing fellowship, growth, and serving the Kingdom with other men. So I decided to start a ministry to and through men in my community— not in my church. I quickly learned that unbelieving men really wanted to be involved. I planned several activities: At the first, one unbeliever came. At the second, ten unbelieving men came. As I began to talk about another event, twenty-five unbelievers said they wanted to attend. What's equally cool is that those men told other men, who in turn told other men.

None of these activities were in a church. One was in a pool hall. One was at a gun range to practice shooting. One was after-hours at a restaurant to play poker. These types of things are a little risky, right? Long-time Christians don't always want to do things that don't quite fit the image of "what Christians do" or "where Christians go." A couple of Christian brothers said they didn't want any part of it because of that. That hurt a little at first, but then I decided that I was in good company. Luke 19:7 relates what the crowd thought of Jesus' visit to the home of Zacchaeus: "And when they saw it, they all grumbled, 'He has gone in to be the guest of a man who is a sinner.'" (ESV)

But what's the end of the story? Zacchaeus was convicted and he repented of his sin. Then Jesus said, "Today salvation has come to this house...For the Son of Man came to seek [go after] and to save the lost." (Luke 19:9-10 ESV) Jesus went to where Zacchaeus was, became his friend, and earned his trust. That friendship opened a door into Zacchaeus' spiritual life.

> **The Son of Man came to go after the lost.**

Help Men Connect

How can we help men get together and build friendships with one another? In order to help men connect, arrange activities where they can do the things they like to do. Events designed for the purpose of making connections can include playing or watching sports, going to a pool hall, playing table games, or getting together to talk over coffee, among many, many other activities.

What the men are interested in is different for every culture, but the goal is the same: to have no specific purpose or agenda beyond the advertised activity. It's just to get together! In Japan, I was told the men go to the hot baths, so that was their church leaders' suggested meeting place. In Zambia, I was told that it would not be considered acceptable to enter a bar in order to play pool, so they did something better: one man in the church bought his own pool table, erected a gazebo around it, and then invited the men in the neighborhood to come and play. (One time, 125 men showed up!)

Can some activities be done in your church building? Maybe. But reaching men through a church may not work. You may need to start by arranging activities for men in facilities or at locations away from the church. You can try activities back at the building later.

To connect with men, you must:

✓ Go where they are

✓ Do the things men want to do

✓ Engage them in the environments where *they* are—not where you wish they were

---

Organize "no-agenda" events. You don't have to share the gospel, a sermon, or even a "thought"; you don't have to invite them to church. Just give men consistent opportunities to get together with other men to do what men enjoy doing. Give them time to trust you. Multiple studies over the years have shown that adult men, for the most part, are lonely. They may have a few acquaintances, but many have no friends at all. According to David Murrow, "Relationships scare a man to death, but they are his deepest need."[124] Mark Greene explains that "If friendships in men's lives seem shallow and transitory, it is because so many of those relationships are emotionally risk free and as such, lacking in authenticity. And authenticity is the glue that holds deeper, more long term friendships together."[125] So we are doing men a great service by helping them in this way. And like my experience with "connect" events for the community, men love it.

In 2018, Abraham Walker started asking men in his neighborhood if they wanted to chat over coffee. He also posted an open invitation on social media. Immediately, 36 men responded. Later, one of the men opened his home for poker nights. He said, "This group has been great to have that camaraderie, especially for activities my wife would never do, like axe-throwing or going to the shooting range... We share ideas, successes, and failures openly and without judgment."[126]

What could you do? Here are a few ideas:

- ❑ Football (Soccer) / American Football / Rugby / Basketball / Baseball / Cricket / Volleyball / Hockey
- ❑ Swimming / Water Polo
- ❑ Hunting / Fishing
- ❑ Barbecue / "Beast Feast" / Bonfire
- ❑ Boating / Motorcycling
- ❑ Flying drones or model airplanes
- ❑ Cards or table games

- ❑ Golf / Driving Range / Tennis / Ping-pong / Corn hole / Horseshoes
- ❑ Bowling / Pool
- ❑ Shooting / Archery
- ❑ Biking / Hiking / Rock-climbing
- ❑ Hang gliding / Parachuting
- ❑ Sports events, races, movies, shows
- ❑ Meet over coffee

For some sports, you could even host tournaments and/or join the local community leagues. But don't form or join a church league—stay out in the world!

There really are many options. Just keep it simple, keep it casual. Don't allow jokes to get off-color, but encourage a little good-humored trash talk, fun, and friendly competition. Just get out there and do something—together.

A Worldwide Need

In Zambia, my friend Mark and I talked to about fifty men at a Man of Valor conference. Zambia, like much of Africa, is a "warm" culture[127] but even so, the men were intrigued by the thirty-plus years of friendship I enjoy with Mark, saying that this was very unusual for them. Mark and I have met weekly almost continually since 1988, when he was single and assisting the youth at the church and I was a young married man with a one year old. At first we studied the Bible along with a few other men. Within months, those men drifted away due to work schedules or locations. He and I continued to meet, and our time evolved to simply meeting with no agenda other than to share life and pray for one another. Differences in life stages or occupations did not affect our friendship.

At the church Mark and I attended, I started what I called "Points of Contact"—POC Groups. I asked sixteen men to be the primary POC for each group, and commit to be at a location of their choosing at the same time and day each week. I specifically told the men that these groups had no agenda. It wasn't to be a Bible study or a counseling group. It was just men getting together to talk—truly, just points of contact! I posted the list of the POCs and their locations. Men immediately responded, and fourteen of the original sixteen groups were flourishing three years later.

> **Points-of-Contact Groups allowed men to get to know and trust one another.**

So, the first thing you need to do to reach men is arrange activities that give them opportunities to build friendships. I suggest that you host several of these first-tier activities for men before you organize a second-tier activity. Men need to learn to trust and enjoy one another first. If they don't, it is unlikely that they will successfully or consistently sustain any other spiritual activity. Murrow says,

> I believe the most valuable spiritual discipline for today's men is the discipline of friendship. This is not to diminish the importance of [Bible reading, prayer, giving, serving, and attending church]. But the men who stay faithful to God are those who walk closely with other Christian men.[128]

2. Grow

Men Want to Improve

Next, offer these connected men opportunities to grow. Men want to improve and get better at living life. Christian men want to grow in their walk with Christ. Now, this is not meant to be growth for simply the sake of growth. We want to help men prepare to make a difference. What we need to offer is an opportunity to grow through personal development so they can do something. But I'm getting ahead of myself.

Unfortunately, the church often doesn't provide teaching specifically for men, on subjects they would be interested in. That's like inviting a clearly thirsty man to your home. You can see that he's dehydrated, so you grab a pitcher to fill a glass for him. But the pitcher is empty!

It is no good being at a church where the pastor can see that men need to know about being a godly dad, about living wisely, about being a godly husband, and wants men to lead in his church and get involved, but does not provide anything to equip the men specifically. Maybe because the pastor doesn't really know his own Bible. Maybe he hasn't realized men need particular training. Either way, he's essentially communicating, "I'm so glad that you are here. Now please go and sit in the back and stay quiet."

> **Often churches essentially tell men: "Please go sit in the back and stay quiet."**

So when I talk about growth, I am referring to teaching the Scriptures to men, men reading the Bible together or studying a book based on biblical ideas and principles. I am talking about offering workshops and studies for men on topics like leadership, finances, fatherhood, working as unto the Lord, leading and influencing the community, loving your wife, or finding your mission.

Make Your Studies Intriguing

Be careful how you promote these studies. Don't merely announce "Men's Bible Study Thursday Night at 7pm." Base everything on scripture, but use captivating titles such as:

Through the Eyes of a Lion	A Dangerous Man
The Root of All Evil	Breaking the Rules
How to Hit a Home Run	How God Makes Men
The Man who Changed Everything	Standing Firm
Stepping Up	A Few Good Men
Stay Alert	How to Lead
Are You Man Enough?	The Ticket to a Successful Life
How to Understand Your Wife	The Finish Line
Living as a Man of Valor	Batter Up
The One Thing That Changes Everything	5 Leadership Skills Every Man Must Know
How to Lead Your Family	How to Take a Risk
How to Make a Difference	How to Manage Money
How to Manage Time	Coaching Your Kids
How to Succeed In Business	How to Follow

How to Craft Your Eulogy	*What is Success?*
A Man of Valor at Work	*How to Make A Difference*
The Confident Man of God	*In The Ring*

Use titles that men will respond to. If you announce a women's study or gathering, a throng will show up—early! Announce something plain-sounding for men, and you'll be preaching to an audience of two: you and the Lord.

Consider providing practical training, such as carpentry, coding, management, welding, mechanics, or farming. If you are a bi-vocational church leader or pastor, bring a man alongside you in your work, if possible. Teach him the job skills and also talk about verses in the Bible. By doing this, you are helping him with both his practical and his spiritual needs.

Additionally, dividing men by age, neighborhood, type of work, commute route, life stage, etc. may be helpful and conducive to gelling. But I'm not convinced it really matters. Men will try out groups based on what works for them, and they'll stay or try another for any number of reasons. I strongly recommend *against* grouping by age. If you do, young men lose the benefit of hearing older men's life experiences, and older men lose the opportunity to mentor.

Location, Location, Location

You can arrange and advertise for groups at your church. Or you could put together small groups of men to meet regularly and study various topics in homes or in coffee shops or restaurants. I'm a big fan of conducting a men's group or get-together in public places because it signals to other men (and women) that men like to get together, enjoy one another's company, and are serious about improving themselves. It is also a witness to everyone that Christian men are studying the Bible. Groups meeting at homes are okay if the group is addressing an addiction or some other less-than-public issue. (Even then, the group host must ensure that the wife and children are not within hearing distance or interrupt. It is vastly important that "what is said in the group, stays in the group," no matter where they meet).

What is said in the group stays in the group.

Judgment-Free Zone

I think the best place for men to learn the truths of Scripture is in a small group where they know, accept, and trust one another. Many have said that the friendships they formed in small groups made all the difference in their lives. And these are not hard to organize. Get a few men together to read the Bible, a book about the Bible or Bible character, or just to talk about life and its challenges. Plan to do it for one hour, and announce start and stop times. Respect the guys' schedules by sticking to the time table. Be committed to the group. Teach in a style men can connect with (for more on this, see Appendices). Ask men in your church and community what topics they'd be interested in.

Over time, as the men build trusting friendships in these groups, they'll start sharing personal matters. They'll confess sin. They'll ask for advice. And transformation will take place.

Give Men Time

Some years ago, I started another men's small group. One of the men in this group went through a painful time because of sickness in his family. The financial burden for their treatment was substantial. It took him four years to disclose that he needed help. In the security and trust of that small group of men, he finally shared how bad things had become in his world.

Be patient with men. It takes time for them to express a need for help, and that's okay. Be hospitable; invite vulnerability; model trust. But don't push. If you do, you might just push men away.

Years after I helped small groups to form, I've had men come to me to thank me for it. I've had men tell me about the impact that a group has had on their lives and marriages. As Murrow explains, "Men who regularly walk with Christian brothers grow deep in faith, strong in service, and extravagant in love."[129] I know of several groups of men who are still meeting together after fifteen years.

When Asked, Men Step Up

Small groups also help to grow new leaders, making the impact go beyond the group itself. I mentioned earlier about the POC Groups. Six weeks after launching, I had a voice mail from the wife of one of the new leaders. Her message was short: "Thank you for asking my husband to be the leader of a men's group. Since he started doing that, he's become a spiritual leader in our home. He takes more time to be with our daughters and reads the Bible with them."

What happened?

When a man is asked to serve or lead, he feels that others perceive him to be a godly, mature man. He thinks, "Other men have a high expectation of me. They think I can lead this study and trust me to be faithful with it." So, he starts to look at the other spheres of his life—his marriage, family, work, and neighborhood—and decides to improve at serving God in those areas as well.

> **When a man is asked to serve or lead, he feels that others see him as a godly, mature man. And he'd best step up!**

But that's not the end of this man's story. A couple years later, his company transferred him to another country, and he started attending a church there. His maturity in Christ was noticed, and he was asked to be an elder. As an elder, he taught in the services from time to time. Later, when the pastor resigned, he was asked to take his place!

His growth in Christ affected his work also. He told me about how he now "inserts the gospel" into business presentations as a matter of course. And every chance he gets, he witnesses to men around him.

All of this happened because I asked him to lead a men's group, and he stepped up to the challenge.

The Key to Building Men: Discipleship Groups

1. Put together a list of your men and group by home or work location. Pick a lead.

2. Help them determine when and where to meet each week.

3. Suggest that they start reading about and discussing one of the men in the Bible (see Chapter 5).

4. Encourage them to talk about what is going on their lives and to pray together.

5. That's it! Let them go—and check in occasionally.

As they read the Bible together and build deep friendships, it won't be long before the men see the value. They will grow in Christ through one another. This brotherhood will change their lives, their homes—and your church. **Bonus:** Assign an older, more mature brother to each group.

3. Serve

Making a Difference

Men want to build friendships with one another. They want to grow, improve, and become better men. They also want to make a difference! They want to have an impact on their families, their communities, and their churches. They want to do something that matters.[130] Men build friendships shoulder to shoulder.[131] Working side by side on something that matters is huge for men—the shared mission, shared camaraderie, even shared competition is powerful. Most importantly, unchurched men are more likely to get involved in a service-oriented environment where there are only men.

For more than ten years, Cedar Run Community Church in Herndon, VA, has been working in Nicaragua, the second poorest country in the Western Hemisphere. To help the intense poverty, the church launched several development projects, including a bicycle shop. Cedar Run collects used bicycles from churches in the United States and ships them to the shop. Church members traveled there and trained local men to repair and restore these bicycles and taught them how to run a business, all the while sharing the gospel. The Nicaraguan men trained other men. In addition to hearing the gospel, all of these men have learned a practical trade. This is something that has an impact, makes a difference, helps men earn a living and provide for their families. CRCC men are doing something that matters.[132]

Committing to pray and provide development resources for men in an international community is an investment in transformation—potentially of an entire community. When your men actively engage in a ministry this big, this visionary—when they see that they can make a difference for the kingdom of God—their involvement impacts their own walk, marriage, family, workplace, church, and community. Engagements like this strengthen your men and your church.[133]

Murrow reports this story about the impact of international assistance on one man:

> Randy was a nominal churchgoer for many years, but he never really came alive in his faith until he took a two-week mission trip to Peru to build a water project in an impoverished village. "I had no idea how real the gospel was until I went on this trip. We depended on God every minute of every day," he says. "He helped us through one tight spot after another." Randy returned from Peru a changed man. Once he realized how powerful and real God is, he began a daily walk with Him. He stepped up to leadership in his church. [He also] returned the next year with a bigger team. Adventures with Christ change men in a way simple church attendance never could.[134]

Men want to do something that matters.

Here's a simple idea closer to home: assign each men's group a needy widow or single mom. Once a month, the men get together to do repairs on her home, assist with financial matters, or help with whatever she needs.[135] Then, a few times a year, bring all these small groups together for a workday at the church or at a public building in the community.[136] Invite other men to join in. Even unbelievers! Some men will only connect with other men through swinging a hammer, shoulder to shoulder.

I heard of a church in an area where few men had work. The church was given an old building and decided to use it to as a training center. Members of the church used their skills and offered training in vocational skills such as welding, electrical, and carpentry. That brought unsaved men in close interaction with saved men who could then share the gospel.

Men want to have an impact.

If all you offer men to do at church is to wipe runny noses in the nursery, don't be surprised if they start leaving. Don't be afraid to bring your men together to do big things! Help out at street and park clean-ups, school repair days, and homes for battered women. These are the types of things men want to do. They want to make a difference. They want to have an impact.

Zigarelli advises, "Fully integrate men into the church by leveraging their strengths. Give them something to do that they're good at. Help them to be that heroic guy who does something."[137]

Murrow says that "productivity fires the imagination of men." He continues:

> Traditional approaches to evangelism leave many men cold. [One church] found that men will gladly witness by serving the community. They [do minor home or car repairs and] say to recipients, "We just want to show you God's love in a practical way." This kind of evangelism gives the church a positive image in the community and motivates people to visit.[138]

What could that look like in your area? What service projects could men do together in their neighborhoods and communities? What could men band together to do in the name of Christ, to show His love in practical ways and bring glory to God?

Here are a few ideas:[139]

- ❑ Job / skills / interview training and coaching
- ❑ Financial counseling
- ❑ Moving assistance
- ❑ Furniture collection & delivery for the poor
- ❑ Food & clothing pantry (fixed or mobile)
- ❑ Bike / car repair & servicing
- ❑ Christmas tree or holiday meal giveaway
- ❑ Community clean-up or
- ❑ Transporting families to visit relatives in prison
- ❑ Free oil changes
- ❑ Free car wash
- ❑ Neighborhood party / barbecue
- ❑ Immigrant & refugee hospitality and shelter
- ❑ Computer repair & give-away
- ❑ Garage cleaning
- ❑ Home repair / painting /

painting of public buildings, streets and walkways, or businesses

- ❑ Yard services (tree trimming, leaf raking, mulching...)
- ❑ Tutoring / mentoring young men, parolees
- ❑ Public restroom cleaning

maintenance for single moms, widows, elderly, prisoners' families, crisis housing centers...

- ❑ First-responder appreciation outings / events
- ❑ Smoke detector battery replacement
- ❑ Tax filing assistance

Men Will Respond

Men will respond if you give them what they need in the context of what they want. There's a progression to CGS: once men have built trusting friendships with one another, they will be more open to gathering in groups to hear the gospel, learn a trade, or study the Bible. But then once these connected friends' are growing and improving together, they will be more likely to help meet other's needs and serve their community. See it? Get them connected, help them grow, help them make a difference.

> ### CGS opens doors for men
> ### to experience abundant life in Christ.

Not all men will come in the door of fun activities. Some may think that's not a productive use of their time. They may want to learn something new and get better at something, and they'll come through that door. Still others may want to serve and make a difference and have an impact. That may be the door for them. Every man is different. That's okay! Offer opportunities to reach men wherever they are, not where you wish they were. If you can get their attention via one of these areas, you'll build credibility and have a better chance of gaining trust and interest in the other areas. Whichever "door" they respond to, it gets them in and involved, so don't focus on one and neglect the other two.

- ✓ Only doing fun connecting activities will eventually get boring.
- ✓ Only offering growth without connection and service will cause men to drift away.
- ✓ Only seeing your men as brawn for service will drag them down over time—they'll feel used. Even if they're okay with being used for a good cause, already-busy men will burn out and leave.

You need all three.

You Have an Opportunity

Men want and need to connect, grow, and serve. We have the opportunity to give them what they want. We can help men build friendships—first with one another, and ultimately with Christ. We can help men find their purpose and prepare them for life's challenges. We can help men make a difference in their home, their church, and their community.

As you begin to think about this, let me advise that it isn't enough to publish or promote your activities from the front of the church, on a website, or on a poster. You have to go up to men and personally invite them. There's nothing more powerful to a man than when another guy looks him in the eye and says, "I want you to come with me."

Don't be too concerned about doing big men's events right away. Just be faithful in the little things. Reach and disciple men on-on-one, and help them disciple other men in the same way. Give men the chance to connect, grow, and serve. That's how you will attract men to your church; that's how they'll stay; that's how they'll become godly leaders in their homes, in your churches, and in your communities. That's how they'll live as men of valor.

Make it Practical

1. Men want to connect with other men in activities that they like and that facilitate conversation and friendship-building. What do they like to do? What would attract them? What events could you plan and host to attract men in your community?

2. Once men are connected in friendship, they need to be provided with opportunities to grow in their spiritual walks and daily lives. What topics would attract men? Who would you need to involve? Do you know of men who are experienced in any of those subjects who could lead or assist? (Consider asking a few of the men in your church or small group, your neighborhood, and your work place what life topics or skills they would like to learn more about. Once you have a list of ideas, brainstorm how you could start classes or workshops based around these topics.)

3. The third thing that every man wants is an opportunity to serve...an opportunity to make a difference and to have an impact. What are some needs in your church and community that a group of men could meet? Do neighborhood schools or other community buildings need to be repaired or painted? Look around you; ask your neighbors, co-workers, and fellow churchgoers. Pay attention to possible projects that you could recruit men from your community and church to help with.

4. When has a personal invitation from another man made the difference for you in choosing to be involved with or attend an event, small group, or service project? When you plan events, do you tend to take the "easy" way by letting advertising do your work for you, or do you take the time to personally invite guys you know?

Notes & References

---

[123] Go to menofvalor.org to read a case study about what has happened in Malawi where church leaders are applying CGS.

[124] Murrow, *Why Men Hate Going to Church*, 213

[125] Mark Greene, "Why men have so much trouble making friends," (Salon 2014) https://www.salon.com/2014/04/12/why_do_mens_friendships_feel_so_hollow_partner/

[126] Jennifer Chen, "Making Friends as an Adult Can Be Hard..." (Yahoo News 2020) https://sg.news.yahoo.com/making-friends-adult-hard-theres-230730014.html

[127] "People from warm cultures tend to build their lives around people and relationships, while those from cold cultures tend to plan in terms of tasks and timelines."
Mrs. Serviette, "Understanding Cultural Differences in Hospitality" (The Serviette 2017)
https://www.theserviette.com/blog/hot-culture-and-cold-culture-hospitality

[128] Murrow, 197

[129] *Ibid.*, 212

[130] "Time is valuable, and [men] want to spend it on something that gets results. Can we blame them?"
Murrow, 39

[131] "Women bond face-to-face, whereas men bond side by side."
Murrow, 212

[132] For more about this ministry, see https://vimeo.com/206706899

[133] For more on this, see menofvalor.org/reachingmen

[134] Murrow, 204

[135] For help setting up a ministry like this, ask New Commandment Ministries: https://newcommandment.org

[136] Workdays at the church are good—as long as that's not all the men do. Get them out in the community!

[137] Zigarelli, *The Man-Friendly Church*, 26

[138] Murrow, 39, 204

[139] For more ideas on reaching the community, see:
- *101 Ways to Reach Your Community* by Steve Sjogren
- *101 Ways to Help People in Need* by Steve and Janie Sjogren
- *The Church of Irresistible Influence* by Robert Lewis

Moving Forward:
The Glorious Mission

Brad Smith

"This God—His way is perfect."

2nd Samuel 22:31 (RSV)

The responsibility for the fulfillment of God's plan for the church throughout the ages starts with men. Murrow makes an intriguing observation: "When the Lord started His ministry, one of His first tasks was to gather twelve men and forge them into a band of brothers. [Was] Jesus ... trying to show us something?"[140]

Women and children will follow the godly example, and strong, Christ-focused leadership of their husbands and fathers. When a man meets Christ, his family is much more likely to follow. Pastor Ross Sawyers believes that "Families are 90% more likely to attend church if the man of the household attends."[141] All indications are that when the father is uninterested or absent from church, the children tend to think that church is for women and children and often stop going when they grow up. They conclude from Dad's absence that going to church is not really a grown-up activity. Unfortunately, mothers' choices generally have much less ultimate effect upon children than their father's choices. "In spiritual matters, children have always followed their fathers."[142] Robbie Low agrees: "It is the religious practice of the father of the family that, above all, determines the future attendance at the Church for the children."[143]

> **The father of the family's religious practice determines kids' future attendance at church.**

Reach the Man and You Reach the Family

My wife pointed out two cases in our own neighborhood that illustrate this. Next door to us lives a family where Mom goes to church, but Dad doesn't. Mom regularly took her daughters with her to church, but as soon as their oldest daughter turned fourteen, she announced that she wasn't going to church anymore—she was staying home with Dad. The family two doors down from us attend the same church. However, in their case both parents go. Their daughter not only continued to be involved in church during her teen years, but also chose to attend a church-based university.

Michael Zigarelli said this about the men-friendly churches he studied: "The pastors of these churches told me that attracting men, while important in its own right, also brings women and children... Get the man and you get the family."[144]

Patrick Morley admits that this approach is hard, but worthwhile: "Pastoring men may not be easy or glamorous, and it's often thankless work. Yet when a man [starts living for Christ, it] will likely change the entire course of his family for many generations to come."[145]

In Acts 16 we find a beautiful picture of this. Paul and Silas shared the gospel with their Philippian jailor, and upon his acceptance of Christ, the man was instantly changed. Then he immediately brought the apostles to his house where they shared Christ with his family. Before the night was through, the entire household had been baptized and was beginning to follow Jesus.

Noah is another example of a father turning the tide of his family's lives. After he completed building the ark, God told him to enter the ark with His family. God said to Noah in Genesis 7:1, "Then the LORD said to Noah, 'Enter the ark, you and all your household, for you alone I have seen to be righteous before Me in this generation.' " (NASB) The statement was not about Noah's family; it was about Noah. But God saved them all from the flood. Because of him. Because of Noah's righteous example and leadership in a generation of depravity, his whole family was saved on the ark.

Even Lot. Despite his sins, failings, and mistakes, on the eve of the destruction of Sodom, the angels of the Lord tell him to take his wife and daughters and leave the city. The angels give Lot specific orders: "...take your wife and your two daughters, which are here..." (Genesis 19:15 NASB) It is Lot who is given the obligation for providing safety for the family. Lot is to lead the way out of Sodom. The agents of God tell Lot to do it. He's in charge. He's responsible.

But sobering Old Testament illustrations show this truth at work in the opposite direction. When four men from the tribe of Levi rebelled against God's chosen leaders, Moses and Aaron, they actually rebelled against God. The Lord responded with a powerful display of His authority and righteous judgment: "The earth opened its mouth and swallowed them up, with their households..." (Numbers 16:32 ESV)

Achan also caused his family's destruction when he stole silver, gold, and a robe from Jericho against God's instructions. It wasn't just the rebellious men who perished for their actions; they also caused the destruction of their whole families. (Joshua 7)

God has given each man a high and serious calling. His actions have consequences for his family's wellbeing, including life or death.

> **God has given each man a high and serious calling. His actions have consequences for his family's wellbeing, including life or death.**

He Promised Floggings, Persecution, and Death

Men are adventurous. They like to take risks. They like danger. They want to do things out in the real world. Not just in the pews. Not just on paper, or on their smart phones. They want to make an impact. They want to brave the odds, break new ground, blaze the trail. Because men are attracted to risk and challenge, it makes sense that the church grows when men are given big tasks.[146] It also makes sense that the church grows explosively where it is persecuted.[147]

In Matthew 10:16, Jesus sent His disciples out "as sheep among wolves." He promised them arrest, floggings, persecution, and even death. He didn't offer that to the women! And far from shrinking away from the risk and challenge that the commission entailed, the men answered the call. That's what men want, and Jesus knew that. They want challenge, leadership, vision, hardship—even the risk of death.[148] And when they get that, they rise up to the challenge—because that's how God made them. This is a key reason we have so much trouble attracting and keeping men in the church: we don't give them something big and great to do!

Men Will Step Up to the Challenge

You may know the story of the missionaries killed in Ecuador in 1956. The Auca Indians attacked and murdered four missionaries. This was big news in the United States at the time. LIFE magazine published the story, and within weeks, 500 men applied to take the place of the five men who were killed—before the mission agency started asking for replacements.[149]

You also know timid Timothy, right? Timid Timothy, the young man that Paul left in Ephesus to build up the church? Church tradition records that later in his life he vehemently, publicly spoke against the pagan worship during one of the city's parades for a Greek god. He started preaching in the midst of the procession. He was grabbed, beaten... and martyred. Timid Timothy became fearless Timothy.

Men want a mission, and the church has the most glorious mission of all time! It should be filled with men! Having something big and impossible to do is what makes men thrive. When they get that, they are affirmed as the men that God wants them to be. And they will rise to the challenge. That's how God made them

No Downside

Reaching and building men has no downside. Having a cadre of godly men benefits them, it benefits their marriages, it benefits their children, it benefits church leaders, it benefits the church, and it benefits the community. Men restored to Christ could mean fewer abortions, fewer widows, fewer single moms, reduced counseling loads, and revived and expanding churches.

Morley writes,

> "Growing men. More workers. Better leaders. Bigger budgets. Restored marriages. Curious youth. A balanced workload. A strong reputation in the community. An increase in first-time visitors. Sound too good to be true?"[150]

Yet this is exactly what we at Men of Valor are hearing from churches in the communities where we've held jumpstart men's discipleship conferences. Due to the increasing number of men of valor in their churches, pastors report spending less time in marriage and family counseling and more time on outreach and teaching. As a result, churches are growing and new churches are being planted.

Will You Catch the Vision?

Proverbs 29:18 says, "Where there is no vision, the people are unrestrained." (NASB) Without vision (truth), men will engage in self-indulgence, they'll lose purpose, direction, and mission... leading to chaos and destruction. Yep.

Years ago, a vision formed in my mind to see an army of men living for Him, obeying His Word, and serving their families, workplaces, the community, and the church. It has begun. The Body of Christ is reaching men! God has blessed Men of Valor International's efforts. But the goal is much bigger than one organization.

I want to place a burning vision in your heart, man of valor! Understand what God made you to be and do. Understand who you are, that you have a high calling and a huge responsibility. Be who you are! The Lord is with you!

And I want to give you, church leader, a burning vision, also. Reach men!

- ✓ If you reach a man, you can reach his family.
- ✓ If you reach a man, you can reach his church.
- ✓ If you reach a man, you can reach his community.
- ✓ If you reach a man—even one at a time—you can reach the world.

"You've tried all the other church-growth strategies. Why not employ the one Jesus used? Go get some men."

—David Murrow[151]

Notes & References

140 Murrow, *Why Men Hate Going to Church*, 213-214

141 Julia DeCelles-Zwerneman, "Where Are All the Men? Exploring the Gender Gap in Church" (Online: Capterra 2016) https://blog.capterra.com/where-are-all-the-men-exploring-the-gender-gap-in-church/

142 Murrow, 145

143 Robbie Low, "The Truth About Men & Church" (Online: Touchstone 2003) https://www.touchstonemag.com/archives/article.php?id=16-05-024-v

144 Zigarelli, "The Man-Friendly Church" (Online: Christianity Today 2018) https://www.christianitytoday.com/ct/2018/june/man-friendly-church.html

145 Morley, *Pastoring Men*, 34

146 "Fellowship Bible Church in Little Rock, Arkansas, models external focus through its small group[s]... After three years, [men] are kicked out into a common cause group that serves the community. Founding pastor Robert Lewis points out, 'That's where men flourish, because men are action oriented.' " Morrow, 203

147 For more, see "Chapter 3: Men: Who Needs 'Em?" of *Why Men Hate Going to Church*

148 "Men have always done the dangerous jobs... Men also do most of the dying for their country." Murrow, 38

149 "The news of this event spread around the world, and organizations like [Missionary Aviation Fellowship] MAF found themselves flooded with applicants who were ready to follow in the footsteps of these men and go to the ends of the earth for the sake of the Gospel. Even today, many of our staff initially came to MAF because they read Jungle Pilot—the story of Nate Saint's life." https://hub.maf.org/location/country/ecuador/it-has-been-60-years "In the years since Saint and his fellows were killed, quite a few Christians—I would estimate several thousand in the overall missionary community—have dedicated their own lives to Christ because of the example of these men. MAF constantly gets applications from people who have been inspired by the story. This is still going on right now." http://www.cowart.info/AucasTheWorstPeopleOnEarth.htm This event also had a direct impact on my family—it spurred John Snavely and his wife Jan to enter the mission field!

150 Morley, 33

151 Murrow, 223

Appendix A

A Bible Study for Men: The Men in the Bible

Try this Bible study with other men. Choose a man in the Bible and find all the verses where he is mentioned. (For example, if you choose Stephen, you will be reading Acts 6 and 7). Read the verses and answer as many of the questions below as you can about each man.

Here are a few to get you started:

Adam (Genesis 1:26-3; 5:1-5)
Gideon (Judges 6-8)
Paul (Acts 9, 13-28)
Gehazi (2nd Kings 4-5, 8:1-6)
Noah (Genesis 6-9)
Titus (2nd Corinthians 6:6-7; 8:6,23; Titus 1:4-6)
Cain (Genesis 4)
Samson (Judges 13-16)
Jonah (Jonah)
Mordechai (Esther)

Nabal (1st Samuel 25:2-42)
Naaman (2nd Kings 5:1-19)
Joseph (Genesis 37-50)
Stephen (Acts 6-7)
Hezekiah (2nd Chronicles 29-32)
Jonathan (1st Samuel 14:1-23; 20:1-17; 23:15-18)
Jacob (Genesis 25:19-34; 27-35)
Elijah (1st Kings 17-19)
Herod (Mark 6:14-28)

1. Who was this man? What kind of work did he do?

2. What can you learn about his character, habits, and attitude?

3. How did he treat others?

4. How did he respond when corrected?

5. Is there anything to admire in this man?

6. Is there anything to dislike about him?

7. How did God see this man? What did God say about this man? (if anything is written)

8. How is this man similar to or different from the ideal man—Jesus?

9. What can you learn from his problems? Do you have any of the problems he had? What did he do about those problems? Should you do anything like what he did?

10. What can you learn from his obedience?

11. What can you learn from his disobedience?

12. What other lessons can you learn from his life?

(Not all questions apply to every biblical account).

Note: You might not be able to study the entire record of a man at one time. For example, for Elijah, read 1ˢᵗ Kings 18:20-40 and talk over how he handled the prophets of Baal. Then the next time you meet, read 1ˢᵗ Kings 19:1-18 about when Elijah was in the wilderness.

Appendix B

<u>Advice for Teaching Men</u>

1. Talk like a regular guy, and pray like a regular guy. Avoid "holy" words, religious repetitions, and flowery language. Avoid feminine metaphors.

2. Use stories.

3. Use stories about men and manly illustrations. Men respond to and are attracted to stories of heroism, beating the odds, achieving victories, standing up to the bad guys, daring, courage, self-sacrifice, danger, ordinary men doing extraordinary things, such as David vs. Goliath, Elijah vs. the Prophets of Baal, or Moses vs. Pharaoh.

4. Always use the Bible—teach what's there, not tempered or gentle, don't soften the message. Let God's Word speak for itself. Be gracious but uncompromising.

5. Highlight the masculine side of Jesus' message: His strength, initiative, action, boldness, directness, and confidence. He knew when to be tough and when to be tender. He demonstrated power under control (meekness).

6. Insert experiences or stories from the work world, sports, or subjects that men in your culture are interested in.

7. Help men understand their calling, mission, purpose, position, and standing before God.

8. Help men to see themselves in the story. You want them to think, "Hmm, maybe I could do that!"

9. Be personal, be real. Share stories, struggles, challenges, when you did things wrong and what you did about it, and when you did things right.

10. Be energetic, lively, enthusiastic, and visionary. Express passion and conviction.

11. Speak about:
- ✓ Brotherhood, one man helping another;
- ✓ Acceptance, being valued and appreciated;
- ✓ Strengths and what they could be (don't always remind men about their weaknesses);
- ✓ Being qualified; and
- ✓ Growing, learning, improving, trying new things.

12. Plan activities (object lessons) to involve men in the message, e.g., tug of war. Ideally, do something unexpected regularly.

13. Keep the message simple: maybe one to three points that they can walk away with.

14. Give a call to action.

Appendix C

Advice For Leading Men's Discipleship Groups

Men's discipleship through men-only small groups and one-to-one mentoring/discipling is the key for men to grow in Christ. No man can live the Christian life alone and hope to succeed; men need one another to stand strong in the battles of life. (Ecclesiastes 4:9-10) This ministry is life impacting for men... but also for the marriages, families, workplaces, neighborhoods—and the church. Ministry to men is crucial!

To Launch a Group, Decide:

1. What day and time will you meet? Will you meet each week or every other week? Whatever you decide, keep to the start and stop time. Respect men's schedules.

2. Where to meet? Church? Home? Restaurant or coffee shop? A restaurant or coffee shop may be more suitable or attractive for the "fringe" guys who either do not go to church or rarely go. They may not be interested in going into a church building. It's a strange place! They may not be interested in going to a home either. A home could mean your wife or kids may interrupt or at least be nearby... and listen in. A restaurant, coffee shop, or deli is a more neutral, comfortable, and familiar setting.

To Lead a Group

Make it:
- ✓ **Informal**: Enjoy it—don't make it tense and pressured.
- ✓ **Relaxed**: Be yourself; be a man, talk like a man.
- ✓ **Not "churchy"**: Don't talk like a pastor; avoid "holy" language.
- ✓ **Comfortable**: Make room for men to talk freely—but don't force them to.
- ✓ **Private**: What is said in the group stays in the group.

Suggested agenda:

1. Open with a brief prayer.

2. Ask everyone how they are doing.

3. Open the Bible and read the section you chose (ideally have one or two of the men read).

4. Answer the questions together; talk about what you discover about men in the Bible... emphasize just how normal the man is.

5. Ask the men what they learned in the study.

6. Close in prayer.

Other guidelines:

First meeting—let the men introduce themselves, let them talk.

If you sense that a man doesn't know the Bible and may not be a believer, meet with him at another time and get to know him, and share the Gospel. Or, he may be a believer but he's not read the Bible much if at all—guide him into the Word.

In time, if it seems right, ask the men for prayer requests, and then pray together. But don't force the men to pray out loud. Ask for volunteers but if you get none, do it yourself. It's okay... in the beginning.

Remember:
Men's discipleship will change *everything.*

Appendix D

Recommended Reading

Men's Discipleship

John Butler, *Gideon: The Mighty Man of Valor*, Scripture Truth, 1992 (and any of the 27 other Bible Biography Series)

Gene Getz, *The Measure of a Man*, Revell, 2016

R. Kent Hughes, *Disciplines of a Godly Man*, Crossway, 2001

Robert Lewis, *Raising a Modern-Day Knight*, Focus on the Family, 1997

Patrick Morley, *How God Makes Men*, Multnomah, 2013

Patrick Morley, *Ten Secrets for the Man in the Mirror*, Zondervan, 2000

David Murrow, *The Map: The Way of All Great Men*, Thomas Nelson, 2010

Tim Shoemaker, *Dangerous Devotions for Guys*, Group, 2009

Gary Smalley & John Trent, *The Hidden Value of a Man*, Tyndale, 2005

Stu Weber, *Tender Warrior*, Multnomah, 1993

Husband & Father

Dr. Emerson Eggerichs, *Love & Respect*, Integrity, 2004

Gary Thomas, *A Lifelong Love*, David C Cook, 2014

Gary Thomas, *Sacred Marriage*, Zondervan, 2000

Gary Thomas, *Sacred Parenting*, Zondervan, 2004

Why Men

Kenny Luck, *Sleeping Giant*, B&H Publishing Group, 2012

Patrick Morley, *Pastoring Men*, Moody, 2009

David Murrow, *Why Men Hate Going to Church*, Nelson Books, 2011; churchformen.com

Leon Podles, *The Church Impotent*, Spence Publishing, 1999

Michael Zigarelli, *The Man-Friendly Church: 7 Churches That Attract Men and the 10 Things They Have in Common*, 2019

Josh McDowell Ministries, "The Father Factor" https://www.josh.org/resources/apologetics/research/

Making an Impact

Vince Antonucci, *Renegade*, Baker Books, 2013

Robert Lewis, *The Church of Irresistible Influence*, Zondervan, 2001

Kirbyjon Caldwell & Walk Kallestad, *Entrepreneurial Faith: Launching Bold Initiatives to Expand God's Kingdom*, WaterBrook Press, 2004

Sam Childers, *Another Man's War*, Thomas Nelson, 2009

David Platt, *Radical*, Multnomah, 2010

Steve Sjogren, *101 Ways to Reach Your Community*, NavPress, 2001

Steve and Janie Sjogren, *101 Ways to Help People in Need*, NavPress, 2002

Owen Strachan, *Risky Gospel*, Thomas Nelson, 2013

Eric Swans & Rick Rusaw, *The Externally Focused Quest: Becoming the Best Church For the Community*, Josey-Bass, 2010

Dedication &
Acknowledgements

This book and Men of Valor International are dedicated first to God. I spent many years praying about who would go and address the needs of men internationally, and it is His leading that has seen both book and ministry come into being.

Secondly, I dedicate this to the men I "hang out with" in the U.S.; my son and sons-in-law; and the men around the world who need to know, believe, and act on the fact that the Lord is with them, because they are mighty men of valor.

I want to thank my daughter Ashley for turning the original conference messages into a first draft. I cannot thank Mary Kay, my wife of forty years, enough for her incredible editing and organization abilities as we labored over subsequent drafts. And thanks to my son Jason, publishing consultant, for final edits, formatting, and guidance.

I also want to thank the many men who have traveled to share the joy of teaching spiritually hungry men—especially Bruce Campbell, Mark Seager, Jesse Taylor, Bill Wilcox, and the late Guy Wilson, all contributors to this book. Men of Valor International has never been about one man; I've had the privilege of teaching alongside some twenty godly men from multiple countries. Thank you, brothers!

Lastly, I am immensely thankful for several men who inspired Men of Valor International to get started: Pastors Mark Seager, John Woodall, and Mike Minter, along with Dan Darby, Hayward Paul, Mike Renner, and Mike Young.

Several brilliant authors had a huge impact on the MOV teachings: John Butler, James Dobson, Gene Getz, Robert Lewis, Aubrey Malphurs, Pat Morley, David Murrow, Gary Thomas, and Stu Weber. I've absorbed so much of their Spirit-inspired writings, and have been so heavily influenced by them, that undoubtedly their concepts and ideas are interwoven throughout this book. I credited them where I was cognizant of that influence but I fear that I missed a few deserved points of acknowledgment as their wise advice is deeply embedded in my thinking, teaching, and writing! I highly recommend that you read their books.

About the Authors

Brad Smith is the executive director of Men of Valor International. He has been involved with men's ministry for more than thirty years. Brad has a B.A. in Bible and Psychology and a minor in communications from Houghton College. Brad created the original MOV training materials for a conference in India in 2004, and has since conducted MOV conferences in over twenty countries. Brad and his wife have three married children and two grandchildren. They live in Virginia.

Bruce Campbell is the executive pastor at Reston Bible Church, Dulles, VA, and has been active in teaching, counseling, and leading small groups for three decades. Bruce serves as senior advisor to Men of Valor International and has taught in MOV conferences in India and Tanzania. Bruce and his wife have four children and fourteen grandchildren.

Mark Seager is the pastor of CityView Church in Ashburn, VA and serves as a senior advisor to MOV. He graduated from Virginia Tech with a BS in Civil Engineering and his first career was as a civil/environmental engineer. He later achieved an MA in Biblical Studies from Moody Theological Seminary. Mark has pastored in four churches, including a congregation in England. Mark has taught in MOV conferences in Zambia and Tanzania as well as teaching MOV material to church leaders in Guatemala and Nicaragua. Even before MOV's inception, Mark has greatly shaped all that is Men of Valor. Mark and his wife have four children.

Bill Wilcox is a retired Navy Captain with twenty-seven years of service as a naval aviator. He is the executive director of Smyrna Ministries International, serving the persecuted church. Bill has served in men's ministries in several churches—most recently as head of the men's ministry at Blue Ridge Bible Church in Purcellville, VA, where he is now an Elder. Bill shared the teaching at an MOV conference in Ghana. Bill and his wife have three children and eight grandchildren.

Guy Wilson worked as a teacher and counselor in Fairfax County, VA, until retirement and then spent ten years in ministry, mostly as assistant pastor and then an active layman. He travelled to five continents on mission trips and taught in Men of Valor conferences in Peru and Paraguay. Guy and his wife have two children and thirteen grandchildren. Guy went home to his Lord in 2021.

Jesse Taylor has a degree in electrical engineering and works as a software programmer in New York City. He has served in various church ministries, and taught in an MOV conference in Paraguay. Jesse and his wife have two children.

About Men of Valor International

Men of Valor International (MOV) changes families and communities by changing men. MOV teaches biblical manhood around the world by leading men's conferences to jumpstart discipleship where there is little or no effort to reach and build men.

An MOV conference covers a man's position in Christ, his priorities, and his practices. Men leave our conferences encouraged and energized because they are learning, often for the first time, how God views men, how much He values them, and His purpose for them. Over the past two decades, God has blessed these men's conferences and has used them to organically establish hundreds of men's discipleship groups in over 25 countries in Africa, Asia, and Central and South America.

MOV has received hundreds of testimonies from men and pastors, sometimes even years afterward, about the impact God's Word has had on them, their marriages, their families, their churches, and their communities. In Malawi alone, over the last six years, over 1,500 men have accepted Christ. Pastors report restored marriages and families, less need for family counseling, growing churches, and new church plants—all through the men that God has called and equipped in the jumpstart conferences.

To request a conference, or a speaker for a men's event, whether in the United States or abroad:

- ✓ Write **info@menofvalor.org**
- ✓ Call **1-844-MEN-VALR**
- ✓ Contact us at **menofvalor.org/request**

Is Your Church Reaching Men in the International Communities You Care About?

When men are changed by God, it changes everything—families, communities, God's Kingdom. Your church is actively involved in international missions, but have you reached the men in those communities? MOV can be your partner to bring a specific focus to reach and build men there. MOV has led over 55 conferences in 26 countries. Change a man: change *everything*.

> **Sponsor an MOV conference where you've invested.**

Foster men's discipleship in that community. And send your men!

An MOV conference:
- ✓ Launches men's discipleship
- ✓ Trains church leaders to reach and build men
- ✓ Restores marriages and families, helps churches to grow, and reaches men through discipleship groups and outreach
- ✓ Initiates and deepens relationships with the believers and the community

After the conference, your men:
- ✓ Pray for these men, their families, churches, and community
- ✓ Conduct a quarterly virtual "check-in"
- ✓ Provide coaching and materials on leading and teaching men to follow God
- ✓ Organize virtual bible studies, a follow-up conference, or other on-site training as possible

Conference sponsorship builds your men, too:
- ✓ Men are often not spiritually challenged. Men need a goal to achieve—a *big* goal. Committing to men in an international community and praying and providing resources for those men is a strategic investment in long-term *community* transformation.
- ✓ When your men actively engage in ministry, in reaching a community for Christ, they too mature in Christ. Knowing that they can make a difference like this for the kingdom of God, it strengthens their walk, marriage, family, workplace, church, and community... and your church!

Sign up for the MOV Newsletter

Stay up to date on how God is using MOV to impact men and their families, churches, and communities—all over the world.

- ✓ Write **info@menofvalor.org**
- ✓ Contact us at **menofvalor.org/signup**

Sponsor a Mission Trip to Reach Men

- ✓ Write **info@menofvalor.org**
- ✓ Call **1-844-MEN-VALR**
- ✓ Contact us at **menofvalor.org/request**

MEN OF VALOR INTERNATIONAL
MENOFVALOR.ORG